Reconsidering the Privileged Powers of Banks

Kozo Torasan Mayumi · Ansel Renner

Reconsidering the Privileged Powers of Banks

Foundations of Sovereign Money, Wealth and Real
Capital for Sustainability

Kozo Torasan Mayumi
The Kyoto College of Graduate
Studies for Informatics
Kyoto, Japan

Ansel Renner
Autonomous University of Barcelona
Barcelona, Spain

ISBN 978-981-99-6057-6   ISBN 978-981-99-6058-3   (eBook)
https://doi.org/10.1007/978-981-99-6058-3

This Palgrave Macmillan imprint is published by the registered company Springer Nature Singapore Pte Ltd.
The registered company address is: 152 Beach Road, #21-01/04 Gateway East, Singapore 189721, Singapore

Paper in this product is recyclable.

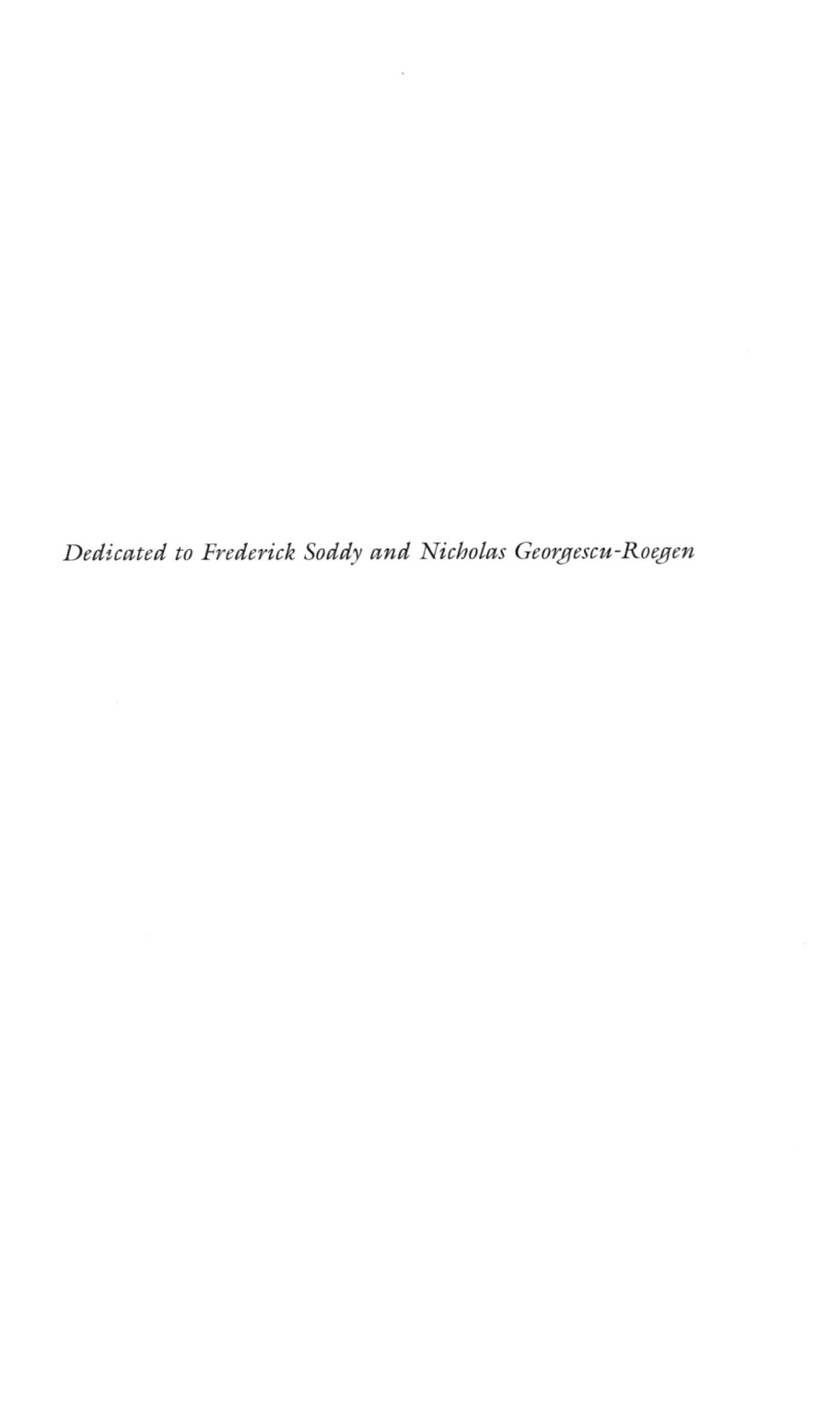

Dedicated to Frederick Soddy and Nicholas Georgescu-Roegen

FOREWORD

Typically, banking, money, and monetary policy are of little importance to most people who are living their everyday lives without much thought to these important issues. However, when there are periods of high inflation or economic uncertainty, people become more concerned and engaged with how the banking industry works and the monetary policies of central banks. These institutions, which many people have very little understanding of, have great control, or, as Kozo Mayumi and Ansel Renner say in this book "privileged powers," over the economy and people's personal economic conditions. Thus, it is vital for people to understand these powers and how they impact their lives.

Mayumi and Renner uncover the privileged powers of commercial banks. Specifically, how banks create profit and productivity out of nothing through money creation using deposits and credit. Both Mayumi and Renner call upon their experiences from previous papers and commentaries published on this subject to provide a well-thought-out and concise explanation of how money is used by both commercial banks and individuals and how their uses are contradictory to the entropy law and negatively impact sustainable and equitable societies.

This ability to manufacture profit through money creation and money interest is the "privileged power" of commercial banks. This power is not available to the individual, where money is used for the exchange of goods and services. However, in both situations, money is, from an individual perspective, a form of wealth. But, when looked at from a public perspective, money is a biophysical debt. As a result, money has a dual nature, one purpose from an individualistic perspective (individuals and commercial banks) and another purpose from a societal perspective. This dual nature impacts sustainable and equitable societies. Mayumi and Renner explain this important concept clearly and concisely, and one cannot underestimate the importance of how the dual nature of money influences sustainable societies.

As Georgescu-Roegen pointed out in his best-known work, *The Entropy Law and the Economic Process*, the economy is for self-preservation, or satisfying basic needs indispensable for survival. Continuing on the point, he explained how the real source of economic value is the value of life for every life-bearing individual. If the economy is looked at through this lens, then the dual nature of money creates a biophysical deficit, entropy, that impacts sustainability. Applying this to banking, there is either the constant creation of money, which creates massive inflation and financial instability, or money is used to create value through scarcity. In either case, entropy increases because neither is compatible with the entropy law, putting a biophysical burden on society.

While the above is an oversimplistic explanation of the dual nature of money, the privileged powers of commercial banking, and the impact on sustainable societies, Mayumi and Renner explain these concepts, with each chapter building upon the next, culminating in a discussion of how society can work together to create a more sustainable and equitable future. This last section of the book is particularly relevant. While many authors will point out the negative aspects of activities and their impact on sustainability, few provide meaningful thoughts or examples on how to actually improve the situation. However, Mayumi and Renner do exactly that in this book, providing several key ideas toward establishing a sustainable relationship between sovereign monetary systems, individual and commercial wealth, and real capital for conscientious development.

This book, as a result, is timely and provides a fresh examination of the dual nature of money. The topic is one that is important to discuss for a sustainable society, for solving interest differences among nations, and developing financial institutions that put individuals less at risk for undesirable financial collapses and catastrophes.

John M. Polimeni
President of the United States
Society for Ecological Economics
Albany, New York, USA

ACKNOWLEDGMENTS

The first author, Kozo Torasan Mayumi, published a related work, *Sustainable Energy and Economics in an Aging Population*, in April 2020. The basic ideas in the book you are currently reading are derived from scattered materials contained in that work. It took us an additional three years of intensive research into issues of sovereign money, wealth, and real capital to elaborate these ideas into the present format. It is now high time that we open a discussion on the privileged powers granted to banks and work toward regaining sovereignty over money systems so that citizens of nations around the world can earnestly strive toward a more equitable and sustainable society.

This book is dedicated to Professors Frederick Soddy and Nicholas Georgescu-Roegen. We, the authors, have been tremendously influenced intellectually by these two greats and extend our sincere admiration for the originality of their penetrating contributions to economic science. Without them, this book could never have been completed. We are convinced that, despite relative neglect during their lifetime in the field of economics, their reputation and influence promise to continue increasing.

Our appreciation and thanks are due to Professor John M. Polimeni of the Albany College of Pharmacy and Health Sciences, the president-elect of the United States Society for Ecological Economics (USSEE). Professor Polimeni has kindly agreed to write a foreword for this book and has provided several important references on the subject of modern monetary theory. We greatly appreciate his time, effort, and helpful inputs.

An expression of gratitude is due to Professors Silvio Funtowicz, Mario Giampietro, Tommaso Luzzati, Roldan Muradian, and Jesús Ramos-Martín, all of whom have kindly written endorsements for the book. Apart from these passages, their moral support has been crucially important along the way.

Chapters 1 and 9 begin with epigraphs taken from the corpus of early Buddhism. Dr. Bhikkhu Bodhi indicated the source of Chapter 1's quotation, which Ms. Isaline Blew Horner, a great scholar of Pali literature, translated. We are similarly indebted to the work of Mr. Michael Olds for his effort on the BuddhaDust compendium. The epigraph used for Chapter 1, a translation by Mr. Frank Lee Woodward, was discovered as a result. We are very pleased to make reference to two great scholars of the Pali literature, Ms. Horner and Mr. Woodward, and are most grateful for their important work.

Certain materials related to Sects. 5.2, 5.4, 5.5, and 8.5 of the Mayumi (2020) book have been reused in a modified format. We are grateful for the permission that Ms. Uma Vinesh of Springer has granted for this purpose.

We would like to thank Mr. Jacob Dreyer, commissioning editor at Palgrave Macmillan, for his unwavering support of this book since the project's inception. This book would have never been published without his sincere effort and support.

Lastly, as is customary but certainly not trivial, we would like to emphasize that we, the authors, assume all responsibility for how we have considered advice and criticism.

CONTENTS

LIST OF FIGURES

LIST OF TABLES

CHAPTER 1

Introduction

Open for those who hear are the doors of deathlessness; let them renounce
their faith.

—Vinayapiṭake Mahāvaggapāḷi (Horner, 1951, p. 9)

1.1 INTRODUCTION

The privilege referred to in this book's title concerns two extraordinary
powers afforded to commercial banks. The first power is the unnatural
ability to create money out of nothing, the second, equally unnatural, is
the ability to breed money from money.

The creation of money out of nothing is a phenomenon most
commonly manifest when demand deposits are added to the current
accounts of bank clients. This money, referred to as "bankmoney"
following Huber (2017), is used primarily as a cashless payment method,
in other words, a way of economic exchange carried out without the use
of physical coins or banknotes. Despite lacking explicit legal authorization, bankmoney, which accounts for the lion's share of the money supply,
has come to be universally accepted as authentic legal tender in modern
states.

The acceptance of bankmoney belies, however, its relatively recent
introduction into financial systems. Its universality is by no means
a foregone conclusion. Macleod (1883, p. 350), a distinguished late

K. T. Mayumi and A. Renner, *Reconsidering the Privileged Powers
of Banks*, https://doi.org/10.1007/978-981-99-6058-3_1

nineteenth-century banking expert from Scotland, was one of the first to remark on what was then something of a novelty: "The express purpose of these banks was to create *credit* [in the form of demand deposits], *incorporeal* entities, created out of *nothing*." Mark (1934, pp. 82–83), continuing Macleod's line of inquiry half a century on, later described in about as lucid terms as possible the essence of money creation by commercial banks: "The banker [...] *makes* money, in the literal sense of the word, by writing up figures in a book as debts. And all that it costs him to *make* his money, is pen, ink, and paper, and the service of the clerk who writes up the figures."

In the natural world, creating something out of nothing is a general and obvious-to-most impossibility. From a natural world perspective, when commercial bankers create money out of nothing, they defy, in a manner of speaking, the law of conservation of energy and matter (the first law of thermodynamics). In generating vast sums of bankmoney at the press of a computer keystroke, bankers achieve the unthinkable. It is in this sense that Macleod and Mark hold bankers in cynical regard, viewing them as miracle workers.

In the United States and the Eurozone, a staggering 95% of the active domestic money supply is bankmoney, "active" meaning that money in savings accounts or otherwise hoarded is excluded from consideration. Huber (2017) refers to the situation that has developed and the immense privilege it entails as a "neo-feudal aristocracy." In the United Kingdom, as of 2011, money created by commercial banks constitutes some 97.4% of the "money supply" (M4) (Ryan-Collins et al., 2012). M4, the broadest conventional consideration of money in the United Kingdom, includes coins, banknotes, time deposits, repurchasing agreements, money market funds, debt securities, and all other deposits at banks or building societies.

The notion of creation "out of nothing" rings surprisingly true when one considers such vast amounts of money produced by commercial banks, offset by relatively minor economic costs to themselves. The phrase may even be taken literally by the more level-headed among bankers. The authors of this book believe, however, that collectively, people have failed to fully grasp the profound significance of banker privilege and the crucial implications that privilege has for the sustainability of societies. Money is purchasing power representing a promise to pay, which can ultimately be exchanged for goods, services, and other economic properties. It is an urgent and critical economic issue for every citizen to question whether the aristocratic privilege of commercial banks is justified.

The second power granted to commercial banks, the unnatural ability to breed money from money, follows a unique legal and institutional arrangement—money, once created from nothing, accrues additional money in tune with a positive interest rate. Money grows over time. As before, the universal expectation of a significant positive interest rate is a relatively recent development in financial systems. Aristotle (1984, p. 1997) condemned taking advantage of such payment in *Politics*, writing that of all modes of money making, "the birth of money from money [...] is the most unnatural." Underpinned by an ethical argument against usury, he perceived the act of interest payment as something against nature—money should be used for exchanging goods and services, not for self-multiplication through the charging of positive interest. In *Divine Comedy*, Dante followed Aristotle and the more general medieval Catholic sense of morality in viewing money as sterile by nature. Usurers, those who would pervert money's sterile nature by breeding it from itself, were placed by Dante on the innermost section of the seventh circle of hell.

Viewed again through the lens of the natural world, commercial banks, in their role as money lenders and having generated money, exhibit a paradoxical ability to sidestep the second law of thermodynamics, otherwise known as the entropy law. It is common knowledge that heat, or energy, tends to dissipate, and material objects, regardless of whether they are man-made or natural, deteriorate over time. This common knowledge, deriving ultimately from the mundane experiences of everyday life, is scientifically articulated in the entropy law. What the law stipulates is that both energy and matter undergo an inevitable *qualitative degradation*—energy scatters, and material objects decompose over time, gradually approaching a state where they can no longer be utilized for human needs.

Consider Japan, for instance, where Article 48 of the Bank of Japan Act asserts that "[t]he Bank of Japan must exchange, without fees, Bank of Japan notes rendered unfit for further circulation due to soiling, damage, or other causes" (MOJ, 2023). Only money, armed with its unnatural ability to self-reproduce, can, in functional terms, escape the entropy law. Degraded money tokens are replaced free of charge by fresh banknotes and otherwise grow with interest over time, all the while maintaining their functional role.

As later demonstrated in Chapter 4, the two unnatural powers granted to commercial banks imply that two units of money appear in the bankers' pockets from an original nothing. Zero can become two within the world of commercial banking! Of course, if economic conditions permit and a continued bullish environment can be anticipated, commercial banks tend toward an increasingly voracious and disproportionate generation of more money than required for the exchange of goods and services. When economic booms subside, commercial banks call in their debts, precipitating a sudden recession. Such boom-recession cycles have become a commonplace monetary phenomenon, elsewhere beautifully chronicled in Aliber and Kindleberger's (1978/2015) classic *Manias, Panics, and Crashes.*

Most economists, whether conventional or heterodox, and the general public, maintain a religious-like faith that monetary phenomena and policy measures related to "depression prevention" have little to do with long-term collectivistic perspectives. The prevailing belief is that monetary phenomena do not fundamentally impact the biophysical dimensions of sustainability.

On the contrary, this book's natural scientific, historical, and institutional analysis reveals profound and substantial connections between monetary phenomena and the biophysical aspects of our social-economic systems and the biosphere. Regrettably, these connections have been almost entirely overlooked in the analysis of the implications of the two unnatural powers of commercial banks.

At a somewhat more general level, this book is mainly concerned with the concept of *dual nature*—a contrast associated with money, wealth, and real capital between individualistic and collectivistic perspectives. The concept is of central relevance for sustainability concerns, opening doors to understanding a largely overlooked essence. Money, wealth, and real capital represent forms of affluence from an individualistic perspective, but regrettably, they create an irrevocable biophysical debt from a collectivistic perspective. As Macfarlane (1978) well described in *The Origins of English Individualism*, individualistic perspectives have become the second nature of the human species in modern times. The individualist mindset prevents us from paying proper attention to the collectivistic views that are otherwise indispensable for establishing a more sustainable and equitable world. It inhibits us from engaging in a process of responsible development. Yet, most people are oblivious to the existence of the dualism and its profound implications for self-preservation. This book aims to enlighten such persons, encouraging them to *abandon their faith in the non-existence of dual nature*, as first suggested in this chapter's epigraph, taken from the *Vinayapiṭake Mahāvagga* among the Early Buddhist scriptures:

> Open for those who hear are the doors of deathlessness; let them renounce their faith.
>
> (Horner, 1951, p. 9)

Renouncing faith in individualistic perspectives is a necessary precursor to accepting the value of collectivistic perspectives toward a more holistic and harmonious paradigm of responsible development (Mayumi & Giampietro, 2014).

These points in mind, three types of dual nature associated with money, wealth, and real capital, along with their implications for more sustainable and equitable societies in the future, are briefly addressed before introducing this book's content chapter by chapter.

First and foremost, the dual nature of money—a fundamental concept for understanding the other two dualities. Money is typically regarded as a measure of an individual's affluence. However, from a broader perspective, money symbolizes a communal debt, as it ultimately represents a promise to pay in the form of existing goods or the production of future goods. Money puts its respective community into long-term biophysical debt. Production, for instance, involves a deficit in terms of entropy as it irreversibly consumes valuable energy and materials, leading to a depletion of exhaustible resources (Georgescu-Roegen, 1971). In fact, since the Industrial Revolution, most of the production process has been freed from direct dependence on land-based renewable resources, temporarily transitioning toward a heavy use of exhaustible resources, such as fossil fuels, for the production of goods and services. For all these reasons, an increase in money can *be seen from a collectivistic perspective* as an increase in future biophysical deficit. We suggest referring to this essential concept as the dual nature of money—money is affluence for individuals but biophysical debt for their community.

The dual nature of money recalls Hardin's seminal article, "The Tragedy of the Commons." Therein it is detailed how individual financial interest generates a tragic turn on the commons, a prime example of biophysical debt to the community. Hardin (1968) addressed the essence of the tragedy of the *commons* through references to *gain, benefit*, and *cost*, common pecuniary considerations in everyday life. He asserts, "each herdsman [in an open pasture] seeks to maximize his *gain*," "the individual *benefits* from his ability to deny the truth even though society as a whole suffers," and a rational person bears a "share of the *cost* of the wastes he discharges into the commons" (Hardin, 1968, pp. 1244–1245, emphasis added). The dual nature of money perfectly mirrors the phenomena associated with the tragedy of the commons, demonstrating the inherent conflict between individual economic welfare and communal long-term sustainability. Among the several global examples of the tragedy of the commons are climate change, habitat loss, and biodiversity loss, each posing a serious threat to sustained net primary production (NPP) in the biosphere.

In recognizing money not only as monetary debt but also, and more crucially for discussions of environmental sustainability, as biophysical debt, social-economic actors can naturally expect a governance structure that deprives commercial banks of their two unnatural powers associated with money issuance and growth. It is vital for states to establish democratic control over new money issuance and distribution in order to create a global economy where biophysical resources can perhaps be sustainably and equitably distributed. As articulated by Huber (2017) and Huber and Robertson (2000), the concept of "sovereign money" should be explored as a legitimate alternative to the current money system, largely dominated by commercial banks. It is of fundamental importance to never lose sight of the fact that money represents debt at the level of the community and can accumulate progressively with a positive interest rate under current legal and institutional settings. Therefore, democratically elected representatives of states must have complete control over the total amount of money and money substitutes (general liquidity) to be issued and deleted, as well as their distribution.

So far, our discussion has proceeded under the assumption that money is used solely within a particular community, such as a given country or nation-state. However, this portrayal of money's dual nature does not address a formidable issue related to the global usage of money and its substitutes, which spans a diverse array of "hierarchically organized" states (Mayumi & Giampietro, 2018). In the lead-up to the collapse of the Bretton Woods monetary management system in 1971, the United States generated a vast amount of money via the banking system to finance the Vietnam War. This action led to a global inflationary trend. Today, several economically powerful entities, including the United States and the European Union, can essentially issue general liquidity at their discretion, often with the active participation or even collusion of privileged banks. This liquidity can be traded on the global market, impacting commodity prices, asset values, and interest rates (or asset returns) in other countries.

Additionally, the discount rate set by the Federal Open Market Committee (FOMC) in the United States, for instance, can cause various repercussions, primarily through fluctuations in the exchange rates of major currencies. Economically smaller countries often find themselves at the mercy of these influences, lacking effective countermeasures. Regrettably, we lack robust and practical tools to address such issues within the current international framework, which the International Monetary Fund and the World Bank uphold. Both of said entities are further strongly suggested to be heavily involved in debt trap creation and, more in general, the borderless activities of commercial banks. We discuss the point later in Chapter 6.

The essence of the dual nature of money lies in the fact that while money is viewed as a form of *affluence* for individuals, it simultaneously represents a biophysical debt for the community to which those individuals belong. On the other hand, producing luxurious goods as a form of wealth and real capital as a form of infrastructure, like railways, involves an entropic process where exhaustible energy and material objects must be irrevocably lost. Hence, the dual nature is also applicable to wealth and real capital. If a strong global orientation toward emphasizing collectivistic perspectives is taken seriously, the idea of the dual nature of money could lead to a significant revision of both the meaning of wealth and the biophysical implications of real capital for sustainability.

The standard definition of wealth encompasses various forms of money substitutes, including equity and other types of financial assets. In practice, these money substitutes are often used to generate additional money substitutes. But money and money substitutes (general liquidity) should be employed exclusively for the exchange of goods and services. In the final analysis, every form of general liquidity represents a form of biophysical debt due to its dual nature. If this biophysical perspective of debt is accepted as tied to the existence of money's dual nature, then the recent trend of rapid expansion of money substitutes ought to be carefully cautioned.

Figure 1.1 illustrates a steady six-decade increase in the ratio of money supply to gross domestic product for the world and four income-based country aggregates. Gross domestic product reflects the market value of goods and services related to national-level economic activity. The measure can be seen as an initial, albeit rough, proxy for wealth and quality of life for the general populace.

The measure should not be regarded as the definitive indicator of a functional economy, however. The primary purpose of an economy is not, per se, the "production of goods and services," as otherwise conventionally claimed in economics. Instead, the true purpose of an economy is the self-preservation of its societal constituents (Georgescu-Roegen, 1971). At the very least, self-preservation demands the satisfaction of basic needs, which primarily rely on biological resources, coming mainly from the biosphere's net primary production. The concept of wealth and the proper role of money are intricate issues tangled up with consideration of Earth's biosphere. In a more sustainable and equitable society than the current one, possessing excessive claims on wealth in terms of general liquidity should not be regarded as some feather in one's hat.

Real capital, the third and final asset form mentioned at the start of this chapter, is generally seen as an agent in the economic production process. In terms of the dual nature of real capital, two points deserve emphasis: (1) the creation of real capital results in a biophysical deficit in terms of an entropy deficit, as useful energy and materials are irreversibly consumed, thereby resulting in fewer exhaustible resources, and (2) real

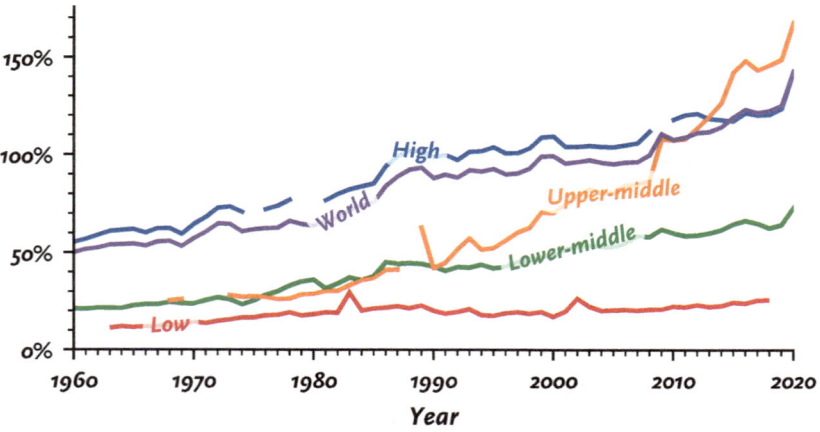

Fig. 1.1 Ratio of broad money supply to gross domestic product (GDP) for low, lower-middle, upper-middle, and high-income economies over the six decades leading up to 2020 (*Data source* World Bank [2023])

capital inevitably deteriorates over time, hence requiring ongoing mainte-nance and disposal practices. Soddy (1926, p. 99) underscored the second point in saying that "by the inexorable laws of thermodynamics, if not of economics, the immense accumulations of the nineteenth century in rail-ways, canals, factories and slum cities, even if they did not get out of date, are all on the same broad highway to destruction. But debts neither get out of date nor wear out; they grow."

Once created, real capital is challenging to convert into consum-able goods—a genuine form of wealth. Soddy (1926, p. 251, emphasis added) notes, "No primitive community would reckon upon eating its ploughs if short of bread. The *financial mentality* of modern man *prevents these elementary considerations from being properly appreciated*." The term "financial mentality" refers here to the prevailing faith in the universal exchangeability of money, and the financialization arms race illustrated in Fig. 1.1 showcases a corollary of such faith.

The ensuing investigation into the powers of banks, the nature of money, wealth, and capital, and pathways of responsible development toward a sovereign money system, proceeds in seven acts. Chapter 2 details the first unnatural power granted to the banking sector—the power to create demand deposits out of nothing. Money in current accounts is now the fundamental cause of financial instability, and money generated through the first power represents the largest fraction of the money stock. Before discussing the process through which modern banking practice developed, three pieces of historical evidence explaining why and how money and credit came into existence are presented. The existence of money as a promise to pay is thereby justified. The development trajectory of the banking sector, culminating in modern times, is then explored, with special attention paid to the practice of *mutuum* in Ancient Rome. Finally, the triangle relationship between commercial banks, central banks, and governments is examined, wherein commercial banks are shown to play a dominant role. The advantage commercial banks gain from the reserve banking system, and their significant involvement in issuing national bonds—compensating for heavy budget deficits typical of economically advanced nations—is scrutinized.

Chapter 3 critically reviews theories on the origins of money interest. The grave consequences of interest rates for discounting practice, especially when allocating exhaustible resources across generations, are discussed. The modern individual accepts without serious debate the prac-tice of discounting based on a positive money interest rate. Our analysis problematizes this acceptance. The entropy law dictates that energy and material objects qualitatively decay over time. Money, being a material object, cannot overcome the entropy law. Coins and banknotes degrade qualitatively per the entropy law. Magnetic devices for storing money as a type of information in computerized systems also decay over time and need to be periodically replaced. The need for an entirely unnatural institutional and legal arrangement thus arises. We argue that while money as a material object decays over time, experiencing structural decline, money as money maintains its functional role over time through the occasional replacement of decayed materials. This reality grants money issuers an unnatural power that guarantees interest payment from money borrowers, justifying the practice of discounting. However, when the practice of discounting is applied to the problem of allocating exhaustible resources among different generations, a serious inconsistency is revealed. In the case of allocating scarce, exhaustible resources, if the discounting practice of conventional economic analysis is employed, the physical quantity of such resources to be allocated steadily diminishes over time. The practice of discounting, based on the existence of money interest, is not compatible with the constraints imposed by the entropy law.

Considering money's fundamental ability to be exchanged for goods, services, money substitutes, or any economic property, it is understandable why all economic entities, including business entities like commercial banks and political entities like nation-states, tend toward an acute desire to obtain the right to issue money that grows per a positive interest over time. This is the basis of the two unnatural powers of money. Emerging from Chapters 2 and 3, Chapter 4 discusses four additional subject matters.

First, it is demonstrated that the present monetary value of all future interest payments on one unit of money principal asymptotes to one additional unit of money. Thus, money issuers can obtain two units of money from zero units of money. The underlying relation is mathematically formalized as the Macleod-Soddy-Allais (MSA) relation, paying proper homage to the contributions of three precursors. On the other hand, if the practice of discounting is to be accepted, it would seem natural to also consider discounting the money loan principal itself. It is shown that if such a scheme of discounting the principal of a money loan is adopted, only one unit of money, not two, would be created when a bank extends a loan. This could dramatically reduce the debt level of societies.

Following the discussion, a case study examination of the balance sheets of Toyota and Sony is conducted, demonstrating that the financial divisions of the two representative producers are extremely lucrative and significant sources of personal profits. The extensive penetration of financial activities into the manufacturing sector is revealed. Finally, the reason why society cannot hope to reach a state of total solvency under the constraints set by the two unnatural powers of the banking sector is presented, along with a revisit of a brilliant analysis made by Mark (1934), some 90 years ago.

Chapter 5 presents the core idea and rationale behind this book—the dual nature of money. Most economists, both conventional and heterodox, as well as the general public, seem to maintain a strong, almost religious-like faith that monetary phenomena and their practical policy implications concerning "depression prevention" have nothing at all to do with long-term collectivistic perspectives for sustainability. On the contrary, our theoretical, historical, and institutional analysis of money presented in Chapters 2 through 4 implies that there are deep connections between monetary phenomena and the biophysical aspects of our society.

As explained in Chapter 2, any form of money is a debt to society with biophysical implications. However, money is customarily seen as a form of wealth from an individualistic perspective—an individual considering money in their coffers as a form of affluence. That is the essence of the dual nature of money. The biophysical debt perspective of money is completely overlooked in conventional economics and, more surprisingly, in heterodox economics.

The debt situation of a select set of countries in terms of external debt per capita and the ratio between external debt and gross domestic product is illustrated. Debt expansion favors economically advanced nations able to generate substantial amounts of debt, a reality that results in an increased burden on economically weaker nations. Under such circumstances, the redemption schemes of national bonds are discussed with the aim of dramatically reducing the careless expansion of national bonds in the future.

If we successfully establish a society in which money is predominantly used to exchange goods and services—thereby minimizing the accumulation of money for money's sake, a situation that potentially ensnares us in a global debt trap—then our contemporary understanding of the meaning of wealth must adapt. Chapter 6 contemplates such a possibility and explores an alternative biophysical theory of wealth, aiming toward a better life. We first discuss how conventional economics often overlooks the stark contrast between biophysical wealth, constrained by the two laws previously mentioned, and financial assets as societal debt, which appear to defy those same laws. Conventional economists frequently and worryingly disregard the biophysical foundations of our economic systems. Perhaps it is high time we formulated an alternative wealth concept compatible with biophysical constraints that acknowledges these two natural laws and steers toward, perhaps, a more sustainable and equitable future.

Chapter 7 addresses real capital and its biophysical burden on society. The dual nature of money suggests that excess financial assets undermine biophysical sustainability. Therefore, the concept of real capital as an agent of production—agents such as machinery, factories, railroads, computer networks, *et cetera*—used to augment the production of goods must be emphasized. Following a brief critical review of capital interest theories proposed in economic theory, we present an alternative biophysical theory of the origin of real capital. The biophysical origin of real capital primarily derives from the expansion of production power for goods and labor-saving efficiency, where properly integrated into the economic process.

Conversely, in the final analysis, all useful energy and materials are ultimately expended during real capital formation and strictly cannot ever be biophysically recovered. Maintaining capital in an efficient state demands additional energy and materials. Moreover, advancements in science and technology often render old capital obsolete sooner rather than later, accelerating the rate at which old capital equipment is replaced, thus further accelerating energy and material consumption. This phenomenon applies to the replacement of old infrastructure with new as well. Real capital's biophysical burden warrants careful consideration for anyone aiming to grasp the concept of sustainability fully. Such consideration, at the very least, necessitates a discussion on the dual nature of real capital.

Chapter 8 proposes a sovereign money system, replacing the unchecked powers currently held by banks. As discussed in Chapter 5, the modern banking sector's money-issuing activities are deeply interconnected with biophysical sustainability. This reality must be recognized and properly understood by every citizen on this planet. In contemporary money systems, commercial bankers carelessly, yet to a predominant degree, control the money supply. When critically reflecting on their unique privileges and working toward reclaiming sovereignty over money systems, it is vital to give a democratically organized new entity full control over the total quantity of liquidity and its issuance and distribution among citizens.

For this purpose, a set of articles concerning nine elements associated with a genuine sovereign money system could be included in constitutions and related legal frameworks. (1) The state establishes a single organization entitled to issue, distribute, and eliminate money. The organization is stipulated in the constitution and democratically managed on behalf of national citizens as sovereign monetary power independent of legislative, executive, and judicial powers. Thus, a singular circuit of money circulation is established. (2) Only the money—coins, banknotes, digital cash, and account money in any form of deposits in the state—created, distributed, and eliminated by the mentioned organization should be accepted as legal tender. (3) This organization must determine the monetary unit of accounting for the official currency. (4) The organization holds responsibility for communicating to the citizenry that money's true societal identity is not merely monetary debt but, more importantly, biophysical debt. (5) The organization must carefully control the total money stock toward a stabilization of the general price level domestically, ensuring the money is mainly used for wealth transactions, as defined in Chapter 6. (6) The organization must pay attention to the distributional economic fairness of money issuance, deletion, and distribution. (7) The level of interest should be carefully reduced to zero to dramatically decrease transactions for increasing "money for money" in the national and international economy. (8) Tax payments and other monetary transactions must be made only with the legal tender issued by the organization. (9) The current accounts of bank customers should be removed from respective bank balance sheets.

After discussing these elements, practical steps toward a sovereign money system and points of caution are covered. The most crucial point is that money wields power over people. Thus, any money issuance, deletion, and distribution decision, even within a sovereign money system, must be thoughtfully arranged and institutionalized. This implies an ongoing iterative process where citizens actively participate in an ever-improving arrangement.

Chapter 9 summarizes the book's essential points and how they interconnect. This summary is interwoven with a discussion on how a nation's political representatives manage money and monetary systems and how we might collectively orient toward establishing a more sustainable and equitable global society. Other matters are discussed toward establishing a harmonious relationship between sovereign money systems, wealth, and real capital for responsible development.

REFERENCES

Aliber, R. Z., & Kindleberger, C. P. (2015). *Manias, Panics and Crashes: A History of Financial Crises* (7th ed.). Palgrave Macmillan. (Original work published 1978).

Aristotle. (1984). Politics. In J. Barnes (Ed.), B. Jowett (Trans.), *The Complete Works of Aristotle* (1st ed., pp. 1986–2129). Princeton University Press (Bollingen Series, 71.2).

Georgescu-Roegen, N. (1971). *The Entropy Law and the Economic Process.* Harvard University Press.

Hardin, G. (1968). The Tragedy of the Commons. *Science, 162*(3859), 1243–1248. https://doi.org/10.1126/science.162.3859.1243

Horner, I. B. (Trans.). (1951). *The Book of the Discipline (Vinaya Piṭaka)* (Vol. 4). Luzac and Company Limited.

Huber, J. (2017). *Sovereign Money: Beyond Reserve Banking.* Palgrave Macmillan. https://doi.org/10.1007/978-3-319-42174-2

Huber, J., & Robertson, J. (2000). *Creating New Money: A Monetary Reform for the Information Age.* New Economics Foundation.

Macfarlane, A. (1978). *The Origins of English Individualism: The Family, Property, and Social Transition.* Cambridge University Press.

Macleod, H. D. (1883). *The Theory and Practice of Banking* (4th ed., Vol. 1). Longmans, Green, Reader and Dyer.

Mark, J. (1934). *The Modern Idolatry: Being an Analysis of Usury & The Pathology of Debt.* Chatto and Windus.

Mayumi, K., & Giampietro, M. (2014). Proposing a General Energy Accounting Scheme with Indicators for Responsible Development: Beyond Monism. *Ecological Indicators, 47*, 50–66. https://doi.org/10.1016/j.ecolind.2014.06.033

Mayumi, K., & Giampietro, M. (2018). Money as the Potential Cause of the Tragedy of the Commons. *Romanian Journal of Economic Forecasting, 21*(2), 151–156.

MOJ. (2023). *Bank of Japan Act (日本銀行法).* Ministry of Justice (法務省), Japan. https://www.japaneselawtranslation.go.jp/en/laws/view/3788#je_ch1at11. Accessed 25 June 2023.

Ryan-Collins, J., et al. (2012). *Where Does Money Come From? A Guide to the UK Monetary and Banking System* (2nd ed.). New Economics Foundation.

Soddy, F. (1926). *Wealth, Virtual Wealth and Debt: The Solution of the Economic Paradox* (1st ed.). E. P. Dutton and Company.

World Bank. (2023). *Broad money (% of GDP)*. The World Bank Group. https://data.worldbank.org/indicator/FM.LBL.BMNY.GD.ZS. Accessed 26 June 2023.

CHAPTER 2

The First Unnatural Power Given to Commercial Banks: Creation of Money Out of Nothing

Banks are nothing but *debt shops*, and the Royal Exchange is the great *debt market* of Europe.

(Macleod, 1883, p. 158)

If it were asked what discovery has most deeply affected the [pecuniary] fortunes of the human race, it might probably be said with truth—*the discovery that a debt is a saleable commodity.*

(Macleod, 1883, p. 200)

2.1 INTRODUCTION

"What is?" questions are both deceptively challenging to answer and, in scientific discourse, notoriously unpopular. The question "What is money?" is no exception. A debate on the topic has been simmering in the background for centuries, at a minimum. While it is not the appropriate time or place to catalog this history, it is useful to highlight the point and embark with a shared understanding of what we mean by "money."

Money is any claim on wealth that is immediately available, without restriction, and broadly accepted as payment. Money is a form of general liquidity, an equivalence class that includes but is not limited to coins, banknotes, and certain time deposits. Which time deposits?

K. T. Mayumi and A. Renner, *Reconsidering the Privileged Powers of Banks*, https://doi.org/10.1007/978-981-99-6058-3_2

17

On this tricky issue, Allais (1987, p. 502) provides a somewhat general economic-perspective criterion:

> the quantity of money held by an operator is the portion of his assets he rightly or wrongly believes *he can use to make his payments immediately and without restriction*. Under this definition, the money supply to be considered as the appropriate one for the analysis of monetary phenomena is the total of assets considered to be available immediately and without restriction *for the purpose of making payments*.

Mitchell-Innes (1913, p. 399), a mainstay of the credit theory of money, complements with a definition of a monetary unit, "[a mere] arbitrary denomination, by which commodities are measured in terms of credit, and which serves, therefore, as a more or less accurate measure of the value of all commodities." Soddy (1934, p. 24), on the other hand, elegantly encapsulates the matter with a memorable one-liner:

> Money now is the *nothing* you get for *something* before you can get *anything*.

Following Huber (2017), money in this book refers collectively to (1) coins, usually issued by a treasury, (2) banknotes, issued by a central bank, (3) central bank reserves, which exist in the current account at the central bank, and (4) "bankmoney," which includes demand deposits and "e-cash" in mobile sub-accounts of bankmoney. Items (1), (2), and (3) are collectively termed the monetary base, totaling a tiny amount compared with bankmoney. The term *general liquidity* refers to liquidity, in other words, money as precisely defined above, plus money substitutes, a category comprising all forms of financial assets, including time deposits, bonds, and equities. Money substitutes are usually created in the secondary monetary and financial markets, originating from the on-lending part of already created bankmoney. Often in this book, where we write "money," it would do just as well to write "general liquidity"—money substitutes included.

Of the four categories mentioned, bankmoney is the one most widely used for cashless payments, where the extinguishing of a monetary obligation involves a money payment. It is important to note that extinguishing a monetary obligation does not necessarily imply a money transfer. The three main alternatives are release, novation, and compensation (Macleod,

1889). Release occurs when a creditor provides a debtor with a formal written receipt for money due, signifying that what was once considered a debt is now viewed as a sort of gift or donation. Novation is a process in which an obligation is extinguished by introducing a new one. This new obligation discharges, pays, and effectively cancels the previous one. The nullification of the preceding obligation serves as the consideration for the new one, providing the key to understanding refinancing processes. Finally, compensation occurs in situations where two individuals are mutually indebted. In such a case, each person may claim that their debt to the other will be offset by the debt owed to them.

Before getting into the concept of credit creation as a demand deposit within the banking system, it is instructive to reflect on the teachings of physics regarding the potential for generating energy from nothing. This consideration will shed light on the privileged status that commercial banks enjoy in the modern banking system. The law of conservation of energy postulates that total energy remains constant before and after any reaction. The law of conservation of mass, while holding for chemical reactions, does not apply to nuclear reactions. This reality is because the binding energy of nucleons (protons and neutrons) is converted into heat energy during a nuclear reaction. Still, importantly, the crucial point is that total energy must be preserved. We cannot create or eliminate energy at will in the natural world.

Even without a sophisticated understanding of the law of conservation of mass and energy, people seem to intuitively grasp from everyday experiences that it is impossible to create energy and material objects from nothing. In stark contrast, it is entirely possible within the banking system for human will to create and erase credit from nothing. Schumpeter (1951, p. 98) echoed Macleod's sentiments from nearly a century prior, asserting that "this creation of means of payment centres in the banks and constitutes their fundamental function."

The creation of money, in a way, challenges the law of conservation (the first law of thermodynamics). The modern credit system indeed represents a remarkably innovative societal mechanism. To underscore the point, within a system of bank ledgers or accounting books on a computerized network, commercial banks possess the extraordinary power to create and extinguish credit at will. This power, though remarkable, is not without detractors. Ruskin, for instance, criticized the perceived misuse of this peculiar economic sorcery in his compendium *Unto This Last*, first published in 1862. In that work, Ruskin (1877, p. 171) states, "Care in nowise to make more of money, but care to make much of it; remembering always the great, palpable, inevitable fact—the rule and root of all economy—that what one person has, another cannot have." Along similar lines, Schumpeter (1951, p. 97 note) remarked on the creation of credit in a fractional reserve system: "while I cannot ride on a claim to a horse, I can, under certain conditions, do exactly the same with claims to money as with money itself."

This chapter discusses the first of two powers granted to the banking sector—the unnatural ability to create demand deposits out of nothing. Money in current accounts is now the primary cause of financial instability, and money generated through this power represents the largest fraction of the money stock (Huber, 2017). Galbraith (1975, p. 5) writes on the subject, "[T]he study of money, above all other fields in economics, is the one in which complexity is used to disguise truth or to evade truth, not to reveal it." The main purpose of this chapter is to reveal to the general public the truth about how bankmoney is created while also reviewing the emergence of the modern money creation process from a historical perspective and the developmental path leading to current banking practices. The process of money creation is relatively simple. Difficulty, however, lies in accepting its simplicity. People tend to believe that the process of money creation must involve a complex and subtle procedure that is too mysterious and delicate for them to comprehend fully. The disproportionate creation of demand deposits is shown to be reinforced by the myth of reserve banking and continuous government debt creation through bond issuance. This "triangle of collusion" among commercial banks, central banks, and governments has become a potent driving force, accelerating the process of creating money and money substitutes—general liquidity.

Before entering on the process along which modern banking practices developed, Sect. 2.2 presents three pieces of historical evidence on the origins of money and credit. First, barter is and was much rarer than commonly believed, involving only instances of interactions with strangers or enemies—situations where reliance on a transaction record was not feasible. Second, the monetary system in its primitive form began to emerge in ancient Babylonian times, represented by devices for recording credit and debt relations. Third, banking activity was initiated as early as around 350 BC in the Roman Republic. Essentially, money represents debts owed to individuals who have provided services to others without yet receiving equivalent service in return. Money is a promise to pay.

Section 2.3 discusses the evolution of the banking sector up to the present time. Banking business began around 350 BC in Rome through agencies called *argentarii*. *Argentarii* created a type of loan known as a *mutuum*. If a person lent money to another person, that money became the borrower's property until the lender demanded its return, a contingent obligation akin to a demand deposit. The fractional reserve banking system is the most evident manifestation of such treatment of deposits. Without any authorized constitutional provisions, modern commercial banks collectively create and extinguish money out of nothing. Thanks to the following two institutional factors, money creation manages a smooth expansion in line with commercial bank initiatives:

(1) the mutual acceptance of credits or debts across the entire commercial banking sector, and
(2) the central bank's readiness to cooperate by reactively creating or absorbing coins, banknotes, and central bank reserves.

Simultaneously, the activities of shadow banking play a crucial role in the circulation of the on-lending money generated by commercial banks. Shadow banking has been a part of the regulated banking system since the 1980s when shadow banks began expanding access to money substitutes (which are not directly related to the bankmoney creation process per se) through securitization, repurchase agreements, derivatives, and other such activities in financial markets. Lastly, we examine a close connection between investment banks and their auditors, such as the relationship between the auditor Ernst & Young and the case of the Lehman Brothers collapse.

Section 2.4 critically examines the close cooperation between commercial banks, central banks, and governments—a triangle in which commercial banks dominate. The general public appears not realize that central banks, such as the Bank of Japan and the United States Federal Reserve Bank, possess a significant degree of autonomy—freedom to operate outside the scrutiny of elected officials. In Japan, for instance, the government authorizes banking licenses and capital requirements for commercial banks without the consent of the National Diet.

Under the reserve banking system, demand deposit creation initiated by commercial banks operates forcefully, resulting in central banks reactively adjusting the amount of central reserve to align with the deposit creation process of commercial banks. The control mechanisms of central banks are, in a sense, secondary and ineffective. We argue that the current reserve banking system is built upon two myths: (1) the myth that the existence of deposits or debts is a function of reserve stock at central banks, and (2) the myth that the prime rate policy of central banks leads directly to a corresponding adjustment, by commercial banks, to the prevailing loan interest rates in the capital market.

Commercial banks are, in fact, exempt from the client money rule, thanks to the myth of the reserve banking system. This system, on paper but not in practice, dictates that commercial banks keep their money and customer money in separate accounts. The close connection between the government, burdened by a continuous budget deficit, and commercial banks must be emphasized. The banking sector plays a considerable role in underwriting sovereign debt on their books and selling the remainder on the open market, thereby securing another lucrative revenue stream.

2.2   Why Does Money Exist

Modern economists generally accept that over the arc of history, barter emerged first, then money, and then credit through the development of the banking system. Adam Smith may be chiefly responsible for this understanding, as evidenced by various statements, for instance, "[W]hen barter ceases, and money has become the common instrument of commerce" (Smith, 1776/1976, p. 36). Samuelson and Nordhaus support the view in their textbook—a cornerstone of undergraduate curricula—stating that as "economies develop, people no longer barter one good for another. Instead, they sell goods for money and then use money to buy other goods" (Samuelson & Nordhaus, 2010, p. 458), and the "financial system is one of the most important and innovative sectors of a modern economy" (Samuelson & Nordhaus, 2010, p. 453). This narrative is misleading.

On the contrary, to overcome the bothersome need for the perfect double coincidence of wants required in barter and to address the shortage of coins due to inferior mining, refining, and minting technology, a credit and debt record system emerged already in ancient Babylonia around 3000–2000 BC (Mitchell-Innes, 1913). This system established a method for postponing the final settlement of economic transactions into the future, thereby overcoming the need for perfect double coincidence.

Let us explore a bit the nature of barter. Barter is a mode of exchange wherein settlement must be finalized at the point of exchange. The goal of barter is to realize a balanced exchange of goods and services among participants. Successful bartering necessitates a perfect match, where each party must offer something of the exact amount required to the other. Barter always requires a perfect double coincidence of wants (Graeber, 2011). However, achieving a double coincidence of wants often proves, in practice, quite challenging.

Anthropological discourse suggests that barter was primarily practiced between strangers who might otherwise have been enemies. Graeber (2011, p. 32, emphasis added), during his presentation of key case studies, notably those of Brazil's Nambikwara and Australia's Gunwinggu, states:

> [What] all such cases of trade through barter have in common is that they are meetings with strangers who will, likely as not, *never meet again, and with whom one certainly will not enter into any ongoing relations.* This is why a direct one-on-one exchange is appropriate: each side makes their trade and walks away.

The credit system is in fact as ancient as money itself. The difficulties of creating standardized coinage due to limited technology made large-scale coin production, and consequently widespread coin circulation, unattainable. To circumvent the necessity for a perfect double coincidence of wants in barter and the scarcity of coins, a *credit and debt recording system* arose in ancient Babylonia using *shubai tablets*, a sort of contract device. The earliest of these tablets, used around 3000–2000 BC, were crafted from dried clay and were about the shape and size of a bar of hand soap. Most *shubai* were used to document straightforward transactions, with the unit of measure being a "she," believed to be a reference to a grain-related unit. To guard against fraudulent tampering, *shubai* were stored in sealed containers. This level of protection is a strong suggestion that *shubai* were not meant as mere records to stay with the debtor. Rather, they were signed and sealed documents given to the creditor, transferable from one creditor to another until the debt was fully settled, at which point the tablet would be destroyed (Mitchell-Innes, 1913).

Medieval Europe offers a second pre-modern instance of a credit system with the use of the tally stick to account for debt. The tally system, like the *shubai* system, was born from *unequal exchanges* that *necessitated* keeping a record of unsettled debt. The tally stick was a tamper-proof device, a stick marked with a series of notches, and was employed during a time of persistent coin shortage and widespread illiteracy. A split tally was typically used to record the bilateral exchange of credits and debts, where each party involved would receive half of a tally stick split lengthwise. When both tally lengths were reunited, a unique and completely identifiable unit was formed. Much of the commerce in medieval Europe was documented using tally sticks, which were used to monitor the purchase of goods, loaning of money, and settlement of debts. Large periodic fairs functioned as clearinghouses, where merchants would congregate with their tally sticks to reconcile their credits and debts (Mitchell-Innes, 1913).

Primitive credit and debt record systems, such as baked clay tablets and wooden tally sticks, were utilized for recording unequal transactions. Despite their primitive nature, they inherently suggest why a money or credit–debt recording system is desirable. It has long been understood that the necessity for money or credit originates directly from unequal transactions, given the difficulty in achieving a perfect double coincidence of wants in the context of barter. It is worth underscoring this point: money or credit, as an instrument, does not serve a direct practical purpose in and of itself. Rather, money or credit represents an abstract right or claim, demanding that another party pay or perform something in the future.

Macleod provides a more precise explanation for the existence of money, worth quoting directly here:

> We have seen that writers of all classes are agreed as to the fundamental *nature of money*. It represents *debts* which are due to persons who have done services to others, and have received no equivalent service in return. It is merely the *right* to demand these equivalent services when they please: and its special function is to measure, record, and preserve for future use these *rights*. If all the services exchanged in society exactly balanced there would be no need for *money*.
>
> (Macleod, 1883, p. 55)

Echoing Macleod, Soddy (1934, p. 25) characterized the essence of money as "merely an ingenious device to secure payment in advance, and in a monetary civilization the owners of money are those who have paid in advance for definite market values of buyable goods and services, without as yet having received them." What Soddy alludes to is that goods

not yet purchased by consumers are created by producers who are entitled to sell those goods and receive a corresponding amount of money.
Hence, money is a promise to pay in terms of present or future goods
and services, reflecting past imbalances that must be addressed. Macleod's
and Soddy's statements imply that money should be used primarily for
exchanging goods and services. They further imply that the amount of
money should not be inflated for the purpose of generating more money,
leading only to an increase in money substitutes without contributing to
the increase of goods and services. The existence of money as a promise
to pay, ultimately exchanged for goods and services, not for other forms
of general liquidity, must be maintained regardless of money's inevitable
structural decay. This topic is of fundamental importance and requires a
more comprehensive analysis, it is addressed in Chapter 3, in discussion
of the second unnatural power of commercial banks.

2.3 The Road to the Present Banking System: Money Creation Out of Nothing

In their discussion of the origins of banking, Samuelson and Nordhaus
(2010, p. 463) assert that "[c]ommercial banking began in England with
the goldsmiths, who developed the practice of storing people's gold and
valuables for safekeeping." Macleod (1883), on the other hand, endorses
Livius, who, in his *Ab Urbe condita libri CXLII*, now available in English
as *The History of Rome*, acknowledged the existence of banking as early
as 350 BC. Macleod (1883, pp. 161–162) affirms that the Romans
initiated banking across Europe as they asserted control over neigh-
boring towns. Local coins brought in by foreigners prompted the Roman
government to establish private agencies called *argentarii* to exchange
foreign money for Roman currency. Over time, *argentarii* broadened
their services to include safeguarding private deposits, without acquiring
ownership. Essentially, they acted as custodians of wealth. Gradually, the
argentarii evolved a novel line of business, which in today's parlance
would indeed be termed "banking." Such business involved accepting
money as personal loans and paying interest on it, thus converting it into
their property and trading with it at their discretion.

Under Roman mercantile law, there were two primary categories of
loans: *commodatum* and *mutuum*. In a *commodatum*-type loan, the
borrower could use the non-consumable loaned object directly without
obtaining outright ownership. Items suitable for such loans included

books and horses. Conversely, a *mutuum*-type loan involved the borrower consuming or otherwise using up the lent object. While the borrower was expected to return to the lender an object similar in kind, the returned object was not necessarily the exact same item. Bread and wine, consumable items, are examples of objects suited for *mutuum*-type loans.

In a somewhat perplexing facet of Roman law, if a person lent money to another, the *money became the borrower's property* until the lender required its return. Intriguingly, in the first large-scale professional banking system known to us, money was treated as a consumable commodity like bread, wine, or meat (Macleod, 1883). If someone deposited money into a bank account, the money became the bank's absolute property until the depositor requested its return. Money loans were treated as *mutuum*-type loans. This treatment perhaps stems from a long-standing banking custom—originating under Roman law and still prevailing today—that views a deposit as a contingent obligation. The banker is not required to retain possession of the deposit until the depositor requests their deposit, such as in cash. This treatment is most clearly manifested in the fractional reserve banking system prevalent worldwide today. While countries like China and India frequently adjust their reserve requirement ratios, most do not. Some nations, including the United States, United Kingdom, Canada, and Australia, have no reserve requirement (0%). Most other developed countries have a reserve requirement of just a few percentage points. Japan, for instance, has a reserve requirement of 0.8%, while in the Eurozone it is 1%. Developing countries typically have slightly higher rates, approximately within 5–15% range (Della Valle et al., 2022).

The treatment of money as a *mutuum*-type loan in Roman mercantile law, along with the use of cash credit akin to money in Scotland, represent significant historical advancements in the realm of finance. These are normative institutions that have become deeply embedded in our political-economic fabric, exemplified in the modern act of money creation. When money is deposited into a bank, the bank acquires an equal amount of deposits as a liability (a liability that only materializes when the customer attempts to withdraw the deposited funds) and that same amount as an asset. What transpires here is that the banker effectively purchases the deposited money from the customer. In return, the bank gives its customer credit in their ledger. This right of action, whether termed credit or debt in banking parlance, is generally referred to as a deposit. It grants banks great capacity to effect monetary expansion.

The epigraph at the head of this chapter eloquently communicates the importance of the discovery:

> If it were asked what discovery has most deeply affected the [pecuniary] fortunes of the human race, it might probably be said with truth—*the discovery that a debt is a saleable commodity.*
>
> (Macleod, 1883, p. 200)

There is little doubt this discovery has immensely impacted the pecuniary fortunes of humanity. On a more specific level, one can precisely say that it has extensively influenced the pecuniary fortunes of commercial bankers—debt shop entrepreneurs.

Pecuniary fortunes represent nothing more than a collective biophysical debt in terms of available energy and materials held by one's neighbors and future generations. This topic is later addressed in a more comprehensive manner in Chapter 5, which underscores the crucial fact that monetary phenomena are deeply interconnected with biophysical sustainability. Due to modern institutional, not constitutional, allowances, commercial banks can create and extinguish money from and into nothing. Entities authorized to issue money often struggle to resist the temptation to issue more. Macleod (1883, p. 285) stressed the rampant use of credit and its grave consequences over 140 years ago: "It is chiefly by the excessive use of *credit* that *over-production* is brought about, which causes those terrible catastrophes called *commercial crises.*"

The creation of debt by the commercial banking system is one of the most perilous aspects when considering national control over money. Case in point, notable, hated debates about how to manage checking accounts in the United States emerged shortly after the stock market crash of 1929 (Phillips, 1995). These discussions gave birth to the Chicago Plan for banking reform, a plan endorsed by Knight and other eminent economists based at the University of Chicago. Intriguingly, Soddy's (1926) book, *Wealth, Virtual Wealth and Debt,* significantly influenced the concepts behind the Chicago Plan. During that same era, approximately, Fisher (1936) penned his work *100% Money,* which provided practical guidelines for overseeing checking accounts in the reserve banking system. Regrettably, the Chicago Plan was never put into effect.

Proposals of 100% money or a fixed reserve ratio—ideas that frequently surface following a financial crisis—fall short of providing satisfactory stabilization for financial systems. This is particularly true when the processes of issuance and deletion of bankmoney are almost exclusively under the control of commercial bankers. Ultimately, the relation between money and credit is not a mathematical function—it hinges on numerous factors. As Macleod (1894, p. 734) pointed out, "*credit* is not a fixed definite function of *money*: but it is, if we may coin the term, a *contingent* function of *money*." The momentum of each type of money or money substitute within the economic system—determined by multiplying the amount of each type of money or money substitute by its respective velocity of circulation—is impossible to pinpoint precisely.

If newly created demand deposits (bankmoney) only circulated among a crediting bank's customers, the circulation would merely entail re-bookings of that bank's overnight liabilities between its customers. However, this scenario is seldom, if ever, the case.

Customers regularly withdraw cash and transfer money to customers at other banks. In the case of cash withdrawal, commercial banks often convert some of their central bank reserve account into cash. Simultaneously, their liability and assets decrease by the same amount. A cashless domestic payment, for example, between Customer A at Bank C and Customer B at Bank D, is achieved in a simple way: suppose Customer A wants to transfer $100 to Customer B. Customer A asks Bank C to transfer $100 from their account to Customer B's account at Bank D. Bank C asks the central bank to send $100 from Bank C's reserve account at the central bank to Bank D's reserve account. The central bank subtracts $100 from Bank C's reserve account and adds that same amount to Bank D's reserve account. A notice is immediately sent from the central bank to Bank D, and from Bank D to Customer B.

The indirect method of transferring deposits from one bank's customer to another bank's customer, described above and shown in Fig. 2.1, is termed *monetary intermediation*. This type of intermediation stands in contrast to *financial intermediation*, which is concerned with the creation of credit and debt relations by non-banks, based on existing demand deposits at commercial banks (see Huber, 2017, pp. 64–67). The essential distinction lies between the role of banks in creating and transferring bankmoney (monetary intermediation), and the role of a wide variety of non-bank financial institutions in taking already existing bankmoney to lend or invest it (financial intermediation). The banking business today

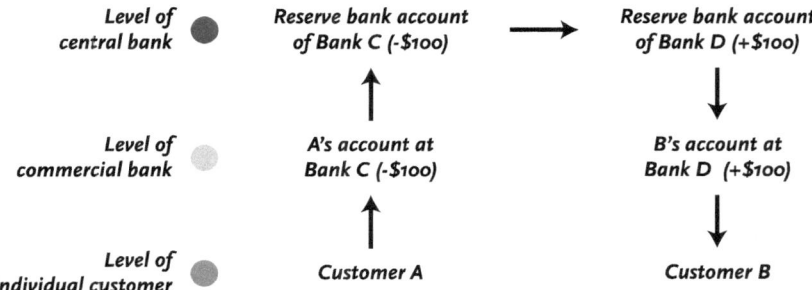

Fig. 2.1 A simple schematic representation of a transfer of money from Customer A to Customer B; the numbers indicated in the figure represent the net balance compared against the initial balance

is primarily about creating as well as temporarily deactivating and reactivating bankmoney. Financial intermediation, on the other hand, has been rapidly expanding since the 1980s.

Money movements between banks often cancel each other out at the end of each day. Those that do not are leveraged by the intraday clearing mechanism, through which the actual amount of central bank reserves used to balance imbalances between different banks is generally a relatively smaller proportion of the total value of the daily transactions (Ryan-Collins et al., 2012). Such a trading practice is fundamental to the concept of a reserve banking system. That is, any commercial bank can manage by keeping just a small fraction of the entire amounts involved in transactions in a current account at the central bank.

Expansion of money creation presupposes the existence of two crucial institutional elements of the cooperative process: (1) mutual acceptance of credits or debts across the entire commercial banking sector, smoothing out intraday imbalances through a clearing mechanism, and (2) the willingness of central banks to cooperate in response to both the creation and deletion of money by commercial banks, reactively creating or absorbing coins, banknotes, and central bank reserves. Demand deposits are predominantly created by market demand, making the banking industry heavily reliant on various non-banking entities willing to undertake debt. These non-banks encompass: (1) households, businesses, and public bodies in need of loans, (2) corporations and governmental bodies issuing fresh equities or bonds, and (3) financial institutions and other monetary investors seeking leverage (Huber, 2017). Additionally, banks increase credit every time they acquire financial and tangible assets for their personal accounts, recording them as assets.

Transactions through which demand deposits are deleted are the reverse of deposit-creating transactions. The amount of money in existence increases so long as the debt held by non-banks exceeds the debt repaid or called in; it decreases when the debt repaid or called in surpasses the amount borrowed by non-banks. However, the expansion of demand deposits is a general trend in the modern economy. New debts are arranged whenever previous debts are successfully repaid, and new bankmoney tends to "show up." Three main channels of demand deposit expansion exist—real estate and mortgages, speculative leverage, and government debt. The yield of these three channels represents, for instance, roughly three-quarters of bank credit across the European Union and the United States (Huber, 2017).

The emphasis in this chapter so far has been on the first unnatural power of the banking sector exercised through debt expansion. Non-banks, including shadow banks, cannot create or delete bankmoney themselves. However, the activities of shadow banking play a crucial role in the circulation of on-lending money already created by commercial banks. While it is important to emphasize the distinction between monetary and financial intermediation, we argue that, in the case of shadow banks, this distinction does not make much sense. Contrary to popular belief, shadow banks do not create demand deposits but rather accelerate the circulation of debts in the form of deposits and bank refinancing activities.

Shadow banking has been an integral part of the regulated banking system for more than three decades, largely increasing access to money substitutes, which do not directly align with demand deposits in terms of securitization, repurchase agreements, derivatives, and other financial market activities. The securitization process, for instance, transforms a set of illiquid loans into a sellable security with a distinct rating in a secondary financial market. It is essential to remember that none of these activities were available to commercial banks before 1980, except for repurchase agreements (Fein, 2013). According to certain economists within the United States Federal Reserve System (the Fed), regulated banking organizations have significantly contributed to the swift evolution of the asset-backed securitization process (Cetorelli & Peristiani, 2012).

Additionally, a sizable portion of recent financial intermediation seems more influenced by regulatory supervision than previously considered.

The fact that traditional banks operate under the watchful eye of banking regulators provides compelling evidence that shadow banking is indeed intimately related to the business area of commercial banks. As typically observed, access to bank deposits as a source of funding for non-bank affiliates of banks is limited by Section 23A of the Federal Reserve Act. This section stipulates that such bank deposits are restricted to approximately 10% of the bank's capital for any single affiliate and 20% of the bank's capital for affiliates in total. However, the Fed itself has encouraged securitization activities by permitting banks to sponsor and guarantee asset-based commercial paper entities, irrespective of the limitations set by Section 23A of the Federal Reserve Act. Essentially, operating subsidiaries of banks are not bound by the abovementioned limits. Shadow banking activities, when undertaken by both banks and their affiliates, have adequate access to both insured and uninsured deposits as a funding source and additional leverage (Fein, 2013). The relaxation of key regulatory requirements by banking regulators further propelled the transformation of banking organizations into shadow banks. Notably, regulators adjusted their capital standards to promote the securitization of residential mortgage loans in a manner that amplified the level of systemic risk across the banking network.

In conjunction with the issue of shadow banks, the auditor's role must be considered. Acting as "public watchdogs," auditors must maintain complete independence from their clients. Auditing is an act that demands absolute fidelity to public interests. Unfortunately, both accountants serving as auditors and their external partners have a strong financial incentive to keep their clients satisfied. The risks to accountant independence became increasingly apparent in the public eye at the start of the twenty-first century when certain auditors were implicated in a wave of major corporate scandals, such as those involving Enron, WorldCom, and HealthSouth (Wiggins et al., 2019).

The case of Ernst & Young (EY) is particularly revealing. EY, employed by Lehman Brothers as an auditor, was perceived as a trusted advisor concerning Lehman's business activities. In other words, EY was trusted beyond merely reviewing Lehman's financial statements. As an investment bank, Lehman habitually employed sale and repurchase agreements (repos) to meet its daily short-term borrowing requirements, borrowing funds on a short-term basis against assets it presented as collateral.

According to the regulations in place before Lehman Brothers' collapse, a repo was reported as a sale or financing *only if the company maintained effective control over the assets used as collateral for the short-term loan*. However, in the Repo 105 transactions, Lehman argued that it surrendered effective control over such collateralized assets since it received only $100 for each $105 in posted collateral.

The "105" in "Repo 105" emerged in this way. According to Wiggins et al. (2019, p. 109), Lehman effectively removed "from its balance sheet the securities transferred as collateral, reducing assets. The cash received was not booked as borrowings, and the obligation to repay/repurchase was not booked as an increase in liabilities." How could such egregious misconduct have been so fortuitously overlooked by the auditors at EY?

The misconduct of Lehman Brothers in essence reminds us of the reverse manipulation seen in the case of "capitalization of costs," or "how to make an expense become an asset," listed as an accounting technique in Smith's (1992) book *Accounting for Growth*. To clarify, "[c]apitalisation is a process by which an item which would otherwise be seen as an expense or debit in the profit and loss account is instead classified as an asset in the balance sheet" (Smith, 1992, p. 101).

2.4   Commercial Banks, Central Banks, and Governments: A Hidden Triangle of Collusion

Regrettably, the misdoings of Lehman Brothers and other such mischievous commercial banks run deeper than mere private sector matters. This section explores a collusive triad formed by a government, its respective central bank, and commercial banks. Within this triad, commercial banks play a dominant role.

The general public may not realize that central banks, in certain respects, function as private entities. The Bank of Japan exemplifies this reality. The vast majority of Japanese citizens may not be aware that the Bank of Japan operates as a type of private company, sanctioned by the Bank of Japan Act, with its shares traded on the JASDAQ in Tokyo. Government securities such as Japanese national bonds are recorded as assets, not liabilities, in the Bank of Japan's accounts. As of June 20, 2019, Japanese government securities exceeded ¥473trn, comprising 84% of the Bank of Japan's total assets and 46% of outstanding Japanese national bonds! These bonds represent a debt to Japan but are considered assets for "private entities," including the Bank of Japan. Therefore, within the current accounting framework, Japanese national bonds at the Bank of Japan can be regarded as wealth. While considering a central bank as a private entity may be conceptually challenging, the Bank of Japan does function essentially as a private corporation. This situation is mirrored in other developed societies, including the United States.

Article 23.1 of the Bank of Japan Act states, "The Governor and the Deputy Governors are appointed by the Cabinet, subject to the consent of the House of Representatives and the House of Councilors" (MOJ, 2023a, art. 23-1). However, if the Bank of Japan were a national organization truly representing democratically elected Japanese citizens, both the Governor and the Deputy Governors would be nominated by these Houses. There is no effective system in place to facilitate rigorous oversight of monetary control by a national organization. Consequently, the central bank carries out monetary control in Japan autonomously. To facilitate this, the Bank of Japan Act stipulates that "[t]he Bank of Japan's autonomy regarding currency and monetary control must be respected" (MOJ, 2023a, art. 3-1). This makes the Bank of Japan independent from the influence of the Diet, Japan's elected representatives. In addition, changes to the articles of the Bank of Japan Act can be made without the Diet's consent, as "[a]ny amendments to the articles of incorporation do not come into effect unless authorized by the Minister of Finance and the Prime Minister" (MOJ, 2023a, art. 11-2). Banking licenses and capital requirements are similarly authorized without the Diet's approval. The Banking Act stipulates both that, "A person may not engage in banking unless licensed by the Prime Minister to do so" (MOJ, 2023b, art. 4-1), and, "[t]he stated capital of a bank must be equal to or more than the amount specified by Cabinet Order" (MOJ, 2023b, art. 5-1). It should now be clear that none of Japanese banking activity is directly controlled by elected representatives. Similar situations are found in the United States and many other contemporary societies.

Neither the Bank of Japan nor the United States Fed can truly claim to represent democratically elected citizens. As mentioned, central bank reserves are employed for short-term interbank transactions to compensate for imbalances between commercial banks. Therefore, the turnover rate ("velocity") of central bank reserves is expected to be significantly higher than that of commercial bankmoney. The velocity of reserve circulation would far exceed that of deposit circulation, leading to a scenario in which vast amounts of demand deposits and a minuscule reserve quantity are compatible. When properly managed, this compatibility is the *raison d'être* of the reserve banking system. However, the fact remains that deposit creation, initiated by commercial banks, is done forcibly, and the central bank reactively responds to such a force by adjusting the amount of central reserve compatible with the deposit creation speed of commercial banks. This is the premise behind cashless fractional reserve banking. Central banks are severely subjected to the ability of commercial banks to create debts, being how the banking sector determines the vast majority of the money supply stock in public and interbank circulation. The quantity of reserves for interbank circulation should be properly regarded as a part of demand deposits or debts created by commercial banks. Central banks have become a crucial and inseparable component of the overall banking sector's activities.

It should be noted that the ratio of central bankmoney varies not only due to legal requirements but also with the spirit of the times. Ryan-Collins et al. (2012, p. 75) report that directly before the 2007–2008 financial crisis, the ratio of central bankmoney, mostly cash in the vault, to bankmoney was roughly 1.25%, rising to slightly over 7% by 2010. A similar trend pre- and post-financial crisis can be observed in the Eurozone and the United States. In summary, central bankmoney in developed countries is but a small, albeit fundamental, fraction of commercial bankmoney.

Part of the reserve banking system seems to be built on a myth that suggests the existence of deposits or debts as a function of the central bank. This myth parallels the notion that banks are supposed to maintain a stock of money that can accommodate the concept of the Roman *mutuum* as a contingent obligation. Commercial banks exploit this reserve banking myth. As the previous data on reserve banking systems worldwide have shown, the reserve ratio is zero or close to zero for most major currency areas. Therefore, commercial banks dodge paying refinancing costs by entirely avoiding interest payments—these banks can create debt without incurring significant refinancing costs. Non-banks, including the general public, on the other hand, must fully finance their businesses, borrowing money with positive interest. The centralized reserve banking system hands commercial banks an incredible, dubious, wholly unearned privilege.

The abovementioned myth concerning the interplay of commercial and central banks cannot be sustained. Under current practices, commercial banks proactively and nearly independently determine their actions, regardless of reserve stock held at the central bank. Misunderstanding about the role of central banks also influenced a faulty rationale behind the Chicago Plan. Proposals for 100% money or a fixed reserve ratio, often presented shortly after a financial crisis, misleadingly fail to entirely address the drawbacks of treating deposits as contingent.

A further myth, pervasive on the point, is that central banks control interest rates—careful adjustments that ripple throughout the economy, both nationally and internationally. However, one can reasonably argue that if a central bank raises or lowers its prime rate, this adjustment does not apply immediate pressure on commercial banks. With fractional reserve banking, where the reserve fraction is usually zero or nearly zero, in developed countries at least, banks can virtually avoid all refinancing costs, given a significant bank turnover. Changes in the prime interest rate have some impact but do not serve as a decisive signal for commercial banks, though they are allegedly critical for determining loan interest rates. This is apparent from the fact that commercial banks nearly entirely control the money supply, through deposit creation.

One last privilege granted to commercial banks related to fractional reserve banking is worth discussing—the *exclusion of client money rule*. Unlike companies and non-bank financial intermediaries, banks are not obliged to follow a client money rule that mandates the segregation of their own money and customer money into separate accounts. For commercial banks, this would mean maintaining these funds in distinct central bank accounts. Yet, all outgoing and incoming payments of a bank are processed through a single operational central bank account, for that commercial bank, irrespective of whether the payment originates from or is headed to customers or is from or to the bank itself. This concept was illustrated in Fig. 2.1. The practice of using a shared account for a bank and its customers greatly facilitates distributed transactions. This significantly benefits the bank's proprietary transactions, which would otherwise necessitate a more expensive reserve base. J. P. Morgan, for instance, comments on this topic as follows:

> Unless otherwise agreed, money received from or held on clients' behalf by a J.P. Morgan Credit Institution in the course of carrying on designated investment business will be held by that J.P. Morgan Credit Institution as banker and not as trustee. Consequently, it will not be subject to the protections provided by the Client Money Rules and as such will not be segregated from the J.P. Morgan Credit Institution's own money and may be used in the course of the J.P. Morgan Credit Institution's business.

(Morgan, 2023)

The misuse of cashless payments by commercial banks, leveraging the reserve banking system, is indeed a troubling practice. Remember that under Roman Law, if a person deposited money into a bank account, that money was considered the absolute property of the banker until the person demanded it back. A similar arrangement persists today, illustrating a remarkable privilege indeed!

Today, one of the main channels through which money substitutes overshoot is public finance, particularly in countries with an aging population. Public finance is a debt consisting mainly of sovereign bonds and treasury bills. Banking consortia act as underwriters for such public debt. The banking sector retains a significant portion of the sovereign debt on its books and sells the rest on the open market—a lucrative source of profit. As a result, more than half of the public debt is funded by newly created deposits originating from new bond issues, and the rest by secondary on-lending of already existing bankmoney (Huber, 2017).

Figure 2.2 illustrates that, due to lax control over the issuance of new bonds in Japan, the balance of total outstanding bonds continuously accrues. This balance includes construction bonds and deficit-covering bonds. Until 1998, outstanding deficit-covering bonds constituted less than ¥100trn. However, post-1998, this value began to increase at a brisk pace. By 2004, outstanding deficit-covering bonds exceeded outstanding construction bonds. In 2019, deficit-covering bonds accounted for over 68% of the total outstanding bonds. Currently, national bonds are issued primarily to offset the constant accumulation of debt. This particular situation in Japan can be accurately described as *running insolvency*. Alternatively, it can be understood as *eternal debt financing*.

Creating national bonds through government deficit is another aspect of the active involvement of commercial banks in the capital market, accelerating the momentum of money substitutes. A close collaboration between the government, the central bank, and commercial banks is yet again observed.

It should be noted that the Bank of Japan is not legally authorized to underwrite newly issued national bonds. However, it has been demonstrated that the Bank of Japan's recent monetary policy—the radical quantitative easing policy that was initiated in April 2013—is not compatible with the original intentions of Article 5 of the Public Finance Act. The volume of national bonds presently held by the Bank of Japan is

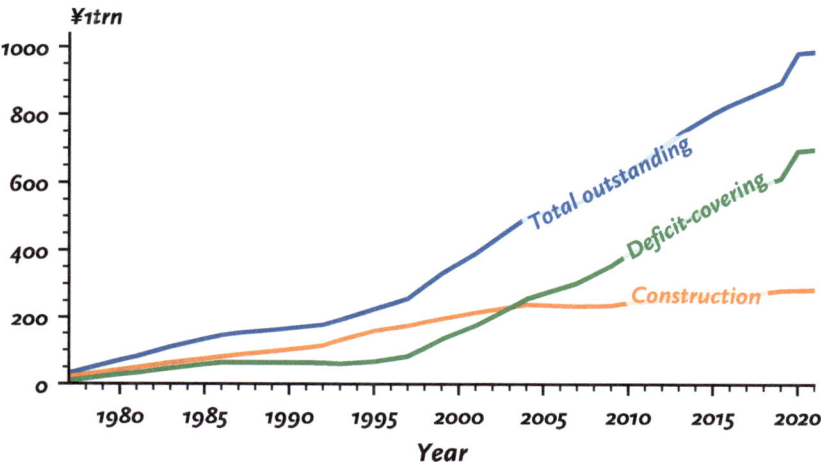

Fig. 2.2 Outstanding national bonds in Japan 1977–2021, detailing total outstanding bonds, construction bonds, and deficit-covering bonds (*Data source* MOF [2023])

greater than that of the commercial banks in Japan. To combat the COVID-19 crisis, from 2020 to the present, Japan has remained heavily dependent on the issuance of national bonds to fill the deficit gap.

2.5   Conclusion

In this chapter, we have traced the history of money creation by banks, leading up to the present demand deposit system. It should be clear to readers that, substantively, bankmoney tends toward endless expansion per two myths. The reserve banking system is built on these two myths: (1) the idea that the existence of deposits or debts is a function of the reserve stock at the central bank, and (2) the idea that the prime rate policy by central banks directly and immediately leads to commercial banks correspondingly adjusting the prevailing loan interest rate on the capital market. These two myths completely ignore that commercial banks can initiate an increase or decrease in the money supply through demand deposit creation, effectively independent of central bank policy associated with the reserve ratio or the prime rate. As shown in this chapter, commercial banks have an *unnatural power to create demand deposits out of nothing*, plus a variety of other related privileges, including the exclusion of the client money rule. Commercial banks also closely collaborate with the government. In fact, the government is heavily involved in the process of creating general liquidity through increasing reliance on the issuance of national bonds to accommodate a quasi-eternal budget deficit. Commercial banks are given the institutional power to underwrite such national bonds after they are issued.

According to a document prepared by the St. Louis Fed, "Supplement to Banking & Monetary Statistics Section 14 Gold," the global gold reserve held by central banks and governments at the end of 1945 was divided as follows: $20.1bn (60.3%) for the United States and $13.2bn for the rest of the world. By the end of 1960, these reserves had shifted to $17.8bn (46.7%) for the United States and $20.3bn for the rest of the world. Given that the United States held more than 60% of the world's gold reserves in 1945, the adoption of the gold standard post-World War II might not seem so unreasonable from their perspective. In retrospect, however, it has become apparent that the gold standard was flawed from the outset. It only related to banknotes and overlooked deposit creation on accounts—a key component of the money supply. Demand deposits (money in bank accounts) evolved into a standard means of cashless payment in bank-managed clearing procedures among companies, government entities, wealthy families, and banks themselves. This leaves one to wonder why the gold standard was adopted in the first place.

Managing the amount of credit creation is indeed challenging. To illustrate this, consider a historical lesson from eighteenth-century Scotland, which demonstrates the emergence of the modern banking system, the appropriate use of a credit system, and the profound influence such a system can wield. The credit system in question was known as cash credit, and its introduction significantly spurred Scotland's wealth accumulation (Macleod, 1883). This system allowed for the creation of a massive quantity of highly liquid, exchangeable property out of nothing, based solely on the will of the bank and its customers. As expected with such an innovative system, the banks in eighteenth-century Scotland typically confined their advances to a reasonable amount and always secured multiple sureties to cover potential losses. "Third-party" members in Scotland—those with superior credit ratings, known as "cautioners" in Scottish law—kept a watchful eye on the proceedings of borrowers and ensured the right of borrowers to review their bank account at any time and, if necessary, to close it.

Interestingly, cash credits were liberally extended across Scotland, including to sectors like agriculture and public works. Here, it is essential to remember that the principle of the "limits of credit" corresponds to the present value of the estimated future product. In agriculture and public works, credit was *employed as productive capital, exactly mirroring the original intended use of money*. The remarkable physical outcomes of this application, which propelled Scotland from the lowest depths of barbarism up to her current proud position over approximately 170 years, are a testament to the influence of cash credit.

To fully comprehend the intricacies of the cash credit system in Scotland, it is crucial to understand the difference between commercial paper and accommodation paper. Commercial paper represents an unsecured, short-term debt instrument issued by a corporation, commonly used for financing accounts receivable, inventories, and addressing short-term liabilities. Commercial paper maturities rarely extend beyond nine months and are usually issued at a discount rate from face value, mirroring current market interest rates. In today's economic climate, commercial paper plays a pivotal role in the capital market, bolstering shadow banking activities backed by commercial banks.

Conversely, the impressive results enjoyed by the Scottish people can be attributed to the use of accommodation paper. This negotiable instrument is signed by one party, the accommodating party, as a favor to another party, the accommodated party. Without receiving any consideration in return, the accommodating party acts as a guarantor for the accommodated party, who remains primarily liable. The purpose of this arrangement is to facilitate the accommodated party in acquiring money or credit. If the accommodated party fails to repay the money lent, the accommodation paper assures that the accommodating party will otherwise settle the debt on the specified date.

Meulen (1917, p. 42, emphasis added), in his work, *Industrial Justice through Banking Reform: An Outline of a Policy of Individualism*, states:

> Whatever effectively announces to the community the desire and ability of the individual to produce a future profit within a given period is a sound credit token, irrespective of what material it may be made, or *by whom issued*.

In extending this perspective, Meulen essentially offers an invitation to commercial banks. The question of to whom the right of money issuance should be conferred becomes a moot point. As sovereign fiat, coins, and notes are legal tender, signifying that they are money which, by legal mandate, must be accepted in debt settlement. Bankmoney, on the other hand, is technically not legal tender. However, it does represent official money, as it is acknowledged by government administrators as a common means of payment, including for tax purposes.

Despite the lack of legislation equating bankmoney with treasury coins and central bank notes, bankmoney is regularly accepted and utilized by all, including public bodies, with the exception of the central bank. To the best of the authors' knowledge, there are no constitutional rules that relate to the interpretation of bankmoney as legal tender. This topic will be explored in greater detail in Chapter 8.

References

Allais, M. (1987). The Credit Mechanism and Its Implications. In G. R. Feiwel (Ed.), *Arrow and the Foundations of the Theory of Economic Policy* (pp. 491–561). Macmillan Press. https://doi.org/10.1007/978-1-349-07357-3

Cetorelli, N., & Peristiani, S. (2012). *The Role of Banks in Asset Securitization* (pp. 47–63). Federal Reserve Bank of New York.

Della Valle, G., King, D., & Veyrune, R. (2022). *Monetary and Capital Markets Department: Technical Assistance Handbook—Reserve Requirements* (pp. 1–31). International Monetary Fund. https://elischolar.library.yale.edu/ypfs-documents/14900

Fein, M. L. (2013). The Shadow Banking Charade. *SSRN Electronic Journal* [Preprint]. https://doi.org/10.2139/ssrn.2218812

Fisher, I. (1936). *100% Money* (Revised ed,). Adelphi Company.

Galbraith, J. K. (1975). *Money: Whence It Came, Where It Went*. André Deutsch, Limited.

Graeber, D. (2011). *Debt: The First 5,000 Years*. Melville House Publishing.

Huber, J. (2017). *Sovereign Money: Beyond Reserve Banking*. Palgrave Macmillan. https://doi.org/10.1007/978-3-319-42174-2

Morgan, J. P. (2023). *Terms of Business—Client Money Rules | J.P. Morgan Securities*. JPMorgan Chase and Company. https://www.jpmorgan.com/disclosures/terms-of-business-client-money-rules. Accessed 25 June 2023.

Macleod, H. D. (1883). *The Theory and Practice of Banking* (4th ed., Vol. 1). Longmans, Green, Reader and Dyer.

Macleod, H. D. (1889). *The Theory of Credit* (1st ed., Vol. 1). Longmans, Green and Company.

Macleod, H. D. (1894). *The Theory of Credit* (2nd ed., Vol. 2). Longmans, Green and Company.

Meulen, H. (1917). *Industrial Justice Through Banking Reform: An Outline of a Policy of Individualism*. Richard J. James.

Mitchell-Innes, A. (1913). What Is Money? *The Banking Law Journal, 30*(5), 377–408.

MOF. (2023). *Financial Materials (財政に関する資料)*. Ministry of Finance (財務省), Japan. https://www.mof.go.jp/tax_policy/summary/condition/a02.htm. Accessed 26 June 2023.

MOJ. (2023a). *Bank of Japan Act (日本銀行法)*. Ministry of Justice (法務省), Japan. https://www.japaneselawtranslation.go.jp/en/laws/view/3788#je_ch1at11. Accessed 25 June 2023.

MOJ. (2023b). *Banking Act (銀行法)*. Ministry of Justice (法務省), Japan. https://www.japaneselawtranslation.go.jp/en/laws/view/3601#je_ch1at7. Accessed 25 June 2023.

Phillips, R. J. (1995). *The Chicago Plan & New Deal Banking Reform*. M.E. Sharpe.

Ruskin, J. (1877). *Unto This Last: Four Essays on the First Principles of Political Economy* (2nd ed.). George Allen.

Ryan-Collins, J., et al. (2012). *Where Does Money Come From? A Guide to the UK Monetary and Banking System* (2nd ed.). New Economics Foundation.

Samuelson, P. A., & Nordhaus, W. D. (2010). *Economics* (19th ed.). McGraw-Hill Irwin (The McGraw-Hill Series Economics).

Schumpeter, J. A. (1951). *The Theory of Economic Development: An Inquiry into Profits, Capital, Credit, Interest, and the Business Cycle*. Harvard University Press.

Smith, A. (1976). *An Inquiry into the Nature and Causes of the Wealth of Nations*. University of Chicago Press. (Original work published 1776).

Smith, T. (1992). *Accounting for Growth: Stripping the Camouflage from Company Accounts*. Century Business.

Soddy, F. (1926). *Wealth, Virtual Wealth and Debt: The Solution of the Economic Paradox* (1st ed.). E. P. Dutton and Company.

Soddy, F. (1934). *The Role of Money: What It Should Be, Contrasted with What It Has Become*. George Routledge and Sons, Limited.

Wiggins, R., Bennett, R., & Metrick, A. (2019). The Lehman Brothers Bankruptcy D: The Role of Ernst & Young. *Journal of Financial Crises, 1*(1), 100–123.

CHAPTER 3

The Second Unnatural Power Given to Commercial Banks: The Origin of Money Interest and Its Implication for Sustainability

But if your theory is found to be against the second law of thermodynamics I can give you no hope; there is nothing for it but to collapse in deepest humiliation. This exaltation of the second law is not unreasonable.

(Eddington, 1928, p. 74)

3.1 Introduction

In the modern age, people usually accept the practice of discounting based on positive money interest without serious deliberation. A prevailing mindset that "money must grow over time" appears to infiltrate all sorts of financial transactions. Money lenders, for instance, are expected to receive the principal amount lent plus additional interest payment on the loan principal. We contend that this additional interest payment, from a physical law standpoint, is unnatural.

At present, all individuals holding monetary assets can earn interest on those assets if they deposit their funds in a savings account. Yet, it is crucial to remember that funds in savings accounts depend first on the creation of bankmoney, in the form of deposits, by commercial banks. Such was explored in Chapter 2. The underlying mechanics of this system dictate that essentially no person can own a savings account without the initial financial bedrock provided by commercial banks, as well as the issuance

K. T. Mayumi and A. Renner, *Reconsidering the Privileged Powers of Banks*, https://doi.org/10.1007/978-981-99-6058-3_3

of coins and banknotes. Furthermore, considering the lending aspects of the system, one should note a striking disparity: the interest rates levied on borrowers generally exceed those offered to savings account holders.

In Chapter 1, it was discussed how Aristotle strongly denounced the practice of usury, being the charging of an unreasonably high-interest rate, or essentially for Aristotle, an interest rate set such that net profits are made on money lent. Leveraging a similar ethical argument, shortly after the stock market crash of 1929, Keynes endorsed two of *The Economic Journal's* symposiums,[1] both discussing the rationale behind charging interest from money borrowers. This chapter provides a more fundamental scientific and institutional analysis of the origin of money interest—an alternative theory of money interest's origins. The discussion also sheds light on an often-neglected yet vital element to consider when allocating exhaustible resources across generations.

It is crucial first to clarify why the fact that money grows over time is unnatural. Section 2.2 of Chapter 2 elaborated on the reasons behind the existence of money. Following the reasoning of Macleod and Soddy, money is used to facilitate final settlement in unequal economic transactions. To fulfill this purpose, the quality of money as money must remain constant over time. Conversely, if the quality of money as money were to fluctuate continually, the function of money in line with its purpose could never be achieved. This is a core reason why precious, less chemically reactive metals like gold and silver have frequently been used in coinage.

Strictly speaking, nothing in our world completely escapes changes in quality. Hot water, for instance, always tends to decrease its temperature, and the heat within dissipates into the surroundings until no more heat is available for human use. Energy always tends to dissipate. Physical entities, either natural or human-made, also undergo constant change through a process of decay. This universal phenomenon is scientifically represented by the second law of thermodynamics—the entropy law. The entropy law dictates that both energy and matter decay over time, degrading their quality until they reach a state where they are no longer available for human use. Money, as a physical entity, cannot escape the effects of entropy. Coins and banknotes degrade qualitatively in accordance with the entropy law. Similarly, magnetic devices storing money as a type of

---

[1] Refer to *The Economic Journal*'s "Saving and Usury: A Symposium" (see Cannan et al., 1932) and "Usury and the Canonists: Continued" (see Dennis & Somerville, 1932).

information in computerized systems also decay over time, necessitating their regular replacement. Thus, the material aspect of money is subject to inevitable qualitative decay. Consequently, an unnatural institutional and legal arrangement is needed to guarantee that money will ultimately be exchangeable for goods and services in the future. One such example can be found in Section 100.5 of the United States Code of Federal Regulations, which stipulates:

> Lawfully held mutilated paper currency of the United States may be submitted for examination in accord with the provisions in this subpart. Such currency may be redeemed at face amount if sufficient remnants of any relevant security feature and clearly more than one-half of the original note remains.
>
> (LII, 2023)

While the material aspect of money decays over time and experiences structural changes, money can still maintain its functional role over time through the occasional replacement of its decayed material constituents.

Before discussing two essential aspects of the unnatural power used to counter the limitations set by the entropy law, Sect. 3.2 provides a brief overview of the emergence of monetary interest from the perspective of conventional economic analysis. Consideration is given to several distinguished economists, including Böhm-Bawerk, Fisher, Gesell, Keynes, and Wicksell. Section 3.3 then presents an alternative theory of the origin of monetary interest. We argue that while money as a material object decays over time, undergoing structural changes, money as money can preserve its functional role through the occasional replacement of decayed material constituents. This arrangement gives money lenders an unnatural ability to expect interest payment from money borrowers.

It is important to note that physicists often reject the idea of material decay as part of the entropic decay process, invoking Einstein's equivalence between energy and matter to ignore material decay. We challenge this dogmatic stance by referencing the works of two thermodynamics giants, Clausius and Planck. Following a thorough examination of Clausius's (1867b) disgregation analysis and Planck's (1945) extensive investigation into the meaning of entropy, we conclude that the diffusion process of matter can indeed be treated as part of a genuine process of entropic decay. This understanding, heterodox as it may be, vindicates our theory of the origin of monetary interest. Section 3.3 demonstrates, firstly, that differentiating between functional decay and material decay provides insights into the emergence of monetary interest. Secondly, it underlines that despite the unavoidable nature of material decay, the functional facet of money is safeguarded through legal and institutional means.

Section 3.4 explores whether the discounting practice, based on the existence of positive money interest and applied to the allocation of exhaustible resources across generations, can be justified from a biophysical sustainability perspective. When allocating scarce exhaustible resources, if the discounting practice of conventional economic analysis is adopted, the physical *quantity of such exhaustible resources allocated consistently diminishes over time*. Metaphorically, one must decrease their rice consumption over time. Naturally, this type of allocation scheme is challenging for people to accept. The discounting practice, based on the existence of money interest, is incompatible with the constraint set by the entropy law. It is necessary to accept the statement of Eddington, the great astrophysicist quoted at the start of this chapter, that no hope should be placed against the entropy law.

Section 3.5 summarizes the chapter's two primary topics and presents the fundamental ideas of Soddy and Georgescu-Roegen. Their work forms the core rationale for writing this book and offers new biophysical foundations from which future economics can be learned.

3.2   A Brief Review of Conventional Economic Analysis of Money Interest

Gesell's "free money" theory considers money as a medium of exchange that should depreciate over time in accordance with commodity depreciation. In this theory, monetary devaluation matches commodity depreciation through the periodic stamping of currency, an act symbolizing partial devaluation. Free money theory does not advocate for negative interest rates; instead, it aims to eliminate the positive interest attributed to money, discouraging unnecessary withholding of money from the market and promoting money's role solely as a means of exchange. However, this theory does not address the specific method of conducting monetary depreciation against various commodities.

Money interest is not an inherent feature of the structural constituent of money. Rather, it emerges from the perpetuation of the functional aspect of money—unnatural in view of physical law. Gesell's free money theory overlooks this essential difference between the structural and functional decay of money. Gesell writes:

> The *physical properties of the traditional form of money* (metal money and paper-money) allow it to be withdrawn indefinitely from the market without material cost of storage [...]. The merchant can therefore force the possessors of wares to make him a special payment in return for the fact that he refrains from arbitrarily postponing, delaying, or, if necessary, preventing the exchange of wares by holding back his money. [....] This special payment, sharply to be distinguished from commercial profit, cannot of course be exacted by the ordinary purchaser [...]. Only the merchant approaching the market as owner of money can exact this tribute.
>
> (Gesell, 1916/1958, pp. 374–375, emphasis added)

Gesell refers to this special payment to money owners as basic interest. Although Gesell rightly focuses on interest rates, he perhaps failed to fully grasp the critical distinction between the *origin* of money interest and the *level* of money interest.

Following Gesell, Fisher demonstrated that the interest rate of any given good cannot turn negative if that good can be stored without significant expense, a condition met by money in the modern institutional setting. On this subject, Fisher (1930, p. 41) stated that "as long as our monetary standard is gold or other imperishable commodity, so that there is always the opportunity to hoard some of it, no rate of interest expressed therein is likely to fall to zero, much less to fall below zero." In making this statement, Fisher, like Gesell, failed to grasp the true nature of money, which certainly does not stem from money's durable structural foundation in materials like precious metals. Fisher, like Gesell, overlooked the key distinction and relationship between material and functional decay and thus failed to explain the origin of money interest.

Fisher and Keynes were contemporaries who both valued Gesell's attempt to eliminate the special advantages given to those who hold money. In his seminal book, *The General Theory of Employment, Interest, and Money*, Keynes investigated the nature of money and monetary interest in relation to commodity-based interests. His analysis included a study of the relationship between a commodity's current price and its future contractual price: "Let us suppose that the spot price of wheat is £100 per 100 quarters, the price of the 'future' contract for wheat for delivery a year hence is £107 per 100 quarters, and that the money-rate of interest is 5 percent; what is the wheat-rate of interest?" (Keynes, 2013,

p. 223). Keynes then concludes that the wheat-own interest rate is -2%, because $1-1.05/1.07 \approx 2$. In reaching this conclusion, Keynes appears to have taken for granted the existence of a positive monetary interest rate that is comparatively higher than the wheat-own interest rate. However, Keynes could not pinpoint why the monetary interest rate exceeded commodity-based interests. Like Gesell and Fisher, his argument does not fully explain the origin of money interest.

Economists have also devoted significant effort to the subject of capital interest (see Böhm-Bawerk, 1890, 1891). According to strict economic logic, the owner of present goods, viewed as capital, must bear an extra cost for their storage to impede inevitable degradation over time governed by the entropy law. Consequently, the owner naturally assigns a greater subjective value to future goods of like kind and quantity. This is because they do not require any extra storage cost in the present, and the owner may choose to enjoy their consumption immediately if desired. The entropy law dictates that perishable goods should be consumed sooner rather than later to circumvent storage costs. However, again due to the entropy law, such economic cost per se cannot strictly or absolutely ensure the lasting quality and form of goods.[2]

Wicksell (1893/1970, p. 108), however, offers an important counterpoint on perishability and economic cost: "This is certainly a great exaggeration." Wicksell implies that Böhm-Bawerk's examples, which include ice and fruit, should not be viewed as exceptions; all foodstuffs are inherently perishable goods. The critical flaw in Böhm-Bawerk's theory seems to be an inadequate consideration of structural decay, which relates to the entropy law. Böhm-Bawerk approached the issue of capital interest as though all goods could be considered durable. Therefore, his theory does not apply to capital interest generally but is only relevant to money loans, wherein the loaned funds are *immediately required* for goods or investment activity.

If Böhm-Bawerk's assertion—that present goods hold a higher subjective value than future goods—depicts the borrower's predicament, it is understandable. In the role of an investor, the borrower must procure present goods as swiftly as possible to benefit from the investment funds yet to be received. Therefore, in monetary terms, present goods must hold greater importance for the borrower than future goods.

---

[2] Unsurprisingly, Böhm-Bawerk did not support his argument by resort to the entropy law. Nevertheless, the thrust is the same where we employ it.

Böhm-Bawerk may perhaps have deliberately refrained from disclosing his implicit belief that positive money interest should be socially accepted, a view he formulated without any theoretical substantiation. Indeed, Böhm-Bawerk was a fervent advocate of the modern financial mindset, subscribing to the principle that "money must grow over time."

3.3   THE MEANING OF ENTROPY BY CLAUSIUS AND PLANCK: A CLUE TO IDENTIFYING THE ORIGIN OF MONEY INTEREST

Certain readers well-acquainted with physics may have raised in Chapter 1 or may raise in this chapter a strong objection to our line of argumentation regarding the entropy law, which, allegedly, is concerned only with energy. Fermi, in his famous text, *Thermodynamics*, states that "thermodynamics is mainly concerned with the transformation of heat [(energy)] into mechanical work and the opposite transformations of mechanical work into heat [(energy)]" (Fermi, 1936, p. ix). On the contrary, two giants of physics, Clausius (1867b) and Planck (1945), directly support our claim—the entropy concept refers to both energy and matter inseparably.

Money in the form of coins or banknotes, as well as in an electromagnetic ("digital") form, if understood from a material perspective, does, in fact, decay over time in dutiful obedience to the entropy law. Every physical entity—from coffee mugs to money—is a compound of a material constituent and a functional component. The functional component indicates a particular purpose for the use of that specific material object, substantively defined.

For nearly all physical entities—except money—the structural and functional elements are inseparable and as the structural constituent decays, its corresponding functional component concurrently decays. Once the structure of a physical entity decays beyond a certain threshold, the entity ceases to fulfill the specific purpose for which it was initially intended (Mayumi, 2019, 2020; Mayumi & Giampietro, 2018; Renner et al., 2021).

To identify a biophysical origin of interest, it is first essential to revisit the perspectives on material dispersion put forth by Clausius and Planck. Clausius (1867b) suggested to measure the degree of dispersion of matter using a then-new variable, *disgregation*. Entropy, in this context, is the aggregate of disgregation and heat dispersion, with the latter receiving the majority of attention in the contemporary discourse on thermodynamics.

Clausius understood disgregation to be more fundamental than entropy in the sense that disgregation can be used to interpret entropy itself in terms of both heat dispersion and material dispersion (Klein, 1969). Although disgregation is generally understood as a relic of times past, it remains highly relevant in our discussion on the origin of money interest. Gibbs (1906) himself strongly endorsed the concept in Clausius's obituary, citing the work of Maxwell and Boltzmann as evidence. Gibbs (1906) also clarified Clausius's intuition by stating that disgregation in a thermodynamic system does not depend on the velocities of a system's particles. In that respect, disgregation differs from the entropy concept, which is commonly understood to refer simply to the dissipation of energy based on the distribution of particle velocities.

According to Clausius (1867a, 1867b), entropy S can be expressed in two terms—heat dispersion (dH/T) and disgregation (dZ). The following relation summarizes:

$$dS = \frac{dH}{T} + dZ. \tag{3.1}$$

In (3.1), it must be emphasized that whereas S is a thermodynamic state function, thus dS an exact differential, H/T and Z are process functions, thus dH/T and dZ are inexact differentials. In other words, the dH/T and dZ terms in (3.1) cannot be represented by a thermodynamic state function—they are path-dependent variables, impossible to quantify separately (Mayumi & Giampietro, 2018). All the same, (3.1) serves to confirm that the concept of entropy is related in a most fundamental way to *both* heat dispersion *and* material dispersion.

Regrettably, Clausius's exploration of material dispersion did not maintain its relevance in the field of thermodynamics for long. Nonetheless, when considering the specific scenario of two perfect gases diffusing, it has consistently been more insightful to interpret the diffusion phenomenon on a material level rather than a thermal one. As Planck suggests in his *Treatise on Thermodynamics* (Planck, 1945, p. 104 footnote, emphasis added), in the instance of the diffusion of two perfect gases, "it would be more to the point to *speak of a dissipation of matter than of a dissipation of energy.*" Planck does not mention Clausius's concept of disgregation, but he firmly grasps the essence of entropy, which must include material dispersion or decay. He further clarifies:

> The real meaning of the second law has frequently been looked for in a 'dissipation of energy.' This view, proceeding, as it does, from the irreversible phenomena of conduction and radiation of heat, *presents only one side of the question*. There are irreversible processes in which the final and initial states show exactly the same form of energy, *e.g.* the *diffusion* of two perfect gases, or further *dilution* of a dilute solution. Such processes are accompanied by *no perceptible transference of heat, nor by external work, nor by any noticeable transformation of energy. They occur only for the reason that they lead to an appreciable increase of the entropy.*
>
> (Planck, 1945, pp. 103–104, emphasis added)

Just as Einstein's mass–energy equivalence has taught us to be flexible in our consideration of energy and matter,[3] and despite the neglect of physicists toward the more general meaning of entropy in favor of an energy dogma, the "dissipation of matter," or disgregation, is indeed a vitally important concept when interpreting the physical meaning of entropy. After all, the entropy law reflects the ubiquitous daily observation that heat tends to dissipate over time and that material objects tend to decay over time. Soddy, a Nobel laureate in chemistry who later made significant contributions to economics and monetary theory, wrote on the matter:

> It is true that twentieth-century science, since Einstein's Theory of Relativity, attempts the fusion of the two laws [(the conservation of energy and matter)] into one. It is possible that energy and matter may be equivalent at a definite exchange ratio, just as Joule showed, a century ago, was the case for heat and work or any other form of energy. If so, one law will do for both [energy and matter]. *But this is yet only a view, for the actual conversion of the one into the other has yet neither been proved to occur, nor can it be practically carried out.*
>
> (Soddy, 1931, p. 30, emphasis added)

---

[3] Breit and Wheeler (1934) made a theoretical calculation of the production of positron-electron pairs as a result of the collision of two light quanta. Such a process, the Breit–Wheeler process, proposing to create matter from energy alone, has yet to materialize. It must be safely recognized that matter cannot be created by energy alone on a large scale on this planet.

Drawing a parallel to Clausius's exploration of material dispersion, Georgescu-Roegen endeavored to create a theoretical foundation for the large-scale phenomenon of material dissipation. Specifically, he strived to encapsulate the dissipation of mineral resources in the economic process in what he termed the "fourth law of thermodynamics" (Georgescu-Roegen, 1977). It is observed that the bulk dissipation of matter amplifies with the scale of economic production, consumption, and disposal, and preserving large-scale material structures poses a formidable challenge in contemporary industrial society. As such, Georgescu-Roegen's fourth law bears significant implications for the sustainable management of concentrated mineral resources. Nevertheless, his fourth law of thermodynamics is not, and cannot be, a physical law, given that the disgregation facet of entropy is not a total differential and, thus, does not lead to a thermodynamic state function.

The inevitable dispersion and decay of material structure, as captured by disgregation, can offer an explanation of *the origin of money interest*. To elucidate this point, call from the top of this passage again to mind that each material object has a physical form (the structural constituent) and a specific function (the functional component). These two aspects, structural and functional, are inseparable. As the physical form of a material object deteriorates due to the entropy law, its associated functional component *concurrently deteriorates*. Once the physical form of a material object has decayed beyond a certain threshold, the object no longer serves the specific function for which it was initially designed.

The uniqueness of money arises from the fact that the functional component can persist independently of its physical form. Structurally speaking, it is self-evident that tangible currencies such as banknotes and coins cannot evade the entropy law. However, when structural decay does transpire (be it low-level entropic or otherwise), the decayed physical form of tangible currency is readily substituted under modern legal arrangements with money issuers, as demonstrated in the cases of Japan and the United States.

The idea of a "cashless economy" assumes that money is pure information and that the second law of thermodynamics does not apply. On the contrary, just like in a "cash economy," digital currency stored on various mediums (magnetic tapes, hard disks, solid-state drives) and transmitted through different channels (fiber optic, twisted pair, coaxial cable) is subject to the entropy law. The replacement of the structural constituent of electronic money occurs more frequently than one might expect in that catastrophic storage failure is just one of the impetus of the structural replacement of digital currency. All electronic storage and transmission of financial data heavily rely on checksums to ensure data integrity, detect bit errors, and either correct those errors or request data retransmission/recopying and replacement. An invalid checksum signals the embedding technology to structurally replace a digital currency token. In summary, the curious ability of money to maintain its function despite inevitable material decay is not rooted in physical law. Rather, it is a legal and institutional arrangement that grants money an entirely unnatural, functionally superior position compared to other material objects.

Over time, as money retains its ability to fulfill its original purpose while material goods lose their capacity to do so, two qualitative gaps emerge—a structural gap and a functional gap. Figure 3.1 illustrates the emergence of such qualitative gaps. The upper left presents a conceptual view of the expanding functional gap resulting from money's defiance of functional decay. In the lower left, the graph is rotated counterclockwise around the origin to provide a more intuitive illustration of money's superior position, resulting from the emerging qualitative gap in function. The two graphs on the left indicate the functional decay gap between goods and money as money. The upper right presents a conceptual view of the expanding *qualitative gap in structure* emerging from institutional arrangements of free structural replacement. In the lower right, the graph is similarly rotated counterclockwise. The two graphs on the right represent the structural decay gap between goods and money as material objects.

As money gradually achieves qualitative superiority over economic goods, *an interest on money emerges*. In this way, the discounting of monetary value in conventional economics can conceivably be justified. However, it is crucial to emphasize once again that the superiority of money—allowing its owner, in principle, to dictate transaction timings with those who need to sell goods to avoid ruinous structural and functional decay of those goods—is a result of institutional and legal arrangements rather than any inherent aspect of money itself.

Scientists should accord due respect and consideration to the general public's everyday experiences and commonsense knowledge. Georgescu-Roegen (1979), in his unique style, endorsed this commonsense counter-argument to energy dogmatists. He continues to stand as an exemplary defender of the general population's admirable observations.

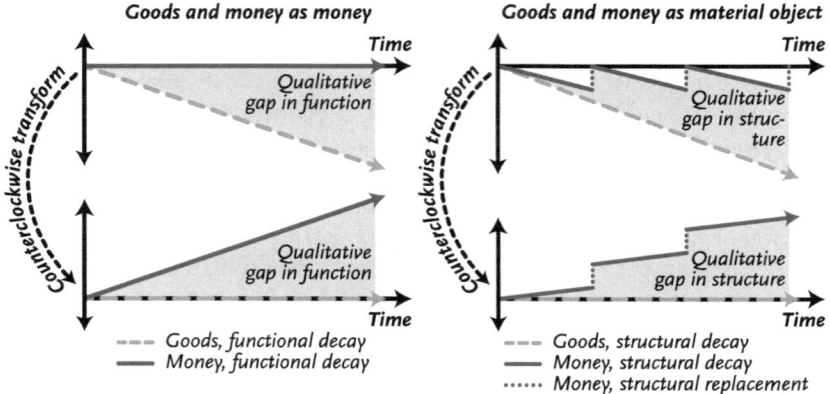

Fig. 3.1 Illustration of the origin of money interest with counterclockwise transforms for clarity, allowing the trends to be more easily read

3.4   Discounting Practices Undermine Sustainability: The Case of the Intergenerational Allocation of Exhaustible Resources

The well-known textbook by Samuelson and Nordhaus (2010, p. 4) asserts, "*Economics* is the study of how societies use scarce resources to produce valuable goods and services and distribute them among different individuals." They further propose that "goods are scarce and society must use its resources efficiently" (Samuelson & Nordhaus, 2010, p. 4). This efficiency criterion necessitates that users of cost–benefit analysis (CBA) in conventional economics adopt a project that maximizes the present monetary value of net economic benefits over a *specified time period*, subject to a set of constraints, following the selection of a specific discount rate.

In line with the efficiency criterion suggested by Samuelson and Nordhaus, we explore the allocation of a specific exhaustible energy resource (such as natural gas) over n years to maximize the present monetary value of net economic benefits, given the total reserve of natural gas $\overline{Q}$ and a positive discount rate r. Without resorting to differential calculus, we can determine an allegedly optimal allocation of natural gas over n years. It is important to keep in mind that the purpose of this exercise is to highlight significant flaws in the efficiency criterion when applied to the intergenerational allocation of an exhaustible resource. Such flaws are made evident when one critically evaluates the discounting practices often uncritically adopted in CBA (see also Mayumi & Renner, 2022).

To properly identify and highlight these flaws without introducing unnecessary complications, we will assume that the demand line for natural gas and the marginal (monetary) cost for extraction remain constant over n years, as shown on the left in Fig. 3.2. From the perspective of conventional economics, demand equals the marginal (monetary) benefit for a representative individual—essentially, a price schedule that a representative individual is willing to pay. The difference between the demand line and marginal cost represents the net marginal benefit (MNB_i), signifying the net monetary benefit gained in year i if an additional, infinitesimal allocation of natural gas is made (hence the term "marginal"). The right side of Fig. 3.2 illustrates the present value of the marginal net benefit ($PVMNB_i$), assuming discount rate r.

$$PVMNB_i = \frac{MNB_i}{(1+r)^{i-1}} = \frac{a - bq_i - c}{(1+r)^{i-1}}$$

Readers are encouraged to understand that if more than q_{i*} of the resource is allocated in each year i, the total present monetary value will decrease. This is the logic of conventional economic analysis! In this case, the scarcity problem does not manifest. However, if $\overline{Q} < \sum_1^n q_{i*}$ the scarcity problem emerges, necessitating consideration of the efficient resource allocation of natural gas over n years.

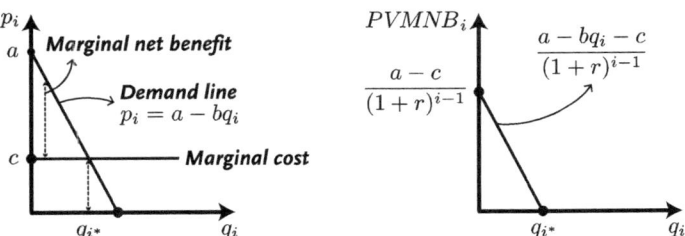

Fig. 3.2 Demand p_i, marginal cost c, and present value of marginal net benefit ($PVMNB_i$) for the period i

How, then, is it possible to find an allocation scheme that maximizes the total present monetary value? The fact that the discount rate r is positive proves essential. A comprehensive mathematical treatment using a recursive method, which aptly reveals the mechanistic view in conventional economics along with an appropriate explanation, is provided in Appendix. For readers less inclined toward mathematics, the solution is presented here without further explanation:

$$q_1 > q_2 > q_3 > \cdots > q_n.$$

This inequality is vital in relation to discounting practice and to the general premise of this book. If the conventional economic rule of discounting—maximizing the present value of the total benefit for the arbitrary years case—is adopted, future generations are doomed to receive a diminishing amount of the exhaustible resource, natural gas, in this example. In certain respects, such a result is a logical consequence of adopting a discounting practice that is...unnatural. We, as a society, must sincerely reconsider whether such a practice of discounting, which most modern individuals accept without deep reflection, is justifiable. The endorsement of the second law of thermodynamics by Eddington, the luminary astrophysics quoted at the beginning of this chapter, must be given full appreciation.

Our analysis of exhaustible resource distribution across generations reveals serious doubts about the capability of conventional economic methods to guide collective decisions, particularly those concerning the intergenerational allocation of resources. It is difficult to expect a hypothetical representative economic agent, optimizing a personal objective function under self-centered constraints, to meaningfully inform collective decision-making processes. However, cost–benefit analysis (CBA), often employed in situations involving collective interests, endorses this individualistic approach. As Georgescu-Roegen (1977) wisely stated, future generations will need to eat and drink just as urgently as the present ones do. Bromley (1990) also argued against the direct adoption of such an individualistic perspective in collective decision-making, asserting that individual-level efficiency has hardly anything to do with group-level efficiency. Jevons (1871/1965), a pioneering figure in neoclassical economics, himself lamented the myopic nature of individual economic agents, while Strotz (1955) demonstrated that the eventual behavior of an economic agent is rarely consistent with their initially calculated "optimal" solution. Indeed, the practice of discounting is only defensible when evaluating money from an individual perspective. Furthermore, the concept of discounting money bears no relevance to the biophysical underpinnings of life, particularly net primary production in the biosphere.

Stiglitz (1997) claims that traditional economic analysis is primarily concerned with just "the next 50–60 years." But how does he rationalize this 50–60 year timeframe? The immense impact of monetary discounting is astonishing when spelled out. In 50 years, $1 depreciates to $0.61 at a 1% discount rate, $0.087 at 5%, and $0.0085 at 10%. In terms of biophysical discounting—discounting of natural resources—the implications of this practice appear incredibly unjust for future generations, particularly given the accelerating pace of change in our contemporary world. The practice of discounting gives rise to significant concerns where the crux of the issue is a clash between individual financial perspectives and collective biophysical viewpoints. This will be discussed in greater detail in Chapter 5, which explores the dual nature of money.

3.5   Conclusion

The two main topics in this chapter encompass an alternative theory of the origin of money interest and a critical examination of the discounting practice for exhaustible resource allocation while accepting the existence of a positive money interest rate.

The differentiation between structural and functional decay is a crucial theoretical aspect when exploring the genesis of monetary interest. We argue that the entropy law, which outlines qualitative change in energy and material objects, can be employed to understand material decay, utilizing Clausius's concept of disgregation. Despite the inescapable reality of material decay, the functional facet of money is legally and institutionally safeguarded. A prime example of such legal structures can be seen in the handling of United States banknotes. Essentially, every nation has a similar institutional setup.

Every physical entity possesses a material structure, or a *structural constituent*, and a specific purpose, a *functional component*. As the structural constituent undergoes decay, per the entropy law, its functional counterpart also deteriorates. In eventuality, the physical object may no longer fulfill the specific role for which it was initially created. However, the functional component is maintained, even if money as a physical object undergoes material decay. Therefore, legal and institutional frameworks afford money, and indeed any form of money or money substitute, collectively termed "general liquidity" and including coins and banknotes, a significantly advantageous position compared to goods in economic exchange.

A qualitative disparity arises and widens as money retains its purpose while other physical entities lose theirs. Only money increases quantitatively over time, in tune with its positive interest rate. In this sense, the discounting of monetary value is justified within conventional economics. The supremacy of money enables its owner, in theory, to determine the timing of transactions with those who must sell goods to curb the structural decay of said goods.

The second topic, the practice of discounting considering positive interest applied to exhaustible resources, is shown to undermine biophysical sustainability. How is it possible to compel the unborn to receive less of an exhaustible resource? Conventional economics uncritically accepts the financialized mentality, which encourages the practice of discounting. A drastic reorientation concerning the problem of discounting practice should be seriously considered by every citizen interested in establishing a more sustainable and equitable future society.

Concerning the second topic, a brief discussion about two greats, Soddy and Georgescu-Roegen, is attempted here. Several fundamental ideas introduced in this book are inspired by their seminal contributions, including ideas in Chapter 2 and this chapter, where the two unnatural powers granted to banks are examined. Neither scholar has been given the attention they justly deserve.

Soddy made remarkable contributions to understanding the role of money and the shortcomings of banking systems, advocating for close scrutiny of the issues that plague our monetary and banking systems. However, economists of his time mocked, generally speaking, his analysis. A notable instance involves the economic historian Higgs, who edited the new edition of Palgrave's *Dictionary of Political Economy* in the 1920s. Higgs critiqued Soddy's work, *Cartesian Economics: The Bearing of Physical Science upon State Stewardship*, stating in the *Economic Journal*: "[I]t is sad to see so distinguished a physicist transformed into a pitiable purveyor of economics fallacies" (Higgs, 1923, p. 101). It seems Higgs may have failed to comprehend the biophysical foundations of economic systems, a concept otherwise eloquently explained by Soddy in his work. If Higgs were alive today, he would perhaps react with astonishment to find that much of Soddy's advice, for instance to discard the gold standard and adopt flexible exchange rates, is now universallys employed. It is a little-known fact that the influential banking reform ideas of the Chicago economists in the early 1930 were largely based on Soddy's proposal for a 100% reserve on demand deposits.

One of the significant proponents of the Chicago Plan, discussed in Chapter 2, Knight supported Soddy's (1926) ideas developed in *Wealth, Virtual Wealth and Debt*, providing a highly favorable review in *The Saturday Review of Literature*: "[I]f this book leads economists to go into [the problems] as they deserve it will render the world a service of inestimable value. [...] The concepts of wealth, virtual wealth (money), and debt emphasize important and neglected distinctions, and in general it is a brilliantly written and brilliantly suggestive and stimulating book" (Knight, 1927, p. 732).

Jevons, one of the four founders[4] of neoclassical economics, from which modern, conventional economics gradually formed, declared that his effort to understand economics was, fundamentally, a "tracing out of the *mechanics of self-interest and utility*" (Jevons, 1871/1965, pp. xvii–xviii, emphasis added). The founders of conventional economics were perhaps in rapture of Le Verrier and Adams's discovery of Neptune, or some such thing, being a discovery contemporary to the founders made by way of paper and pencil operations and the equations of Newtonian mechanics. On the other hand, Georgescu-Roegen (1975, p. 348) criticized the "indiscriminate attachment to the mechanistic dogma." Even today, conventional economists perceive the economic process as a mechanical analog consisting of principles of energy and mass conservation and an optimal strategy of maximization or minimization. The dire consequences of this perspective are highlighted in Sect. 3.4, considering the case of exhaustible resource allocation.

In systems interpreted through the lens of classical mechanics, energy and matter entering a process emerge in precisely the same quantity, adhering to the principle of conservation. Naturally, the analysis of mechanics, concerned with changes in locomotion, often leads to unrealistic descriptions and conclusions when applied to the economic process. Among the highly questionable assumptions are: (1) the economic process is reversible, (2) the future path of the economic process is

---

[4] The four fathers of neoclassical economics are identified with frequency as Jevons, Gosses, Menger, and Walras.

predictable, (3) variables in the economic process are under human control, (4) an initial equilibrium is always recoverable after a perturbing external force is removed, and (5) the economic process is circular and cannot possibly affect the environment.

Georgescu-Roegen's work stands in opposition to this epistemology, instead relying on the entropy law as a theoretical edifice. Life, in essence, is an entropic process. Organisms maintain their highly ordered structures by absorbing low entropy from their environment to compensate for continuous internal entropic degradation. From a biophysical perspective, the economic process is also an irreversible entropic process, taking in low-entropy energy and matter and expelling high-entropy energy and matter into the environment. A radically different perspective on the economic process is required where these observations are taken into account: (1) the economic process is irreversible, (2) the future path of the economic process is uncertain due to entropic indeterminacy, (3) the economic process is not always under human control, (4) the economic process is continuously changing and frequently disrupted by unexpected events, and (5) the economic process is not an isolated self-sustaining system and cannot proceed without continuous energy and material exchange with the environment—an exchange that irrevocably alters the environment.

Georgescu-Roegen's insightful analytical ability allowed him to identify the analytical fallacy of the mechanistic epistemology of conventional economists. Georgescu-Roegen, eminent as he was and despite his substantial contributions, was never seriously considered for such recognition as the Sveriges Riksbank Prize in Economic Sciences, though his contributions were no doubt substantial. For the established practitioners of conventional economics, to bestow such an honor on Georgescu-Roegen would be equivalent to signing their own professional obituaries—a clear impossibility. Politics aside, the contributions of Soddy and Georgescu-Roegen, which emphasize the importance of the second law of thermodynamics, must receive due attention from both conventional and heterodox economists and, more importantly, from the general public. The public should be aware of the profound connection between monetary phenomena and biophysical sustainability in relation to entropy.

Appendix 3.A

Continuing the discussion in Sect. 3.4, an allocation scheme that maximizes the total present monetary value is given full mathematical treatment in this appendix. Discount rate r is assumed positive, and the 2-year case is considered first.

If half of $\overline{Q}$ is allocated to each year, an inequality $a - \frac{b\overline{Q}}{2} - c > \frac{a - \frac{b\overline{Q}}{2} - c}{1+r}$ is obtained, namely, $PVMNB_1 > PVMNB_2$. Remembering that each $PVMNB_i$ ($i = 1$ or 2) is a decreasing function of q_i, as was shown in Fig. 3.2, more natural gas allocation to the first year, represented by $\Delta q_1 > 0$, and less natural gas allocation, represented by $\Delta q_2 = -\Delta q_1 < 0$, will increase the total monetary benefit for two years. During this process, $PVMNB_1$ decreases and $PVMNB_2$ increases, finally reaching equality: $PVMNB_1 = PVMNB_2$. Let the difference between $PVMNB_1$ and $PVMNB_2$ be referred to as d_2.

$$d_2 = a - \frac{b\overline{Q}}{2} - c - \frac{a - \frac{b\overline{Q}}{2} - c}{1+r}$$

is a constant. The absolute values of the slopes of $PVMNB_1$ and $PVMNB_2$ are b and $\frac{b}{1+r}$, respectively. To completely fill the gap d_2, changes in q_1 and q_2, in other words Δq_1 and Δq_2, where Δ represents a marginal change, must satisfy the following two conditions:

$$d_2 = b\Delta q_1 - \frac{b\Delta q_2}{1+r} \tag{3.A.1}$$

$$\Delta q_1 + \Delta q_2 = 0. \tag{3.A.2}$$

The latter condition comes from the total reserve of natural gas, given at the level of $\overline{Q}$. It is straightforward to solve this linear equation with two unknowns, Δq_1 and Δq_2. So, for the 2-year case, the maximum present value of the total benefit is reached when $PVMNB_1 = PVMNB_2$ is realized.

Assuming that recursive procedures are similarly conducted up to the case of $n - 1$ years, we can now solve for the case of n years. First, allocate equally $\overline{Q}/n$ to each year. Then, because r is positive, the following inequality relations must be fulfilled.

$$a - \frac{b\overline{Q}}{n} - c > \frac{a - \frac{b\overline{Q}}{n} - c}{1+r} > \cdots > \frac{a - \frac{b\overline{Q}}{n} - c}{(1+r)^{n-1}}$$

so

$$PVMNB_1 > PVMNB_2 > \cdots > PVMNB_n.$$

However, assuming that the case of $n-1$ years has already been solved, we can establish the following inequality:

$$PVMNB_1 = PVMNB_2 = \cdots = PVMNB_{n-1} > PVMNB_n.$$

Let the difference between $PVMNB_i$ and $PVMNB_n$ ($i = 1, 2, 3, \ldots, n-1$) be d_n, which is a constant. It is possible to make all the $PVMNB_i$ terms equal by filling the gap d_n, by solving the following linear equation with n unknowns: Δq_1, Δq_2, up to Δq_n.

$$d_n = b\Delta q_1 - \frac{b\Delta q_n}{(1+r)^{n-1}}$$

$$d_n = \frac{b\Delta q_2}{1+r} - \frac{b\Delta q_n}{(1+r)^{n-1}}$$

...

$$d_n = \frac{b\Delta q_{n-1}}{(1+r)^{n-2}} - \frac{b\Delta q_n}{(1+r)^{n-1}}$$

and

$$\Delta q_1 + \Delta q_2 + \cdots + \Delta q_n = 0.$$

The recursive procedure presented here reminds us of the basic principle nearly always used in mechanics. Feynman (2011, §4–5), the acclaimed 1965 winner of the Nobel Prize in Physics, states the essence of mechanics using marginal changes: "This approach is called *the principle of virtual work*, because in order to apply this argument we had to *imagine* that the structure moves a little—even though it is not really *moving* or even *movable*. We use the very small imagined motion to apply the principle of conservation of energy."

In our case, what is conserved is the total reserve $\overline{Q}$ and the constraint is represented by the relation $\Delta q_1 + \Delta q_2 + \cdots + \Delta q_n = 0$. So, our procedure is exactly the same as the mechanical application of conservation of energy to the exhaustible resource allocation problem across generations.

To repeat, the maximum present value of total benefit is realized when all $PVMNB_i$ terms are equalized:

$$PVMNB_i = \frac{a - bq_i - c}{(1 + r)^{i-1}}.$$

However, since the discount rate r is positive

$$\frac{a - bq_i - c}{(1 + r)^{i-1}} = \frac{a - bq_{i+1} - c}{(1 + r)^{i}} < \frac{a - bq_{i+1} - c}{(1 + r)^{i-1}}$$

and comparing the first term and the third term, we obtain

$$\frac{a - bq_i - c}{(1 + r)^{i-1}} < \frac{a - bq_{i+1} - c}{(1 + r)^{i-1}}.$$

Multiplying both sides by $(1 + r)^{i-1}$ and rearranging the two numerators, noticing the term $-b$ is negative, we obtain the final result, $q_i > q_{i+1}$ for $i = 1, 2, \ldots, n - 1$. That is

$$q_1 > q_2 > q_3 > \cdots > q_n.$$

References

Böhm-Bawerk, E. V. (1890). *Capital and Interest* (W. Smart, Trans.). Macmillan.

Böhm-Bawerk, E. V. (1891). *The Positive Theory of Capital* (W. Smart, Trans.). Macmillan.

Breit, G., & Wheeler, J. A. (1934). Collision of Two Light Quanta. *Physical Review, 46*(12), 1087–1091. https://doi.org/10.1103/PhysRev.46.1087

Bromley, D. W. (1990). The Ideology of Efficiency: Searching for a Theory of Policy Analysis. *Journal of Environmental Economics and Management, 19*(1), 86–107. https://doi.org/10.1016/0095-0696(90)90062-4

Cannan, E., et al. (1932). Saving and Usury: A Symposium. *The Economic Journal, 42*(165), 123–141. https://doi.org/10.2307/2223770

Clausius, R. (1867a). On Several Convenient Forms of the Fundamental Equations of the Mechanical Theory of Heat. In T. A. Hirst (Ed.), *The Mechanical Theory of Heat with Its Applications to the Steam-Engine and to the Physical Properties of Bodies* (pp. 327–376). John Van Voorst.

Clausius, R. (1867b). On the Application of the Theorem of the Equivalence of Transformations to Interior Work. In T. A. Hirst (Ed.), *The Mechanical Theory of Heat with Its Applications to the Steam-Engine and to the Physical Properties of Bodies* (pp. 215–266). John Van Voorst.

Dennis, L., & Somerville, H. (1932). Usury and the Canonists: Continued. *The Economic Journal, 42*(166), 312–323. https://doi.org/10.2307/2223851

Eddington, A. S. (1928). *The Nature of the Physical World*. Macmillan.

Fermi, E. (1936). *Thermodynamics*. Dover.

Feynman, R. P. (2011). *The Feynman Lectures on Physics* (3 vol., New Millennium ed.). Basic Books.

Fisher, I. (1930). *The Theory of Interest*. Macmillan.

Georgescu-Roegen, N. (1975). Energy and Economic Myths. *Southern Economic Journal, 41*(3), 347–381. https://doi.org/10.2307/1056148

Georgescu-Roegen, N. (1977). The Steady State and Ecological Salvation: A Thermodynamic Analysis. *BioScience, 27*(4), 266–270. https://doi.org/10.2307/1297702

Georgescu-Roegen, N. (1979). Myths About Energy and Matter. *Growth and Change, 10*(1), 16–23. https://doi.org/10.1111/j.1468-2257.1979.tb00819.x

Gesell, S. (1958). *The Natural Economic Order* (Revised English ed., P. Pye, Trans.). Peter Owen Limited. (Original work published 1916).

Gibbs, J. W. (1906). Rudolf Julius Emanuel Clausius. In *The Scientific Papers of J. Willard Gibbs* (pp. 261–267). Longmans, Green, and Company.

Higgs, H. (1923). Frederick Soddy, M.A., F.R.S. Cartesian Economics: The Bearing of Physical Science upon State Stewardship. *The Economic Journal, 33*(129), 100–101. https://doi.org/10.2307/2222927

Jevons, W. S. (1965). *The Theory of Political Economy* (5th ed.). A.M. Kelley (Reprints of Economic Classics). (Original work published 1871).

Keynes, J. M. (2013). *The General Theory of Employment, Interest and Money* (Vol. 7, A. Robinson & D. Moggridge, Eds.). Cambridge University Press (The Collected Writings of John Maynard Keynes).

Klein, M. J. (1969). Gibbs on Clausius. *Historical Studies in the Physical Sciences, 1*, 127–149. https://doi.org/10.2307/27757297

Knight, F. H. (1927). Review of "Money: Wealth, Virtual Wealth and Debt" by Frederick Soddy. *The Saturday Review of Literature*, p. 732.

LII. (2023). *31 Cfr § 100.5—Mutilated Paper Currency*. Legal Information Institute. https://www.law.cornell.edu/cfr/text/31/100.5. Accessed 25 June 2023.

Mayumi, K. (2020). *Sustainable Energy and Economics in an Aging Population: Lessons from Japan*. Springer (Lecture Notes in Energy). https://doi.org/10.1007/978-3-030-43225-6

Mayumi, K., & Giampietro, M. (2018). Money as the Potential Cause of the Tragedy of the Commons. *Romanian Journal of Economic Forecasting, 21*(2), 151–156.

Mayumi, K., & Renner, A. (2022). Misapplication of Conventional Economic Analysis to Climate Change from the Post-normal Science Perspective: The

"Social Cost of Carbon" Myth. *Frontiers in Climate*, *4*. https://doi.org/10. 3389/fclim.2022.865514

Mayumi, K. T. (2019). Money, Credit and Interest in Light of Unconventional Perspective. In *Nonviolent Political Economy*. Routledge.

Planck, M. (1945). *Treatise on Thermodynamics* (3rd ed., A. Ogg, Trans.). Dover.

Renner, A., Daly, H., & Mayumi, K. (2021). The Dual Nature of Money: Why Monetary Systems Matter for Equitable Bioeconomy. *Environmental Economics and Policy Studies*, *23*(4), 749–760. https://doi.org/10.1007/s10 018-021-00309-7

Samuelson, P. A., & Nordhaus, W. D. (2010). *Economics* (19th ed.). McGraw-Hill Irwin (The McGraw-Hill Series Economics).

Soddy, F. (1926). *Wealth, Virtual Wealth and Debt: The Solution of the Economic Paradox* (1st ed.). E. P. Dutton and Company.

Soddy, F. (1931). *Money Versus Man: A Statement of the World Problem from the Standpoint of the New Economics*. Elkin Mathews and Marrot.

Stiglitz, J. E. (1997). Georgescu-Roegen Versus Solow/Stiglitz. *Ecological Economics*, *22*(3), 269–270. https://doi.org/10.1016/S0921-8009(97)000 92-X

Strotz, R. H. (1955). Myopia and Inconsistency in Dynamic Utility Maximization. *The Review of Economic Studies*, *23*(3), 165–180. https://doi.org/10. 2307/2295722

Wicksell, K. (1970). *Value, Capital and Rent*. A.M. Kelley (Reprints of Economic Classics). (Original work published 1893).

CHAPTER 4

Lucrative Financial Activities and Their Close Relation to the Solvency of Society

For money was intended to be used in exchange, but not to increase at interest. And this term interest, which means the birth of money from money, is applied to the breeding of money because the offspring resembles the parent. Wherefore of all modes of making wealth this is the most unnatural.

(Aristotle, 1885, p. 19)

4.1 INTRODUCTION

Reflecting on money's fundamental ability to be exchanged for goods, services, and alternative forms of general liquidity, it appears natural that all economic actors, including business entities such as commercial banks and political entities such as nation-states, tend toward an acute desire to obtain the right to issue money—in particular, money that grows in tune with a positive interest rate over time once created. Building on the foundation set in Chapters 2 and 3, this chapter contributes four additional points to the story.

Section 4.2 considers the issue of how much interest payment can be expected to accumulate, theoretically, from one unit of principal. The theory and its mathematical formalization were historically investigated by three greats—Macleod, Soddy, and Allais, to which homage is paid by initializing the archetypical mathematical form as "the MSA relation." The MSA relation formally illustrates the temptation strongly felt by those

67

K. T. Mayumi and A. Renner, *Reconsidering the Privileged Powers of Banks*, https://doi.org/10.1007/978-981-99-6058-3_4

entitled to issue money to issue evermore. The institutionalized nature of this relation allows the banking sector to obtain two units of money out of nothing as *present value*—one unit of money generated as principal and one unit of money generated through interest payment.

Section 4.3 then proposes an alternative loan redemption scheme, standing in contrast to the MSA relation and following one of Soddy's (1934) bright ideas. If the practice of discounting is acceptable, why not discount the loan principal as well? The resulting scheme would generate a situation where total interest still approaches one but where loan principal approaches zero. In such a situation, one unit of money would create only one unit of money, and, in this way, a dramatic debt reduction could be realized.

Any type of interest rate function of time, so long as it is always positive, satisfies both the MSA relation and the discounting loan principal scheme. This mathematical fact derives from the tacit agreement among bankers and economists that any form of capital as purchasing power—assuming a continuous growth of monetary equivalent over time—can be regarded as the present value of the sum of all future interest payments over an infinite time horizon. Sections 4.2 and 4.3 jointly imply that there cannot exist a universally justifiable theory capable of determining a "proper" rate level for both money interest and capital interest. The emergence of the positive interest phenomena is, in this sense, indeed unnatural—only justified by the modern financial mentality, hegemonic, and previously described.

The steady growth and dominance of the financial services sector is a highly conspicuous trend in contemporary society, particularly notable post-World War II. Section 4.4 examines this trend within the corporate world, reflecting on the balance sheets of two representative Japanese "manufacturers," Sony and Toyota. It is not well recognized that the operating income of both companies largely derives from their respective financial divisions. Sony, for instance, is involved in the business of life insurance, non-life insurance, and banking. Toyota arranges car loans, car lease contracts, and car insurance. The balance sheet status of both producers is assessed in relation to the quantitative easing policy of the Bank of Japan, a policy that began in 2013 and ushered in a significant, unfortunate increase in the monetary base.

Taken as a set, Sects. 4.2 through 4.4 contribute to our understanding of the structural foundations of the modern financial privileges granted to the banking sector and other related sectors. These privileges ultimately undermine the possibility of a solvent societal whole. Section 4.5 reveals that contemporary society faces two perennial paradoxes due to the existence of the two unnatural powers. These paradoxes are indeed serious. On the one hand, to increase investment in society's prolonged prosperity, debt must be expanded. On the other hand, efforts toward solvency lead to a painful contraction of the money supply and the potential bankruptcy of society as a whole in the long run (Mark, 1934). The paradoxical nature of this existential predicament is primarily addressed when attention is paid to the following: loans for solvency are repaid in money, or money substitutes, and further loans cannot be extended unless the banking sector creates more money or money substitutes. The critical aspect is that the banking sector and its affiliates tightly control the money stock.

4.2 Present Monetary Value Over Continuous Time and the Macleod–Soddy–Allais Relation

In the natural gas allocation case study presented in Sect. 3.4, the present value of the marginal net benefit for the $(t + 1)^{\text{th}}$ year was discounted by the factor $(1 + i)^t$ where i is the fractional rate of money interest per annum. Therefore, one unit of money in the $(t + 1)^{\text{th}}$ year can be said to have a present value equal to $(1 + i)^{-t} \cdot (1 + i)^{-t}$ is the discount factor for the discrete-time case. But what is the analogous discount factor for the continuous time case?

Dividing a year equally into two periods modifies the previous relation, such that the present value equals $\left(1 + \frac{i}{2}\right)^{-2t}$. If we generalize this procedure, dividing a year equally into k periods instead of the special case of two periods, the present value is equal to $\left(1 + \frac{i}{k}\right)^{-kt}$.

Substituting $K = \frac{k}{i}$ in the expression above, the new expression of the present value of one unit of money is obtained, that is

$$\left(1 + \frac{1}{K}\right)^{-iKt}.$$

If the division process of one year is repeated, meaning K approaches infinity, the following expression, using the Euler's number, $e =$

$\lim_{K \to \infty} \left(1 + \frac{1}{K}\right)^K$, is obtained

$$\lim_{K \to \infty} \left(1 + \frac{1}{K}\right)^{-iKt} = \lim_{K \to \infty} \left[\left(1 + \frac{1}{K}\right)^K\right]^{-it} = e^{-it}.$$

In this way, for the case of continuous time, we can transform the monetary value at the beginning of the year t into the present value by multiplying by the discount factor e^{-it}, assuming interest rate i does not change with time.

Let us consider this case, where interest i is constant. The discount factor e^{-it} can be used to obtain the present monetary value from the monetary value at time t. In this case, the present value of future interest payment (PVFIP) between the initial point 0 and a final point t_f can be calculated using the discount factor e^{-it}:

$$PVFIP = \int_0^{t_f} ie^{-it} dt.$$

The integration of ie^{-it} is $-e^{-it}$ and, substituting t_f and 0 into t in the term $-e^{-it}$, we get

$$PVFIP = \int_0^{t_f} ie^{-it} dt = -e^{-it_f} - \left(-e^{i \times 0}\right) = 1 - e^{-it_f}. \qquad (4.1)$$

where t_f approaches infinity, $PVFIP$ asymptotes to 1 in the case of a constant interest rate. In other words,

$$PVFIP = \int_0^{\infty} ie^{-it} dt = 1.$$

The same final result can be obtained where the interest rate changes over time. For a precise formulation, see Appendix A. To briefly summarize the assertion, wherein with the constant interest rate case we have the term e^{-ix}, in the changing interest rate case we have the term $e^{-\int_0^x i(\tau) d\tau}$. $PVFIP$ between an initial point of time 0 and a final point of time t_f

can be represented as

$$PVFIP\left(0, t_f, i(x) : x \in \left[t_0, t_f\right]\right) = \int_0^{t_f} i(x)e^{-\int_0^x i(\tau)d\tau}\,dx \qquad (4.2)$$

and

$$PVFIP(0, \infty) = 1. \qquad (4.3)$$

The final form shown in relation (4.3), which is a plugging in of values into (4.2), being (4.1) solved over the infinite time horizon, is named here the Macleod–Soddy–Allais (MSA) relation. This naming pays tribute to the work of the three pioneers who first explored its intricacies. The crux of the MSA relation is that it maintains validity, independent of the functional form of the interest rate over time, provided the interest function $i(t)$ remains always positive.

Relations (4.1) and (4.2) exhibit a swift expansion over the initial time periods. However, their growth over time exhibits a noticeable deceleration due to their inherent exponential decay term—essentially, an increasing form. For instance, relation (4.1) entails that the present value of future interest payment (PVFIP) for a 5% interest rate stands at 0.39 in ten years and 0.63 in twenty years. This implies that the present value of total interest received is 39% of the principal in ten years and 63% in twenty years. It is imperative to understand that such hefty interest payment on money exists solely due to the institutional superiority bestowed upon money issuers. There is no inherent justification for interest payments to follow an exponential pattern like the one embedded in the MSA relation. This pattern ultimately empowers money issuers to virtually double their principal from nothing at present value.

Our discourse must now circle back to money's violation of the first and second laws of thermodynamics. From this standpoint, money, conjured from nothing, can be seen to elude functional decay. Owing to money's capacity to grow exponentially, in line with the MSA relation, money issuers are heavily incentivized to offer loans by generating demand deposits as frequently as reasonably feasible. Loan provision is seldom a solitary act. Typically, a new and different contract for additional debt is signed soon after a loan or bond is fully repaid. In such a framework, it appears impossible to prevent the relentless emergence of new money and money substitutes, the general liquidity, in today's global economy.

The MSA relation can be considered a fundamental catalyst of instability in current monetary and financial markets. It is a driver that propels market participants toward asset bubbles (associated with the widespread creation of superfluous assets) and toward insolvency (a condition far more severe than running solvency). The MSA relation posits that the present value of a perpetual flow of interest on one unit of principal equals one unit, and, beginning from any initial time t_0, remains equivalent to one unit *regardless of future interest rate level* fluctuations, provided $i(t)$ remains positive. Succinctly put, this allows money issuers to add one unit of interest payment to their one unit of principal, *ceteris paribus*, thereby creating two units of present monetary value from nothing. Unsurprisingly, entities with the authority to issue money often find it challenging to resist the allure of releasing increasing amounts of money debt, ultimately with a portion into their own coffers, given allowing circumstances. The MSA relation encapsulates the quantitative essence of this temptation.

According to the second law of thermodynamics, structural constituents must inevitably undergo qualitative decay. Chapter 3 explored how money, unlike economic goods, can circumvent functional decay, leading to a qualitative disparity between money and goods over time. The prestigious position bestowed upon money issuers, which includes both private financial institutions and governments—both of which are capable of creating one unit of principal from nothing and procuring an additional unit of money in the form of interest payment—is indeed remarkable. Soddy (1931, p. 25), as paraphrased by Daly (1980, p. 474), stated: "The ruling passion of the age is to convert wealth into debt in order to derive a permanent future income from it—to convert wealth that perishes into debt that endures, debt that does not rot, costs nothing to maintain, and brings in perennial interest." Soddy's contention was that such a conversion is an illusion borne out of the dual nature of money and the fallacy of composition. Although an individual can subsist on the interest from the debt they own, a community as a whole cannot survive on the interest from its members' collective indebtedness.

In the context of national bonds—where the community is a nation and money is loaned to the state—annual interest is ultimately paid by the taxpayer to bondholders. A significant portion of those interest payments is returned to banks in exchange for their services in creating new money as bank credit and transferring it to bondholders using their bonds as collateral security. In this manner, a substantial portion of taxes ultimately ends up with banks. Quantitative easing policies, whereby bonds are bought directly from banks, offer an additional opportunity for banks to generate more credit, often resulting in a preposterous situation.

Describing the scene a century past, Bilgram (1921, p. 765) wrote, "The sum total of debts on which interest must be paid amounts to probably more than four times the amount of currency in use, inclusive of deposit currency (I do not know where to obtain reliable and complete statistics on this subject), hence the yearly interest payments absorb more than one quarter of all currency."

Figures 4.1 and 4.2 show a part of the modern-day picture. The top pane of Fig. 4.1 displays the broad increase in general government debt among the G7[1] countries since 2005. It is important to remember that government debt is generated through the issuance of national debt instruments, such as treasury bills, notes, and bonds, and to note that the G7 collectively accounts for a bit over one-quarter of the world's gross product. In 2021, the last accounting year, all but Germany had a gross government debt larger than their gross domestic product. Government debt does not, of course, encompass "debt" in general. To this point, the bottom pane of Fig. 4.1 shows private sector debt. Considering the G7 as an aggregate, private sector debt is roughly twice general government debt and, on average, in recent years, stands at more than twice the gross domestic product. Figure 4.2 shows interest payments on general government debt as a percentage. The top pane relates to gross domestic product, and the bottom pane relates to government expenditure. The former coordinate averaged 2.0% for the bloc in the five years leading up to and including 2020, while the latter averaged 6.4%. Data for private sector interest rates and payments are highly variable and context-dependent, making it too difficult to estimate here.

By the end of 2020, there were roughly $2trn in circulating United States currency. Over the period from 2016 to 2020, on average, $517bn was paid per annum in terms of interest on United States government debt—almost exactly the "one quarter" estimate Bilgram made a century ago, considering not debt in general but just the government fraction. It is worth noting that among currencies, the United States dollar has a

---

[1] The G7 is comprised of Canada, France, Germany, Italy, Japan, the United Kingdom, and the United States.

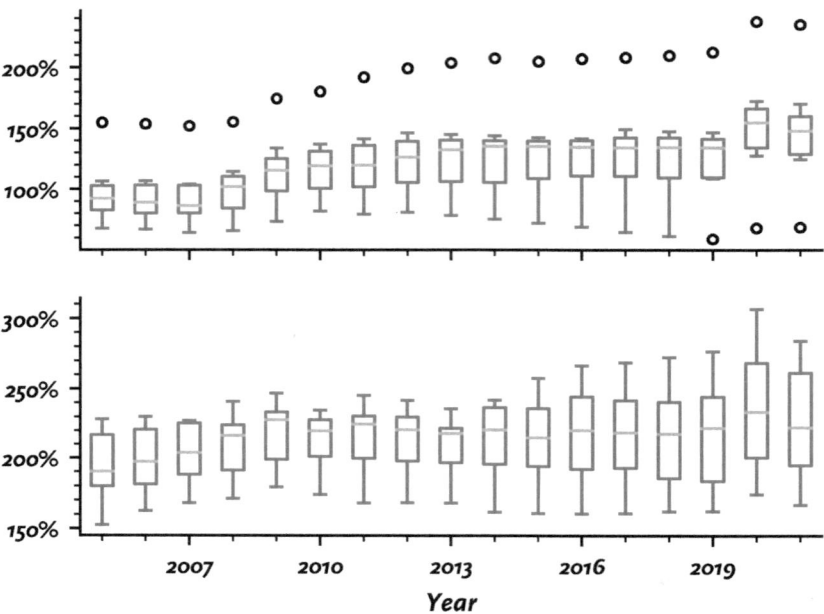

Fig. 4.1 For the G7 countries, general government debt (percent of gross domestic product) on the top, with the topmost outlier being Japan and the bottommost outlier being Germany, and private sector debt (percent of gross domestic product) on the bottom (*Data source* OECD [2023a, 2023b])

disproportionately large presence internationally.[2] The case of low-income countries caught in severe debt trap is often considerably worse. Bilgram's (1921, p. 765) grim warning of the situation provoked is just as, if not more, relevant today as it was a century ago: "[T]he business world must submit to one of two evils: either a continually increasing indebtedness that can never be canceled, or a reduction of the money in circulation. The first cannot continue indefinitely, and the second causes a depression of business."

---

[2] Estimates point toward roughly half or a bit more (increasing) of United States dollars are circulating abroad (Judson, 2017).

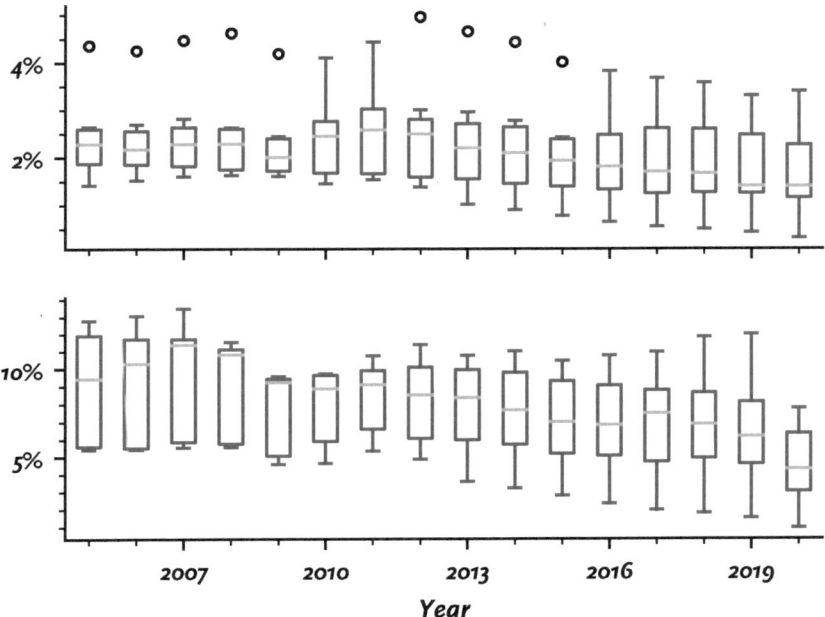

Fig. 4.2 For the G7 countries, interest payments (percent of gross domestic product) on government debt on the top and interest payments (percent of government expenditure) on government debt on the bottom (*Data source* World Bank [2023a, 2023b, 2023c])

4.3 DISCOUNTING THE LOAN PRINCIPAL: AN UNCONVENTIONAL IDEA

Soddy (1934) proposed an intriguing alternative to paying monetary loan interest that implicitly followed Gesell's free-money theory. The basic idea behind Soddy's proposal was that if discounting is to be accepted, the monetary value of loan principals must also be discounted. For example, at the end of the first year of a $100 loan, the loan principal was proposed to be discounted per its anticipated value. Assuming a 5% interest rate, the principal would be reduced to $95 after a year, and the second year's interest would be 5% of that $95, the third year's interest 5% of $90.25, and so on. Soddy's alternative is as brilliant as it is simple and leads to a dramatic reduction of debt stock across society.

At the time of proposition, Soddy considered the case of a constant value interest rate. If the more general case where the interest rate is a function of time is considered, a most intriguing point is revealed. Consider variables:

(1) A, the principal at the beginning,
(2) G, the fraction of the original principal A already redeemed by discounting the principal,
(3) t, the time in years, and
(4) $i(t)$, the rate of interest per cent per annum at time t.

First, note that at a constant interest rate i the interest payment accruing is $idt = (t + dt)i - ti$ over the time period $(t, t + dt)$. Where the interest rate is a function of t, the interest accruing AdG over the time period $(t, t + dt)$ is equal to the principal A multiplied simultaneously by the fraction of A not yet paid as interest, $(1 - G)$, and by the value corresponding to $(t + dt)i(t + dt) - ti(t)$, which represents the change in the interest payment accruing.

Relegating the full mathematical derivation to Appendix B, we have:

$$AdG = A(1 - G) \times \{(t + dt)i(t + dt) - ti(t)\}. \qquad (4.4)$$

The profound implication of (4.4) is that, for the complete redemption of a loan principal of one unit of money, a debtor must pay back only one unit of money instead of the current—assuming an infinite time horizon—two units of money, thereby dramatically reducing money payments to the banking sector.

The fraction of the original principal A already redeemed by discounting the principal between t_0 and t_f, $G(t_0, t_f)$, is

$$G(t_0, t_f) = 1 - e^{-\{t_f i(t_f) - t_0 i(t_0)\}} < 1. \qquad (4.5)$$

Relation (4.5) shows that the fraction of the original principal A already redeemed by discounting the principal between t_0 and t_f grows nearer and nearer to one but can, in fact, never reach one, regardless of the form of the interest function over time. Furthermore, $G(t_0, t_f)$ is dependent only on the initial and final points in time, independent of the path over which the interest function changes in time. (4.5) highlights a common analytical essence between its derivation and the derivation of the MSA relation, illustrated in Sect. 4.2.

With G representing the fraction of A already paid as interest, $\lim_{t \to \infty} G = 1$, assuming $i(t) > 0$ at all times. In this way, the accumulated interest in the presented lending scheme cannot exceed the principal A, implying that the inequality $G < 1$ holds for any finite time horizon. Parallel to the evolution of G over time, we also have that $\lim_{t \to \infty} A(1 - G) = 0$. Hence, in the case of relation (4.5), it is not possible to add one unit of interest to every one unit of loan principal over an infinite time horizon, as was the case with the MSA relation. In other words, while in the case of the MSA relation the principal is maintained intact over time, in (4.5), the principal approaches zero due to the discounting of the principal. If a loan redemption scheme such as that presented by (4.5) were to be used in the modern global economy, it would dramatically reduce the superior position accorded to debt issuers, regardless of whether any given loan is ultimately extinguished by money payment, release, compensation, or novation. Such a scheme could provide a valuable starting point for those economic communities wishing to significantly weaken the mechanism that incentivizes the actions of debt issuers and buyers of monetary assets. This could thereby reduce the substantial quantity of irrelevant monetary assets and the extent of asset bubbles, along with their associated vast sustainability concerns. In a globalized world, after all—and as will be discussed later in Chapter 5—money and monetary assets are biophysical debt at the level of the global community.

4.4   The Financial Divisions of Sony and Toyota: A Most Lucrative Business

The significant growth in the finance sector post-World War II stands out as a notable trend in industrial society. Figure 4.3 provides a time series dataset on the finance sector in the United States from 1947 to 2017, expressed as a percentage of gross domestic product. Aside from a brief period following the Lehman Brothers collapse in 2008, a share of more than 6% of the gross domestic product has been consistently maintained since the early 1990s. The Office of National Statistics in the United Kingdom documents a similar pattern, where the finance sector has held a share of over 5% of the gross domestic product since 1990. These trends reflect a broader phenomenon of financialization in the corporate world, a subject further explored in the subsequent sections considering the cases of two Japanese companies, Sony and Toyota.

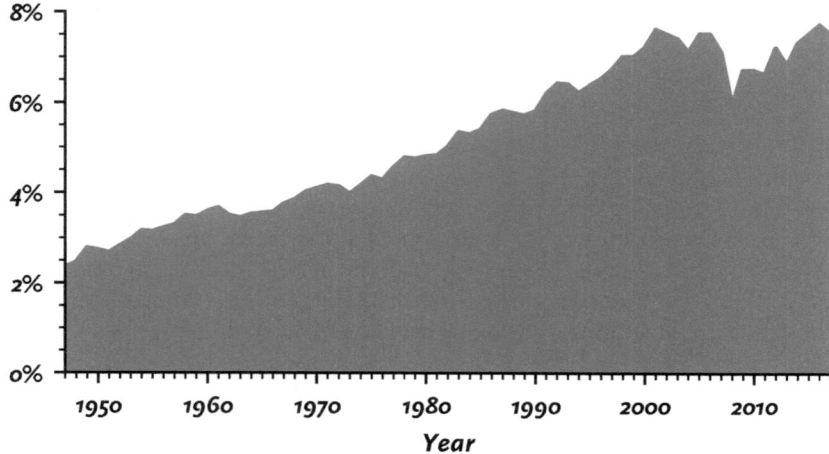

Fig. 4.3 Percent share of gross domestic product in the finance and insurance sector in the United States, 1947–2017 (*Data source* BEA [2018])

Before getting into the balance sheets of the two Japanese companies, traditionally viewed as manufacturing entities, it is necessary to understand the Bank of Japan's quantitative easing policy. This policy, initiated in April 2013, involved the Bank purchasing outstanding national bonds from the banking sector. The objective was to provide non-financial business sectors with increased liquidity for investments.

Figure 4.4 illustrates the government bond holdings of the Bank of Japan and domestic commercial banks in Japan from 2014 to 2019. As of early 2014, the Bank of Japan's national bonds totaled ¥187trn, whereas commercial banks held national bonds worth ¥652trn. A reversal in this trend became evident post-2014. By 2019, the Bank of Japan held national bonds worth ¥463trn, a roughly 150% increase from its 2014 value. In contrast, commercial banks held ¥395trn in national bonds, amounting to just 60% of their 2014 holdings.

Regrettably, the Bank of Japan's policy did not materialize as intended. The monetary base, comprised of cash and reserves in current accounts at the Bank of Japan, soared, as demonstrated in Fig. 4.5. Figure 4.5 represents Japan's monetary base from 1970 to 2019, showing a remarkable increase in monetary base following the implementation of quantitative easing policy in April 2013. Specifically, monetary base rose from

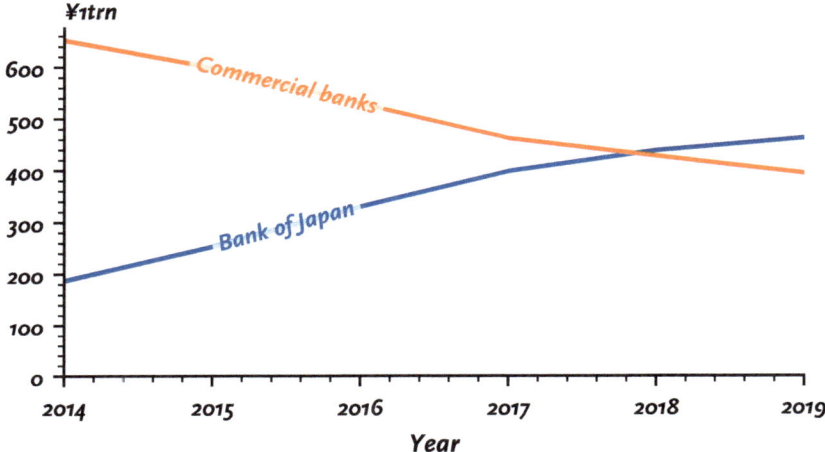

Fig. 4.4 Government bond holdings of the Bank of Japan versus domestic commercial banks, 2014–2019 (*Data source* BOJ [2022])

¥131.9trn in 2013 to ¥499.8trn in 2019, marking a 280% increase over six years.

As was noted in Chapter 2, Japan's reserve requirement is less than 1%. Under the extremely low-interest rates throughout the period considered, the banking and financial sectors exploited the situation to earn relatively higher interest payments. This was accomplished by depositing additional liquidity into the Bank of Japan's current account, failing to provide non-banking business sectors with the intended liquidity. As of May 7, 2019, domestic deposits in current accounts with the Bank of Japan were held by 124 private banks, 251 credit unions, 13 trust banks, and 4 governmental banks, along with 50 foreign banks.

An important question arises: where did the additional liquidity created by the Bank of Japan's quantitative easing policy flow? We argue that such liquidity found its way into the stock market, generating stock market bubbles. The Nikkei Index indeed rose from 17.5k in December 2014 to 26.6k in December 2020, marking an increase of more than 50% (Nikkei, 2023). Although the Bank of Japan's original objective for the quantitative easing policy was not fully met, there was a fortunate consequence for Japan's export-oriented business sectors. Despite counter quantitative

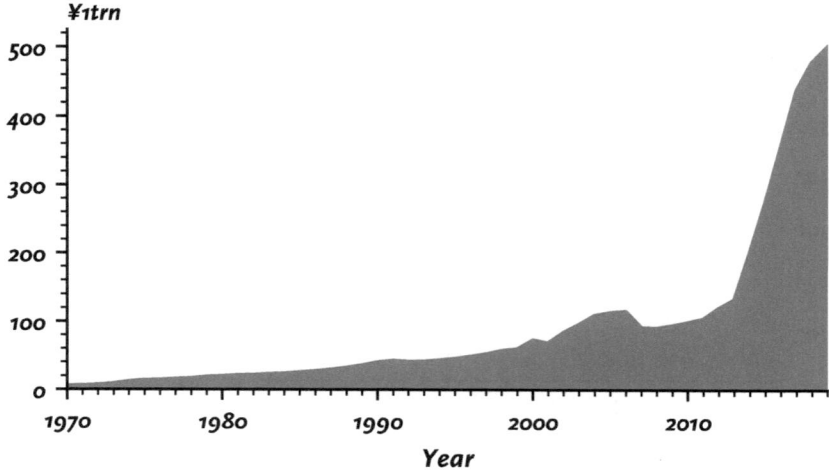

Fig. 4.5   Monetary base for Japan, 1970–2019 (*Data source* BOJ [2022])

easing measures implemented by several economically influential coun-tries and regions between 2013 and 2019, aiming to prevent a surge in the value of their respective currencies, the Japanese yen exchange rate against the United States dollar fell significantly during the same period. Figure 4.6 depicts this trend. Before the initiation of quantitative easing, from 2011 through the latter half of 2012, the yen-dollar exchange rate hovered around ¥80 to $1. However, in October 2013, the exchange rate climbed to ¥98 to $1, and from March 2015 through January 2016, the exchange rate hovered around ¥120 to $1.

Overall, the approximately 50% rise in the purchasing power of the United States dollar against the Japanese yen after 2013 resulted in a period where the general price level of Japanese products for a United States citizen decreased by 50%, all else being equal, thereby stimulating imports from Japan. These changes in general price levels were observed across a broad spectrum of products and companies, including Sony and Toyota. This and the Bank of Japan's consistent quantitative easing resulted in windfall profits in many instances.

The significance of these trends is often not fully understood by the general public, nor is the extent to which the corporate world has become financialized and how profitable financial operations can ensure stable

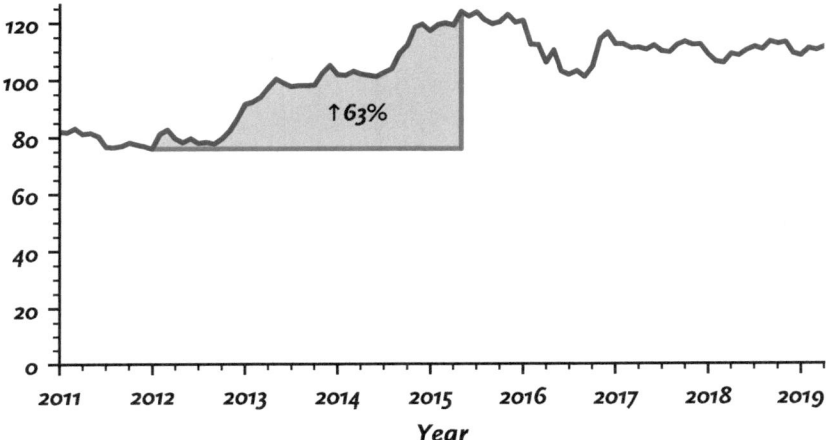

Fig. 4.6 Exchange rate of the Japanese yen to the United States dollar, 2011–2019, where it should be noted that the slight appreciation of the yen against the dollar in 2016 was largely attributed to the yen's perception as a safe haven currency in light of the United Kingdom's decision to leave the European Union ("Brexit") (*Data source* WSJ [2023])

income streams in the face of external disturbances such as exchange rate fluctuations. Many people are surprised to discover that the financial divisions of both Sony and Toyota contribute a substantial portion of the companies' operating incomes. Operating income is an accounting metric that quantifies the profit generated from a company's operations after deducting operating expenses such as wages, capital depreciation, and the cost of goods and services sold. In contrast, sales and operating revenue represents all money received by a company, including the sales of products and services.

Sony has four primary divisions: (1) consumer products and devices (CPD) and networked products and services (NPS), (2) pictures, (3) music, and (4) financial services. The financial services division is further split into life insurance, non-life insurance, and banking businesses, with the life insurance sector being the most significant. Toyota also has three divisions: (1) automotive, (2) financial services, and (3) other. Figure 4.7 and Fig. 4.8 present a time series for Sony and Toyota's different business divisions, focusing on two key indicators: operating income and the percentage share of operating income against sales and operating revenues.

From 2010 to 2017, Sony's financial services division emerged as the most impactful division, both in terms of absolute operating income and the ratio of operating income to sales and operating revenues. The division reported an operating income of ¥119bn (15%) in 2010, which increased to ¥179bn (15%) in 2017. On the other hand, Toyota experienced a decline in this ratio, falling from 30% in 2010 to 14% in 2017. Despite halving in relative terms, the operating income remained substantial, totaling ¥358bn in 2010 and ¥286bn in 2017. The financial services divisions of both Sony and Toyota are closely interconnected, highly profitable, and largely independent of the Bank of Japan's quantitative easing policy. For instance, automobile manufacturers such as Toyota typically

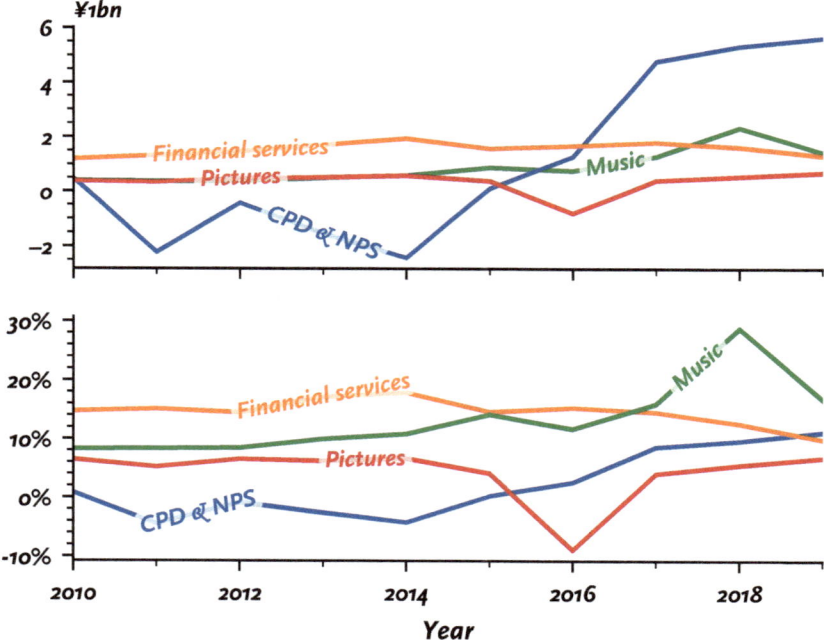

Fig. 4.7 Operating income (in billions of Japanese yen) on the top and the ratio of operating income to sales and operating revenues (percent) on the bottom for Sony since 2010 (*Data source* Sony [2023])

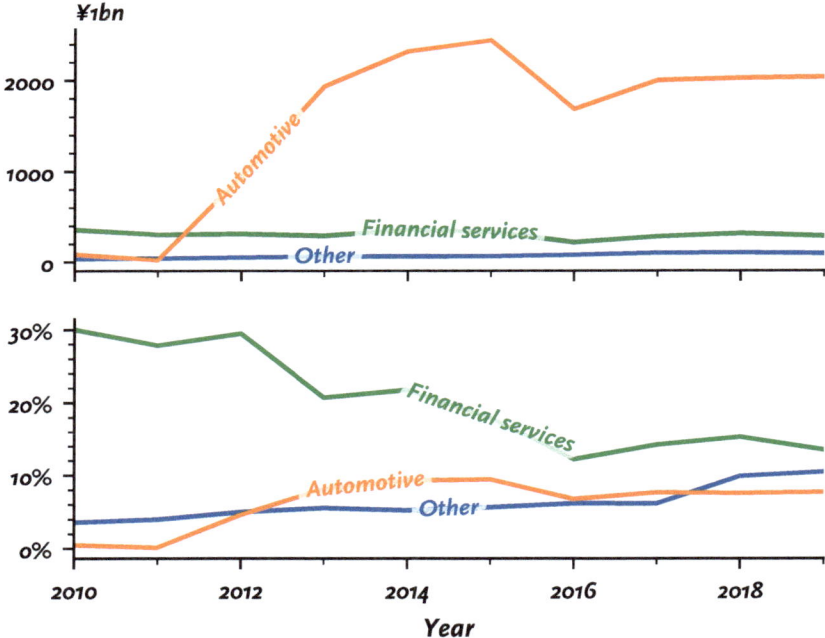

Fig. 4.8 Operating income (in billions of Japanese yen) on the top and the ratio of operating income to sales and operating revenues (percent) on the bottom for Toyota since 2010 (*Data source* Toyota [2023])

facilitate new or used car loans, refinancing of existing cars, car lease contracts, and car insurance. To turn a profit, car manufacturers leverage data, acquired at little cost, on individuals and companies seeking loans, leases, and insurance contracts. They then extend attractive proposals to these entities, capitalizing on their advantageous fund-procurement conditions.

Regarding Fig. 4.7, an observable trend from 2011 to 2014 is that before and shortly after the implementation of quantitative easing, Sony's operating income for the CPD and NPS division was negative. This division's average operating income deficit was ¥1.7bn during that period. However, the favorable exchange rate of the yen allowed Sony's CPD and NPS division to maintain a positive operating income from 2015 to 2017, which gradually increased from ¥119m in 2015 to ¥39bn in 2017. It is unlikely that this increase in Sony's operating income within the CPD and NPS division, starting in 2015, is directly related to qualitative product improvements. Regardless of the Bank of Japan's monetary policy, Sony's financial services division, specifically the insurance sub-division, held the largest share of the company's operating income, representing 48.8% of total operating income in 2010 and 57.6% in 2016. In the 1980s, Sony was a "rising sun" in the global electronics industry. The conglomerate has since evolved into a distinct entity that often does not generate income from its production division. The ratio of operating income to sales and operating revenues for Sony's financial services division surpassed that of all other company divisions.

Less than two years before the Bank of Japan's quantitative easing, Toyota's automotive division earned ¥860m in 2010, and ¥216m in 2011. Due to the favorable exchange rate of the Japanese yen against the United States dollar, the division's operating income post-easing soared to ¥23bn in 2014. Conversely, Toyota's financial services division maintained relative stability in operating income from 2010 to 2017, fluctuating between ¥2.2bn and ¥3.6bn, averaging at ¥3.1bn. The division's share of Toyota's total operating income was a substantial 74.7% in 2010! Following the Bank of Japan's quantitative easing and a significantly devalued yen, Toyota's automotive division recovered financially, with its share of total operating income climbing to 84% in 2017. While the sale of electric vehicles has indeed catalyzed significant growth in the automotive market and contributed considerably to Toyota's increased operating income, it seems unlikely that the surge in operating income beginning in 2015 is closely associated with qualitative improvements of the automotive division's products. The ratio of operating income to sales and operating revenues for Toyota's financial services division has consistently been the highest among all company divisions, far surpassing any other division. Monetary factors, such as exchange rate fluctuations, profoundly influence the financial solvency of manufacturing companies, separate from "progress" tied to technological innovations.

4.5   Dynamics of Solvency, Running Solvency, and Bankruptcy: Revisiting Mark's Innovative Analysis of Inescapable Debt Trap for the Whole of Society

The banking sector can theoretically create two units of money out of nothing. This reality is a consequence of the two unnatural powers discussed in Chapters 2 and 3. The MSA relation is the theoretical manifestation of the interest payment maximum—one unit of additional money from one unit of principal. The privilege given to the banking sector is indeed extraordinary.

A comprehensive examination of collective monetary debt trap for society, stemming from the two powers of the banking sector, is presented in the following. It is framed in relation to the ideas proposed by Mark (1934) nine decades ago. Revisiting his innovative analysis of the stark contrast between individual business solvency and the collective solvency of society is worthwhile as it facilitates a full appreciation of the true nature of the two unnatural powers, which have led to inescapable debt trap at the societal level, despite the many efforts of individual economic entities to maintain solvency. The general existence of this inescapable debt trap may be due to the biased individualistic perspective that money and money substitutes are wealth. This view drives people to seek opportunities to acquire ever more money. As demonstrated in Chapter 2, all forms of money are debt, clearly and convincingly stated by Macleod (1883, p. 55), and worth repeating here: "We have seen that writers of all classes are agreed as to the fundamental *nature of money*. It represents *debts* which are due to persons who have done services to others, and have received no equivalent service in return." It should also be noted that Macleod's analysis strongly suggests, in principle, that money should be used to exchange for goods and services, not for creating or acquiring more money or money substitutes. Aristotle's views on breeding money from money, stated at the beginning of this chapter, echoes this spirit.

In fact, it is easy to see why an individual economic entity's potential for solvency does not automatically lead to societal solvency. This is particularly true if most existing money stock in a given society is derived solely from the commercial banking sector—a reality not only in Mark's time but also today. Complete societal solvency would entail the disappearance of all bank deposits! If loan repayment for society as a whole surpasses a certain point, the total existing bank deposits tend to shrink more rapidly.

Mark (1934, p. 95) understood the nature of the two unnatural powers examined in Chapters 2 and 3, and Sect. 4.2 of this chapter:

> As the banks are now the sole issuers of new money, and have already issued more than nine-tenths of all the money in existence, it is obviously impossible for society to pay back more than is issued (i.e., total loan plus interest), *without having further recourse to the banks themselves.*

Further recourse to the banks naturally entails the road to societal insolvency—a servitude-like dependence on the banking sector.

Before concluding this chapter, let us revisit the key points of Mark's rationale. The two most important aspects for every economic entity to remember are: (1) all forms of money and money substitutes in existence are debt, and (2) it is impossible for society as a whole to pay back more than the existing money without creating, in the banking sector, additional debt, given that most of the money supply is created in the form of demand deposits as loans by the banking sector. Paradoxically, despite the efforts of individual economic actors to repay debt governed by a positive interest rate, society can only remain prosperous, as a whole, by increasingly indebting itself. The burden of interest payment is indeed a monstrous parasite for society.

Why exactly can society as a whole not escape the debt trap paradox, ultimately leading to the collapse of collateral security in the hands of the banking sector? Much has changed between the present day and the context in which Mark wrote, particularly in capital markets, the scale of transactions involving investment banking activities, and the variety of new financial products such as derivatives. However, the core argument provided by Mark remains valid.

Mark's (1934, p. 97) classification of economic entities (excluding the banking sector) into three categories, depending on the degree of monetary and financial viability, is also suitable for us to consider here in the modern context.

A. *Solvency* is when an economic entity can cover all administrative and distributional obligations, not tied to any bank overdraft or loan liability, from its gross profits. Alternatively, solvency is when the entity can cover these two charges from gross profits, and the market value of its financial assets can cover bank overdraft and loan liabilities.

B. *Running solvency* occurs when the realization of an economic entity's total capital assets at current market value, not book value, does not sufficiently cover its total liability—this does not necessarily result precipitate bankruptcy.

C. *Actual* or *potential bankruptcy* is when an economic entity cannot cover all administrative and distributional obligations. In this scenario, the entity might resort to disposing of its capital assets, which the banking sector would then appropriate.

The rentier class, referring to people living solvent on unearned income from interest or return on investment acquired or inherited, belongs to Class A. Wage and salary earners with sufficient income, independent of bank loans and other forms of monetary debt, also belong to Class A. If these individuals enter into loan contracts with the banking sector, they may eventually be categorized as Class B or Class C. For instance, the Japanese government, with its eternal budget deficit due to an aging population and sluggish economic growth perennially covered by the issuance of national bonds, is a good example of a political entity belonging to Class B, borderline Class C. Voluntary bankruptcy refers to a situation in which a party that cannot pay its debts decides to petition the court for bankruptcy. In this case, the debtor initiates the bankruptcy process on their own, as opposed to being compelled to do so by their creditors. In 2021, over 68,000 people in Japan filed for voluntary bankruptcy. These individuals belong to Class C.

All bank deposits in circulation are the deposit liabilities, for the banking sector, of Class B and Class C. Conversely, some parts of the complex cross-indebtedness within Class B and Class C can be canceled out on the surface of the bookkeeping procedures of accounting. However, an uncleared debt liability always exists, which can be referred to as the *residuum* of the liability. Such residuum, the industrial liability, must be held by the banking sector and economic entities in Class A. In relation to deposits and industrial liabilities, what Class B and Class C can do at most is increase these types of liabilities when society is in a boom period or perhaps default during a recession. Nothing more can be done. Of course, there are always transfers of economic entities over time between the three abovementioned classes. Nevertheless, the debt situation in Class B and Class C remains unchanged—these two classes are perpetually incapable of escaping debt trap. Unfortunately, the banking sector strongly prefers to maintain such a situation indefinitely, into the sunset as it were.

The banking sector uniquely plays two roles. The first role is that of the holder of all deposit liabilities. The second is that of the holder of industrial liabilities, which include the interest paid to the banking sector as owners of the deposit liabilities and the acquired collateral security from defaults or bankruptcies of Class B and Class C—the number and scale of which, regrettably, is tending to increase rapidly in modern times. The secret behind this scenario can be readily revealed. Classes A through C all stem from the progressive issuance and circulation of demand deposits created out of nothing and the interest payments on these deposits, embodying the dual powers of the banking sector. Furthermore, numerous fictitious elements appear on balance sheets due to, for instance, the concealment of insolvency, understatement of outstanding drafts and money advanced, overstatement of earnings and cash in hand, and understatement of profits, as beautifully exemplified by Smith (1992). No individual in a society can accurately ascertain the society's overall financial status, and the society as a whole cannot free itself from debt trap as long as the two powers of the banking sector remain intact, institutionalized by governments and central banks, as previously discussed in Chapter 2.

Thus, a given society's monetary and financial viability is maintained through the seamless circulation of fictitious bank loans, which exist based on faith alone. No one can make a genuine monetary appraisal of the sum total of financial assets, which is debt to the whole of society. The three classifications suggested by Mark (1934) become indistinct when one attempts to make capital asset valuations based on market conditions—a concept many fail to grasp properly.

4.6   CONCLUSION

The case studies of Sony and Toyota examined in this chapter demonstrate how fluctuations in exchange rates significantly influence corporations' balance sheets, even those typically regarded as operating outside the finance sector. One prevalent strategy corporations use to insulate themselves from such influences is conducting their own financial operations—entire divisions devoted to pecuniary matters that repeatedly prove highly profitable year after year.

In parallel with this trend of corporate financialization is the narrative of derivatives—contracts that derive their value from an underlying asset, a form of monetization procedure wherein, often, the underlying asset exists primarily for the express purpose of money generation. Readers may recall that overleveraging related to mortgage market derivatives was a significant factor in the 2007–2008 financial crisis. Figure 4.9 illustrates the impressive growth of the global daily turnover of foreign exchange and over-the-counter derivatives, from $1.3trn per day in 1995 to $12.7trn per day in 2022. In relation to global gross product, these figures represent 4.3% per day in 1995 and 12.5% per day in 2022, down from a peak of 14.9% per day in 2019. This significant expansion of the derivative market is closely connected to another megatrend of financial expansion—the growth of shadow banking activities, operations that exist outside the traditional banking sector but are nevertheless supported by it.

A fourth and final aspect of pecuniary expansion can be found in the story of private debt. Figure 4.10 illustrates the trend in household debt and non-financial corporation debt for a selection of thirty-nine countries since 1995. In the most recent year accounted for, 2021, the average level of household debt as a percent of national gross domestic product was 62%. For non-financial corporations, that figure was 152%. Earlier in this chapter, in our discussion of the MSA relation, we encountered in inferential form the enormity of the second unnatural power of banks, where the present value of future interest payments over the infinite time horizon is one no matter the interest rate, as long as interest remains positive. Armed with an understanding of the two unnatural powers of banks, Fig. 4.10 should hardly come as a surprise.

Likely, the only chance we have at durably tempering such ubiquitous and concerning financialization megatrends, including but not limited to the four mentioned, is for societies at large to reflect on the basic nature of money and understand the proper meaning and arrangement of sovereign money systems. Ahead of Chapter 8, which discusses sovereign money systems in a systematic manner, this chapter contributes to a clearer understanding of the peculiar characteristics of the modern arrangement and presents an unconventional loan discounting formula, which could act to radically mitigate debt trap and free various actors from their current state of running solvency—fueled nowadays, to a predominant degree, by flows of fictitious money.

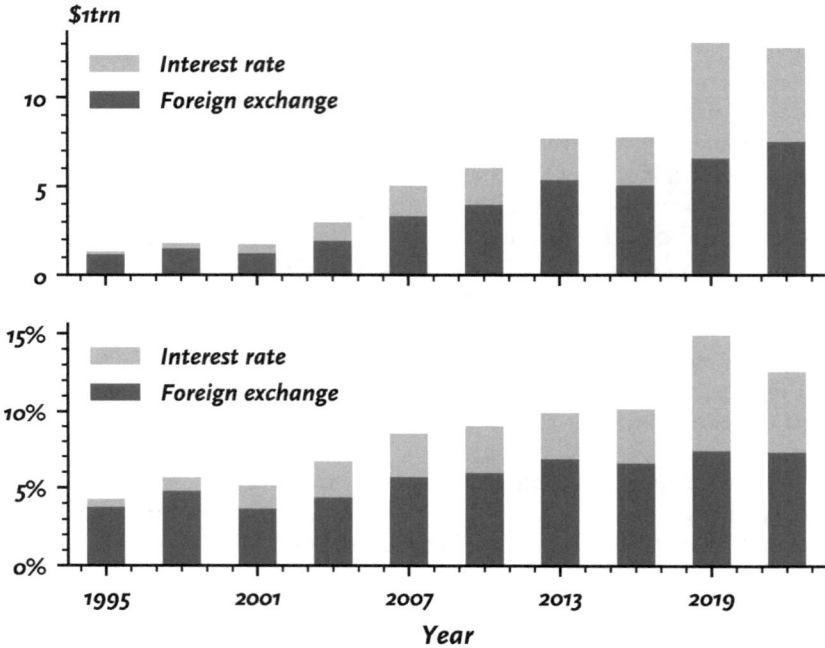

Fig. 4.9 Global daily turnover of foreign exchange (FX) and over-the-counter (OTC) derivatives in absolute monetary terms (top pane) and as a percentage of annual gross domestic product (bottom pane) following the Triennial Bank Survey 1995–2022 (*Data source* BIS [2022] and IMF [2023])

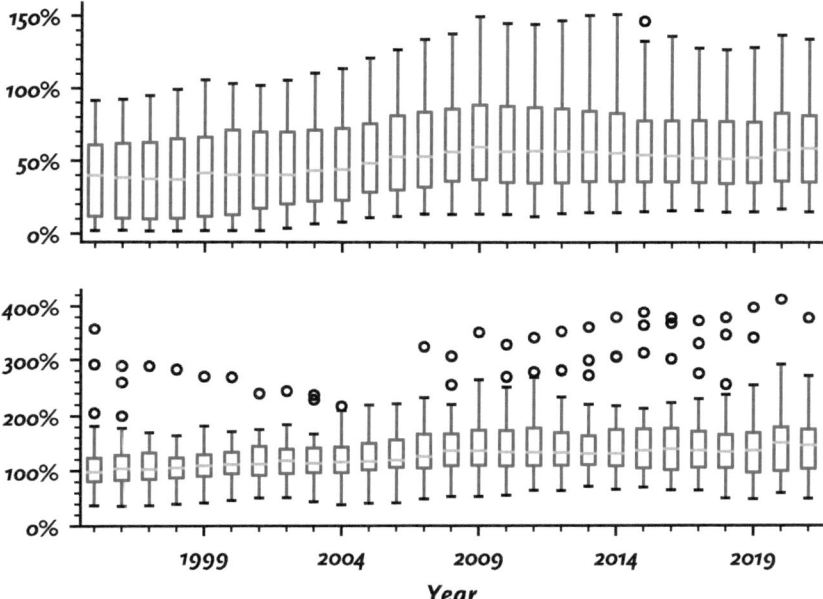

Fig. 4.10 Private debt as household debt (all instruments) on the top, and non-financial corporation debt (all instruments) on the bottom, as percent of GDP for thirty-nine[3] countries, 1995–2022 (*Data source* IMF [2022a, 2022b])

Appendix 4.A

The present value of future interest payment (PVFIP) between an initial point of time t_0 and a final point of time t_f can be represented

$$PVFIP\big(t_0, t_f, i(x) : x \in [t_0, t_f]\big) = \int\limits_{t_0}^{t_f} i(x) e^{-\int_{t_0}^{x} i(\tau)\mathrm{d}\tau}\,\mathrm{d}x. \qquad (4.\mathrm{A}.1)$$

[3] The thirty-nine countries considered are Austria, Belgium, Brazil, Bulgaria, Canada, Chile, Colombia, Croatia, Cyprus, Czech Republic, Denmark, Estonia, Finland, France, Germany, Greece, Hungary, Ireland, Israel, Italy, Japan, Republic of Korea, Latvia, Lithuania, Luxembourg, Malta, Mauritius, Mexico, Netherlands, Norway, Poland, Portugal, Romania, Russian Federation, Slovak Republic, Slovenia, Spain, Sweden, Switzerland, Turkey, United Kingdom and United States.

Defining $g(x) = \int_{t_0}^{x} i(\tau)d\tau$, note that $g(t_0) = 0$ and $g(t_f) = \int_{t_0}^{t_f} i(\tau)d\tau$. Note also that $i(x)dx = dg$. Substituting $g(x)$ and dg into (4.A.1), we have that

$$\int_{g(t_0)}^{g(t_f)} e^{-g}dg = \left[-e^{-g}\right]_{g(t_0)}^{g(t_f)} = -e^{-g(t_f)} + e^{-g(t_0)} = 1 - e^{-\int_{t_0}^{t_f} i(\tau)d\tau}.$$

(4.A.2)

As $t_f \to \infty$, (4.A.2)'s final form shows that

$$1 - e^{-\int_{t_0}^{\infty} i(\tau)d\tau} = 1$$

and

$$PVFIP(t_0, \infty) = 1.$$

The critical point of the MSA relation is that it remains valid independently of the functional form of interest rate over time so long as the interest function $i(t)$ remains always positive.

APPENDIX 4.B

In his proposal, Soddy considered the case of a constant-value interest rate. The more general case of an interest rate allowed to vary over time is considered in the following, using variables:

- A, the principal,
- G, the fraction of the original principal A already redeemed by discounting the principal,
- t, the time in years, and
- $i(t)$, the rate of interest per cent per annum at time t.

It must first be noticed that with a constant interest rate i, the interest payment accruing is $idt = (t + dt)i - ti$ over the time period $(t, t + dt)$. Suppose the interest rate is a function of t. In that case, the interest accruing AdG over the time period $(t, t + dt)$ is equal to the principal A multiplied simultaneously by the fraction of A not yet paid as interest $(1 - G)$ and by the value corresponding to $(t + dt)i(t + dt) - ti(t)$ that represents the change in the interest payment accruing.

Whence

$$AdG = A(1 - G) \times \{(t + dt)i(t + dt) - ti(t)\}$$

from which we obtain

$$(t + dt)i(t + dt) - ti(t) = \left(i(t) + t\frac{di(t)}{dt}\right)dt.$$

It is then possible to obtain the final form

$$AdG = A(1 - G) \times \left\{i(t) + t\frac{di(t)}{dt}\right\}dt. \tag{4.B.1}$$

Integration of (4.B.1) leads to

$$1 - G = e^{-\int_{t_0}^{t_f}\left\{i(u) + u\frac{di(u)}{du}\right\}du}. \tag{4.B.2}$$

Integration by parts of the latter part of the exponent in (4.B.2) further leads to

$$\int_{t_0}^{t_f} u\frac{di(u)}{du}du = t_f i(t_f) - t_0 i(t_0) - \int_{t_0}^{t_f} i(u)du$$

and (4.B.2) can be transformed into

$$G(t_0, t_f) = 1 - e^{-\{t_f i(t_f) - t_0 i(t_0)\}}. \tag{4.B.3}$$

Relation (4.B.3) shows that the total interest accruing grows nearer and nearer to the principal but can, in fact, never exceed the principal, regardless of the form of the interest function over time. Furthermore, the total interest accruing depends only on the initial and final points in time, independent of the path over which the interest function changes over time.

REFERENCES

Aristotle. (1885). *The Politics of Aristotle* (Vol. 1, B. Jowett, Trans.). Clarendon Press.

BEA (2018) *National Income and Product Accounts: Table 6.16D: Corporate Profits by Industry (GDPbyInd_VA_1947–2017)*. Bureau of Economic Analysis, United States Department of Commerce. https://www.bea.gov/sites/default/files/2018-04/GDPbyInd_VA_1947-2017.xlsx. Accessed 26 June 2023.

Bilgram, H. (1921). The Quantity Theory Scrutinized. *Journal of Political Economy, 29*(9), 757–766. https://doi.org/10.1086/253393

BIS. (2022). *Download Bis Statistics in a Single File ('full_der_otc_tov_csv.zip')*. Bank for International Settlements. https://www.bis.org/statistics/full_data_sets.htm. Accessed 26 June 2023.

BOJ. (2022). *Statistics (統計)*. Bank of Japan (日本銀行). https://www.boj.or.jp/statistics/index.htm. Accessed 26 November 2022.

Daly, H. E. (1980). The Economic Thought of Frederick Soddy. *History of Political Economy, 12*(4), 469–488. https://doi.org/10.1215/00182702-12-4-469

IMF. (2022a). *Household Debt, All Instruments*. International Monetary Fund. https://www.imf.org/external/datamapper/HH_ALL@GDD. Accessed 26 June 2023.

IMF. (2022b). *Nonfinancial Corporate Debt, All Instruments*. International Monetary Fund. https://www.imf.org/external/datamapper/NFC_ALL@GDD. Accessed 26 June 2023.

IMF. (2023). *Gdp, Current Prices*. International Monetary Fund. https://www.imf.org/external/datamapper/NGDPD@WEO. Accessed 26 June 2023.

Judson, R. (2017). The Death of Cash? Not so Fast: Demand for U.S. Currency at Home and Abroad, 1990–2016. In *War on Cash: Is There a Future for Cash? International Cash Conference*. Island of Mainau, Germany.

Macleod, H. D. (1883) *The Theory and Practice of Banking* (4th ed., Vol. 1). Longmans, Green, Reader and Dyer.

Mark, J. (1934). *The Modern Idolatry: Being an Analysis of Usury & The Pathology of Debt*. Chatto and Windus.

Nikkei. (2023). *Historical Data (Nikkei 225)*. Nikkei Incorporated. https://indexes.nikkei.co.jp/en/nkave/archives/data. Accessed 26 June 2023.

OECD. (2023a). *Private Sector Debt*. Organisation for Economic Co-operation and Development. https://stats.oecd.org/index.aspx?queryid=34814. Accessed 26 June 2023.

OECD. (2023b). *Public Sector Debt, Consolidated, Nominal Value*. Organisation for Economic Co-operation and Development. https://stats.oecd.org/Index.aspx?DataSetCode=QASA_TABLE7PSD. Accessed 26 June 2023.

Smith, T. (1992). *Accounting for Growth: Stripping the Camouflage from Company Accounts*. Century Business.

Soddy, F. (1931). *Money versus Man: A Statement of the World Problem from the Standpoint of the New Economics*. Elkin Mathews and Marrot.

Soddy, F. (1934). *The Role of Money: What it Should Be, Contrasted with what it Has Become*. George Routledge and Sons, Limited.

Sony. (2023). *Materials | Financial Information (資料 | 財務情報)*. Sony Financial Group Incorporated (ソニーフィナンシャルグループ株式会社). https://www.sonyfg.co.jp/ja/financial_info/results/. Accessed 26 June 2023.

Toyota. (2023). *Financial Results (決算報告)*. Toyota Motor Corporation (トヨタ自動車株式会社). https://global.toyota/jp/ir/financial-results/index.html. Accessed 26 June 2023.

World Bank. (2023a). *Broad money (% of GDP)*. The World Bank Group. https://data.worldbank.org/indicator/FM.LBL.BMNY.GD.ZS. Accessed 26 June 2023.

World Bank. (2023b). *Interest Payments (% of Expense)*. The World Bank Group. https://data.worldbank.org/indicator/GC.XPN.INTP.ZS. Accessed 26 June 2023.

World Bank. (2023c). *Interest Payments (current LCU)*. The World Bank Group. https://data.worldbank.org/indicator/GC.XPN.INTP.CN. Accessed 26 June 2023.

WSJ. (2023). USD to JPY | Japanese Yen Historical Prices. *Wall Street Journal*. https://www.wsj.com/market-data/quotes/fx/USDJPY/historical-prices. Accessed 26 June 2023.

CHAPTER 5

The Dual Nature of Money: Pecuniary Individualistic Perspectives Endanger Collectivistic Perspectives for Biophysical Sustainability

Thus money, so far from being rightly regarded as a part of national wealth, is rightly regarded as a part of the national debt, the claims of individuals on the national wealth, exactly like Consols or War Loan except that, being repayable in wealth on demand in every market, it does not and need not bear interest like a debt repayable, if at all, in the future.

(Soddy, 1926, p. 82)

5.1 Introduction

Seasoned economists will recall Lucas Jr.'s bold assertion during his 2003 presidential address to the American Economic Association, where he declared that the "central problem of depression prevention has been solved, for all practical purposes, and has in fact been solved for many decades" (Lucas, 2003, p. 1). A few years later, the world economy suffered its most significant economic meltdown in nearly 80 years, so it appears prudent to view Lucas Jr.'s stance as one of profound over-confidence. As Aliber and Kindleberger (1978/2015) have phrased it, financial explosions and collapses are a "hardy perennial" of economies. The empirically observed pattern of recurring financial crises is likely to continue unabated far into the future.

K. T. Mayumi and A. Renner, *Reconsidering the Privileged Powers of Banks*, https://doi.org/10.1007/978-981-99-6058-3_5

97

On the other hand, from our perspective, both mainstream and heterodox economists, as well as the general public, seem to maintain a strong, almost religious-like belief that monetary phenomena and their practical policy implications for "depression prevention" have nothing whatsoever to do with long-term collectivistic perspectives. This suggests that monetary phenomena have no fundamental influence on the biophysical dimensions of sustainability. Quite the opposite! The theoretical, historical, and institutional analysis of money provided in the previous three chapters suggests that there are deep connections between monetary phenomena and the biophysical aspects of our society. However, these connections have largely been overlooked in the discourse and analysis surrounding the role of money.

This chapter addresses the dual nature of money. As initially explained in Chapter 2, all forms of money represent debt at the societal level—both biophysical debt and, trivially, monetary debt. From the perspective of any given individual, however, it is more common to consider money as a form of affluence—a representation of wealth. The near-total disregard for collectivistic perspectives associated with monetary phenomena, particularly when viewed through a biophysical lens, hampers sustainability ambitions (Mayumi, 2020; Mayumi & Giampietro, 2018; Renner et al., 2021). The idea of money as biophysical debt is completely overlooked not only in mainstream economics but, more surprisingly, in heterodox economics as well. We live in an era where individualistic perspectives are dominant—in a paradoxically "globalized" world rooted firmly in the principles of individual property rights, political and legal liberty, direct individual communication with God, and so forth (Macfarlane, 1978). While we should not disregard the valuable lessons and substantial benefits derived from these sentiments, ignoring the collective counterpart could have grave consequences.

The rest of this chapter is structured as follows. Section 5.2 discusses the dual nature of money. Money is a promise to pay, ultimately in terms of goods and services. Owners of money are entitled to receive goods and services in the future in exchange for their money. However, from a biophysical perspective, every stage of the economic process—production, distribution, consumption, and disposal—requires valuable energy and materials. This results in the depletion or dilution of the remaining stock of fossil fuels and rare mineral resources for future generations. In an "empty world," a world in which the global economic system is not at capacity, there is neither a shortage of natural resources nor sink capacity. Unfortunately, our current global economic system situates us squarely in a "full world," as argued convincingly by Daly (2005). In our world, the availability of resources, especially but certainly not exclusively the supply of oil and gas, is far from guaranteed. The warnings of peak oil by voices like Campbell (2000), and those indicating that environmental loading is threatening climate conditions, such as the IPCC (2014), generate fodder for concern. In our increasingly financialized world, we must realize the deep implications of the dual nature of money for biophysical sustainability.

The following text introduces the dual nature of money. Section 5.2 reveals the fallacy of the double-entry bookkeeping convention, a widely used accounting scheme that effectively conceals the collectivistic reality of the dual nature of money. Three case studies are discussed—Black-Rock, the Bank of Japan, and the United States Treasury. Section 5.2 also discusses the debt situation of a select set of countries in terms of external debt per capita and the ratio between external debt and gross domestic product. The expansion of debt favors economically advanced nations that can generate substantial amounts of debt. This reality results in an increased burden on economically weaker nations.

Japan serves as an excellent example of such a dynamic due largely to its persistent budget deficit and a looming increase in social security payments caused by an aging population and the sluggish growth of gross domestic product (Mayumi, 2020). Of course, the demographics of many other nations are not far behind.[1] It would be wise for all to take note of the forces Japan is battling against. To temporarily circumvent the shortage of national budget, the Japanese government has repeatedly resorted to issuing national bonds. This action has the side effect of increasing biophysical debt in the future due to the dual nature of money. Section 5.3 describes this situation in detail. Section 5.3 then presents a redemption scheme for national bonds that can dramatically reduce their careless expansion. The logic behind such a redemption scheme was already briefly touched upon in Sect. 4.3, the case of discounting

---

[1] In the OECD, the average fertility rate has fallen below 1.6 children per woman, down from more than 2.8 children per woman just five decades ago. The current rate remains well below the approximate 2.1 children per woman needed to maintain a stable population (the "replacement rate"). South Korea has a shocking rate of less than half the OECD average and China, with a population of roughly 1.4bn and a fertility rate only slightly greater than half the replacement rate, is running full-throttle into a massive demographic cliff. See OECD (2023).

loan principal. Every nation, indeed, every region of the world economy, should seriously reconsider the capital biophysical sin of a careless expansion of national bonds and general liquidity. Section 5.4 concludes and discusses miscellaneous issues associated with the dual nature of money, lightly touching on ideas of sovereign money, which will be discussed fully in Chapter 8.

5.2   The Dual Nature of Money

Money is a promise to pay and is ultimately employed by individual possessors to trade for real goods and services (Wilson, 1934). Viewed through this lens, any economic entity has a robust impetus to issue money if permitted or to acquire the capacity to issue money. This propensity, and indeed this comprehension of money issuers' incentives, is sufficient on its own to explain why the stock of general liquidity tends toward constant expansion, given a conducive environment for those issuing money. Understanding money in this way is at the heart of the financial instability intrinsic to the modern economic system. Today, people derive benefit from the issuance of various forms of general liquidity, such as credit cards or reward cards. Credit is virtually indistinguishable from traditional money in almost all applications, even though people rarely acknowledge this equivalency or reflect on its implications. While printing currency in one's basement is a felony offense, numerous private economic entities, including banks and financial corporations, generate vast quantities of money and money substitutes. Many private entities, like investment banks, produce money substitutes without fully grasping the biophysical debt that this entails at a societal level. Paradoxically, at the community level, whether regionally or globally, money and its substitutes represent biophysical debts destined ultimately for exchange for goods and services. Assertions such as, "Traditional coin currencies were free of debt" (Huber, 2017, p. 13), are misleading in two aspects. First, as demonstrated in Sect. 2.2 ("Why Does Money Exist?"), any form of money presumes the existence of a debt to be resolved in the future. Second, such monetary debt must ultimately be settled in terms of goods and services, which demand accessible energy and material resources subject to the constraints imposed by the entropy law.

From a natural sciences viewpoint, all goods and services are produced at the cost of valuable energy and materials—production increases total entropy more than would occur without production (Georgescu-Roegen,

1971). Consequently, economic production typically involves a deficit in biophysical terms as a certain quantity of exhaustible resources is irretrievably consumed. Irreversible biophysical loss is not confined to the production process and, furthermore, nature does not offer a check-out line for humans to pay for the exhaustible resources they extract. Royalties on exhaustible resources are human constructs, not nature's.

Conversely, resources in situ, being irreproducible and nearly irrevocably lost once consumed, cannot possess any production cost on which to base a pricing mechanism (Georgescu-Roegen, 1979). However, all contemporary economic processes of production, distribution, consumption, and disposal inexorably diminish the exhaustible energy and materials available to future generations. Real capital created by economic processes, like basic infrastructure, also inevitably deteriorates over time at a rate commensurate with its size and scale. This decay engenders additional irreversible biophysical debt through its implication of the necessity for maintenance and renewal processes. Due to these factors, an increase in money can be regarded, from a *community standpoint*, as an *increase in future biophysical liability*.

The discussions thus far in this chapter point toward the notion of the dual nature of money—two opposing perspectives on money and its essence. Whereas money is perceived as a form of wealth from an individual's perspective, from a collective viewpoint, money is both a representative and an instigator of biophysical debt. Acknowledging this dual nature of money emphasizes the urgency with which global communities must thoughtfully reassess certain facets of their political and financial institutions, presuming that a degree of restraint is deemed beneficial and that we have the desire to preserve our communal biophysical integrity.

So, just as readily as it is considered a part of national wealth, money must also be considered a part of national debt. Money at the national level represents the total of individual claims on national wealth. The question then arises: how is it possible to have interest on money? We will soon see that defending such a practice is not trivial *prima facie*, and indeed, the concept is no stranger to robust, level-headed criticism, such as that levied by Soddy (1926) in *Wealth, Virtual Wealth and Debt*, unamusingly on the eve of the Great Depression.

It is important to highlight that the concepts of *individual* and *communal* are contextual, their meanings only understandable in relation to each other. It is perhaps most natural to consider the individual perspective to be that of a single person and the community perspective to be that of their embedding clique. Nevertheless, a nation, viewed as a community in one analytical context, could be considered an individual in another, such as in the interaction between a nation and a larger economic bloc or within the framework of the global economy as a whole. This relativism, although intriguing, should be momentarily set aside. Instead, the reader is encouraged to understand that acknowledging money's dual nature is crucial to prevent the unnecessary expansion of the money stock and ensure biophysical sustainability, a concept hitherto largely neglected.

Soddy was perhaps the earliest scholar to grasp the dual nature of money clearly. In his words: "National securities and money are both wealth from the standpoint of the individual owner and [...] debt from the standpoint of the community" (Soddy, 1926, p. 222). Any individual economic entity, be it a person, company, commercial bank, or even a country, regards all forms of money as abstract representations of wealth, registering their money as an asset on their balance sheet. On the other hand, the presenter of money or a money substitute is entitled to a certain amount of goods and services or to the replacement of the original money form with another form of money provided by the receiver. This entitlement does not necessarily depend on whether the presenter categorizes such money as an asset or a liability. As long as the receiver of the money is confident in the market validity of the received money, a final exchange for goods and services or a different form of money is feasible. For instance, when a consumer presents cash for a coffee at a cafe, the cafe owner is unlikely to care whether that cash is the presenter's personal asset or a bank liability: a cup of coffee is served regardless.

Both the general population and economists usually perceive the creation of securities, such as government bonds, as the creation of debt. However, it is noteworthy that individual economic agents who hold government bonds in their portfolios often view them as wealth, not debt. Take, for instance, BlackRock, the world's largest investment management company, which managed close to $8trn in assets as of 2020. For BlackRock clients who hold government bonds among their managed "financial assets," these bonds represent genuine personal monetary wealth.

Let us consider another fundamental example of the dual nature, as demonstrated by the Bank of Japan's balance sheet. Surprisingly to many, the Bank of Japan operates somewhat like a private company, with shares traded on the JASDAQ in Tokyo. The Bank's accounts, inclusive of government securities like Japanese national bonds, are categorized as assets, not liabilities. National bonds, therefore, constitute a form of wealth for the Bank of Japan as an individual entity. Conversely, as of September 30, 2020, Japanese government securities held by the Bank of Japan exceeded ¥530trn, equating to 57% of outstanding Japanese national bonds (BOJ, 2020). From a communal perspective, these national bonds represent a debt to Japan. More critically, in terms of sustainability, Japanese national bonds can be seen as potential biophysical debt, triggering entropic processes that accelerate natural resource exploitation, among similar concerns.

A third, more grandiose example is perhaps more useful still to grasp the importance of dual nature in international political economy. As of February 2021, outstanding United States Treasury securities amounted to $7.1trn. Naturally, the United States views this sum as a debt. Conversely, the major foreign nations[2] that hold these United States Treasury securities perceive the same sum as an asset individually. *A conventional accounting scheme based on the double-booking entry convention is oblivious to this collective reality.* To reiterate, when an individual pays for a coffee at a cafe, the cafe owner is indifferent to whether the money is the customer's personal asset or a bank liability: they serve a cup of coffee regardless.

Similarly, whether items like United States Treasury securities are recorded as an asset or a liability, the mere presence of debt necessitates the provision of a tremendous quantity of future goods and services. From a global viewpoint, such a scenario is dire, not only precipitating repeated financial crises but also provoking more general crises of sustainability. In the global context, the primary driver of the recent surge in government debt has been the substantial monetary measures implemented to address the COVID-19 crisis. These measures amounted to approximately $7.5trn in 2020 alone, according to the International Monetary Fund (IMF, 2020). Such initiatives encompassed a massive infusion of new general liquidity into the worldwide economy, predominantly through the issuance of government bonds, among other instruments.

---

[2] Japan held $1.3trn, China $1.1trn, the United Kingdom $459bn, Brazil $259bn, India $204bn, France $108bn, Germany $74bn, Sweden $41bn, *et cetera* (USDT & FRB, 2021). Each of the listed countries considers the respective amount as an asset.

While the dual nature of money is not a particularly difficult concept to grasp, where explained directly, it seems not to be duly recognized by the general public or economists, mainstream or heterodox.

The discussion advanced thus far serves to assure readers that all individual economic entities face a strong temptation to obtain issuing rights for *any form of general liquidity* with a positive return, acknowledging that the ultimate purpose of such general liquidity is its exchange for a certain amount of goods and services. This reality is one of the fundamental drivers of post-industrial financialization in the global economy, a process that has led to a situation where, in the United States over the past decade, for example, a full 24–28% of the total domestic corporate profits were generated by the financial[3] sectors (BEA, 2018). Moreover, corporations in "non-financial sectors," such as those in manufacturing, are frequently seen to generate well over half their operating income from financial activities.

The above points are so critical to the discussion of money and global sustainability that they warrant rephrasing. Individuals typically regard money as a claim to wealth. However, money is also a collective biophysical debt at the community level since it entails a promise to pay in terms of either existing wealth or the production of future wealth. Ultimately, money places communities as wholes into long-term biophysical debt[4]: (1) the production of real capital entails a biophysical deficit in terms of entropy since useful energy and materials are irrevocably consumed, thereby resulting in fewer exhaustible resources, and (2) real capital unavoidably decays over time, necessitating upkeep and disposal.[5]

The first point on biophysical debt is, in particular, well-recognized by biophysical analysts. For instance, it is underscored by Soddy (1926, p. 118), who comprehended money as exchangeable for wealth and wealth itself as "a form or product of energy or work which enables or

---

[3] The United States Bureau of Economic Analysis's definition on "financial" consists of finance, insurance, banking, and other holding.

[4] Biophysical debt in the most general sense is generated whenever real capital is produced due to the fact that the production of real capital entails an entropy deficit (Georgescu-Roegen, 1971). Monetary debt is an abstract negative quantity of money that defies interpretation in physical terms.

[5] The decay and deterioration of real capital, for example buildings and infrastructure, must be managed and addressed by the surrounding economic community. The creation of purchasing power is therefore an extremely delicate business—it dictates the quality and quantity of biophysical debt received by an economic community.

empowers life." Soddy also took great care to highlight the second point on biophysical debt, evidenced by his observations that the immense accumulations of infrastructures, such as "railways, canals, factories and slum cities [are] all on the same broad highway to destruction" (Soddy, 1926, p. 99). Furthermore, he pointed out that the "material counterpart of the tendency of energy to flow is the tendency of materials to change" and that "[l]iability to rot, decay, catch fire, suffer slow deterioration is thus an *essential* quality of [physical] wealth" (Soddy, 1926, p. 116). Concerning both the first and the second points, the sharp distinction between biophysical debt and monetary debt should be emphasized: monetary debts are "subject to the laws of mathematics [(increasing at a compound interest rate)] rather than physics" (Soddy, 1926, p. 70).

For Soddy, wealth represents the physical flow of goods and services that contribute to a decent life, echoing the ideas of Ruskin. In 1926, Soddy characterized the portion of the monetary aggregate *intended for the exchange of goods and services* as "virtual wealth." He asserted that other forms of money, such as financial assets, ought to be minimized and emphasized the necessity of maintaining a delicate balance between physical and virtual wealth (Soddy, 1934).

We maintain that Soddy's concept of wealth, viewed as a flow of material goods and services, offers invaluable insights for future discussions on sustainability. Consequently, we give due attention to the issue of wealth in connection with biophysical sustainability in Chapter 6.

In Fig. 5.1, which illustrates the debt situation of a select group of countries in terms of external debt per capita and the ratio of external debt to gross domestic product (GDP), there is a cluster in the lower-left section comprising countries with comparatively low-external debt measures. Conversely, countries exhibiting progressively higher levels of external debt are scattered upward toward the right. Despite Greece's high-external debt to GDP ratio—a point of severe criticism levied by several larger European economies, such as Germany—the United Kingdom's ratio, at 329%, is considerably higher. The capacities of Greece and the United Kingdom to manage their external debt are evidently regarded differently. However, as the dual nature of money highlights, money embodies a debt at the community level, irrespective of the identities of the creditors or borrowers. In the context of Fig. 5.1, the "community" could be interpreted as the global economy.

A fundamental capability required by any country aiming to navigate conditions of indebtedness is the ability to issue money, a commodity

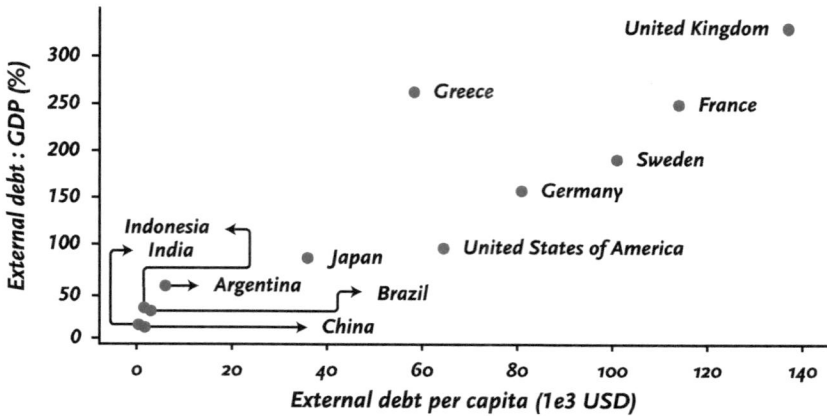

Fig. 5.1 External debt per capita and relative to gross domestic product (GDP) for twelve major economies as of 2020 (*Data source* UN [2019] and Trading Economics [2021a, 2021b])

consistently traded on the international financial market. Although Greece can increase its debt within the framework of the global economy, it cannot assume the role of a debt issuer without approval from economically influential countries like France and Germany. These countries themselves are grappling with significant debt situations within the European Union.

More than 80 years ago, Mark keenly noted our global addiction to debt and monetary return in his book, *The Modern Idolatry: An Analysis of Usury and the Pathology of Debt*:

> It is important, therefore, to realize that *we are all usurers*—from the child who deposits his mite in the penny savings-bank to the international syndicate of money-lenders which operates through the Bank for International Settlements and the League of Nations machinery at Geneva—and that the universal adoption of this evil and disruptive principle, against the teaching of all the highest philosophical and religious examples, is ratified by common consent and full legal authority.
>
> (Mark, 1934, p. 3)

In the present day, the proverbial "We" take for granted that unearned income is an easily justified, indeed, most natural thing. This justification is irresistible to virtually all members of modern, individualistic society, being a society where there are a variety of ways of acquiring unearned income. Tragically, this reality does not pay due attention to the dual nature. As Popper (1945, p. 3) aptly remarked, however, "The future depends on ourselves, and we do not depend on any historical necessity." It appears most timely and urgent for all citizens to grasp the essence of the dual nature of money so that we can avoid situations where "We" engage in usury.

5.3 A STRATEGY TO DRAMATICALLY REDUCE UNNECESSARY OUTSTANDING NATIONAL BONDS

The incentive to create new money is extraordinary. Private minting or counterfeiting is, of course, strictly prohibited, but a poor definition and conceptualization of money allows for considerable room for maneuvering. As explored by various contemporary works such as Huber (2017) or Ryan-Collins et al. (2012), most money in the present global financial system is bankmoney. According to Huber (2017), bankmoney is money on account as a form of demand deposit, created, for example, by commercial banks every time they credit a non-bank customer account. Huber (2017) estimates that roughly 95% of the active domestic money supply in the eurozone is bankmoney. Ryan-Collins et al. (2012) estimate that figure to be 97% for the case of the United Kingdom. It now seems timelier than ever for the citizens and governing apparatuses of fiscal communities to concern themselves with regaining sovereignty over money issuance and distribution.

In anticipation of a more involved discussion on sovereign money in Chapter 8, this section focuses on a national bond redemption scheme, the baby form of which was originally proposed by Soddy (1926). The redemption scheme proves to be as crucial as ever in the modern day. Due to a rapidly aging population—a relative shrinkage of the economically active population coupled with sluggish growth of gross domestic product—Japan, for example, has been issuing an enormous quantity of national bonds, a specific type of money substitute.

Previously, in Chapter 2, Fig. 2.2 illustrated Japan's record of bond issuance through a time series on the balance of outstanding bonds comprised of construction bonds and deficit-covering bonds. Until 1998, the value of outstanding deficit-covering bonds was less than ¥100trn. However, this value started to increase significantly after 1998. By

2004, the value of outstanding deficit-covering bonds surpassed that of construction bonds, and by 2021, these bonds made up more than 70% of the total outstanding national bonds issued in Japan.

To fully comprehend the gravity of this situation, it is critical to understand Article 5 of Japan's Public Finance Act. This article prohibits the Bank of Japan from underwriting public bonds at the time of new bond issuance. However, it does not forbid the Bank of Japan from underwriting national bonds *after they have been issued*. The Bank often misuses this power to underwrite already issued national bonds, with a notable instance being the implementation of its quantitative easing policy, which started in 2013. A number of other central banks around the globe operate similarly.

Table 5.1 presents a series of significant general account budget statistics for Japan spanning the last three decades. The table suggests that approximately 8% of the general account budget has been spent on national bond interest payments in recent years. Although the interest payment on the balance of outstanding bonds is more or less obtained by multiplying the balance of outstanding bonds by the weighted average of the interest rate on national bonds, 8% of the general budget is certainly a substantial amount. Moreover, considering distributional inequality, the ratio of the weighted average interest rate to the savings account interest rate is extraordinarily high in modern times—830 × in 2021, compared to a meager 14.3 × in 1989. National bond owners enjoy certain privileges compared to less wealthy individuals—those with no option but to deposit only a small fraction of their earnings into their savings accounts, with lower-interest rates, hoping for a decent life.

In such a situation, revisiting Soddy's compound scheme for national bond redemption seems appropriate. Compound redemption implies that a national government repurchases national bonds from private owners and receives interest payments on the portion of the national bonds it has redeemed. These interest payments are intended to be used for additional redemption of the principal, and income tax is levied on the portion that has not yet been redeemed. On the surface, this scheme may appear unfairly harsh on national bond owners. However, the existence of money's dual nature dictates that due consideration should be given to taxing unearned income.

Table 5.1 Japanese general account budget statistics 1989–2021, detailing the balance of outstanding bonds, general account budget, interest payment on the balance of outstanding bonds, weighted average of interest rate on national bonds, interest rate on saving account, and the ratio of the interest rate on national bonds to that on saving account

		1989	1997	2005	2013	2021
¥1trn	Balance of outstanding bonds	161	258	527	744	990
	General account budget	66.3	78.4	85.5	100	106.6
	Interest payment	10.6	10.6	7	8.1	8.5
%	Interest on national bonds (1)	6.16	4.02	1.42	1.15	0.83
	Interest on saving account (2)	0.43	0.1	0.02	0.02	0.001
	(1)/(2)	14.3	40.2	71	57.5	830

Data source MOF (2023)

Soddy, in his work, considered the simple case of a constant interest rate. Nevertheless, the general case, where the interest rate $i(t)$ is a function of time t, is worth exploring. In addition to the following line of thought, see Appendix for a complete mathematical argument.

(1) G where $0 < G < 1$ is a part of the principal B of a bond that has been redeemed. The national government is supposed to receive an interest payment on G and use such interest payment to redeem the principal further.

(2) Income tax p where $0 < p < 1$ is imposed on the part of the principal B that is not yet redeemed, the part $(1 - G)$.

If interest rate $i(t)$ is a function of time t, the interest accruing on the principal of one unit over time period $(t, t + dt)$ is shown to be $f(t)\Delta t$ where $f(t) = i(t) + t\frac{\Delta i(t)}{\Delta t}$.

Intuitively speaking, the first term, $i(t)\Delta t$, is the interest payment over the time period $(t, t + \Delta t)$ if the interest rate were fixed and the second term, $t\Delta i(t)$, is an additional interest payment associated with the change in the interest rate $\Delta i(t)$.

Therefore

(1) $BGf(t)\Delta t$ represents the total interest payments on BG over the period Δt. The government uses those payments toward redeeming the part not yet redeemed.

(2) $pB(1 - G)f(t)\Delta t$ represents the rate of income tax p imposed on all interest payments and $B(1 - G)f(t)\Delta t$ the amount owners of bonds receive over Δt. This amount is also used for the redemption of national bonds.

(3) $B\Delta G$ represents the sum of the two parts $BGf(t)\Delta t$ and $pB(1 - G)f(t)\Delta t$.

Canceling B from both sides, the following differential relation is obtained:

$$Rf(t)dt + p(1 - R)f(t)dt = dR. \qquad (5.1)$$

While it is possible to obtain a general solution to (5.1), given any functional form for the interest rate $i(t)$ and the income tax rate p, the simpler case of a constant interest rate is instead provided:

$$G(t) = \tfrac{p}{1-p}\{e^{i(1-p)t} - 1\} \qquad (5.2)$$

where $G(0) = 0$, meaning that, at the initial point, no redemption is yet made.

Introducing the relation $\frac{1}{i} = T$, where variable T is the period of years in which the principal is redeemed by accumulated interest payment, (5.2) can then be rearranged in the form

$$\tfrac{t}{T} = \tfrac{1}{1-p}\ln\left(\tfrac{1}{p}\right). \qquad (5.3)$$

Note that ln denotes natural logarithm.

Figure 5.2 shows the relation between $\frac{t}{T}$ and p. Given a tax rate p, the vertical axis, $\frac{t}{T}$, represents how much time, in terms of T, is required to redeem a national bond completely. As the reader might already suspect, the higher the tax rate, the shorter the time needed to make a complete redemption.

Splitting G into terms G_1 and G_2, where term G_1 represents the interest earned on the redeemed part G and term G_2 represents the income tax on unearned income from the part of national bonds not yet

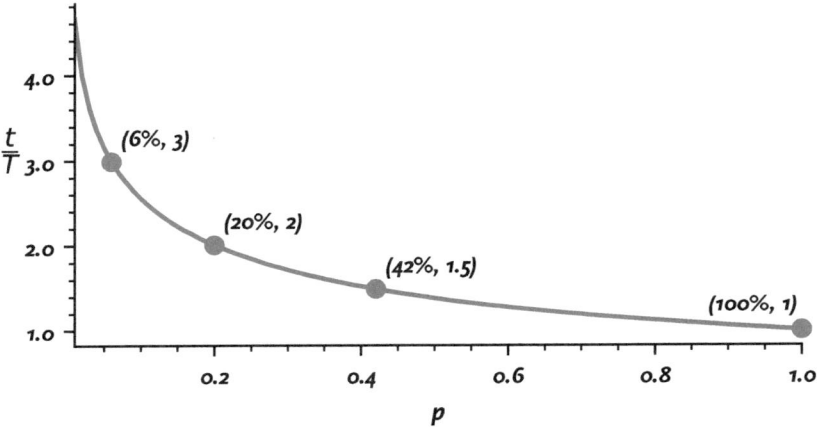

Fig. 5.2   The relation between complete redemption time $\left(\frac{t}{T}\right)$ and income tax rate (p)

redeemed, $(1 - G)$, the following three relations may be obtained:

$$G = G_1 + G_2,$$

$$\frac{dG_1}{dt} = iG,$$

and

$$\frac{dG_2}{dt} = ip\{1 - G\}.$$

where $G = 1$, a complete redemption case, the final forms of G_1 and G_2 would be as follows:

$$G_1 = \frac{1}{1-p}\left\{1 - \frac{p}{1-p}\ln\left(\frac{1}{p}\right)\right\} \tag{5.4}$$

and

$$G_2 = \frac{1}{1-p}\left\{\frac{p}{1-p}\ln\left(\frac{1}{p}\right) - 1\right\}. \tag{5.5}$$

Following (5.4) and (5.5), a graphical representation of terms G_1 and G_2 as they vary depending on the income tax rate p is shown in Fig. 5.3. As p increases, the interest earned on the redeemed part, G_1, decreases.

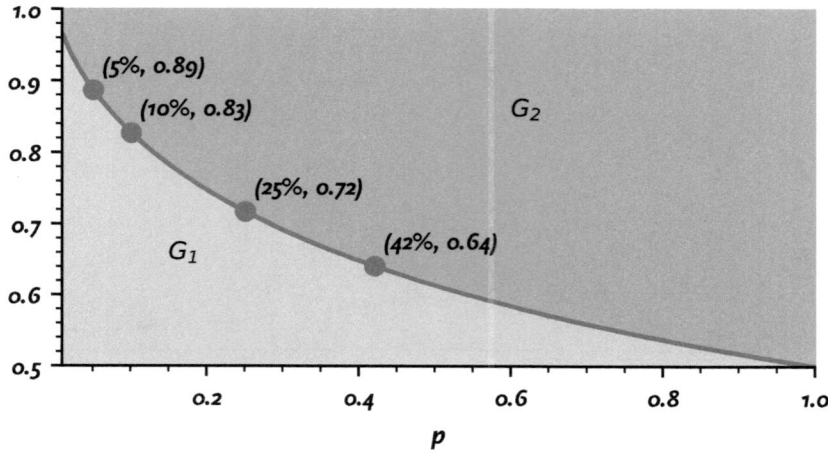

Fig. 5.3 The relation between the part redeemed by interest (G_1) and the part redeemed by income tax (G_2), following income tax rate p

Should a national bond redemption scheme, such as that outlined in (5.4) and (5.5), be implemented in modern economies, it could dramatically reduce the privileged status granted to debt owners, regardless of how a given bond is ultimately settled, be it by money payment, release, compensation, or novation. This scheme may serve as a valuable starting point for economic communities seeking a way to significantly weaken the mechanisms that incentivize the actions of debt issuers and buyers of monetary assets. Consequently, the scheme would reduce the overwhelming volume of irrelevant monetary assets and the magnitude of asset bubbles and their associated vast sustainability concerns. After all, in a globalized world, all monetary assets constitute biophysical debt for the global community. As expressed by Soddy (1931, p. 25) and paraphrased aptly by Daly (1980, p. 474):

> The ruling passion of the age is to convert biophysical wealth into debt in order to derive a permanent future income from it—to convert biophysical wealth that perishes into debt that endures, debt that does not rot, costs nothing to maintain, and brings in perennial interest.

Soddy's argument was that this conversion is an illusion, achievable only by disregarding the combined significance of money's dual nature. An individual can live off the interest on the monetary debt they own, but a community, as a unified entity, cannot sustain itself on the interest from the shared biophysical indebtedness of its members.

5.4 CONCLUSION

Keynes (1930, p. 130, emphasis added) once asserted in his *A Treatise on Money*, "Thus when we are concerned with the wealth of a part of the total system under consideration, whether the part is an individual or a country, we have a fourth category, namely, the net balance of claims on money, which we will call *loan capital*." Keynes adheres here to the conventional economist worldview whereby money is a component of wealth, and its net balance of claims constitutes wealth. He never did pay adequate attention to the dual nature of money, completely disregarding the biophysical considerations associated with money.

Contrastingly, Macleod (1883, p. 35, emphasis added) postulates that money's "function is to represent the *debts* which arise from *unequal* exchanges among men: and to enable persons who have rendered services to others, and have received no equivalent from them, to obtain that equivalent or satisfaction from someone else." His perception of money corresponds to the concept of virtual wealth as proposed by Soddy. Virtual wealth, money being the canonical example, represents a promise to pay in terms of goods and services already delivered by society as a whole but not yet disbursed in biophysical terms.

Just over a century ago, Soddy (1922, p. 30, emphasis added) fully acknowledged the dual nature of money and the perils of an excessive financial sector expansion in his work, *Cartesian Economics*:

> You cannot permanently pit an absurd human convention, such as the spontaneous increment of debt [(*compound interest*)], against the natural law of the spontaneous decrement of wealth [(*due to the entropy law*)]. [...] [T]he significant and distressing fact is that this absurd law, with the concentration of money in the hands of trusts and combines of financiers, now tends to operate more and more fully every day.

Note that our discussion does not address potential international agreements that could deter an excessive expansion of the global money supply. In the current flexible exchange regime, any modification in the prime interest rate implemented by any major currency triggers substantial implications for the exchange rates of all other primary currencies, as well as shifts in investment decisions by corporations and individual financial agents. Furthermore, exchange rate adjustments inevitably result in capital transfers among those seeking global financial investment opportunities. While no one realistically knows how to manage such situations, we do understand that without international cooperation, any national decision on a new money supply system will swiftly face failure. The downfall of the Bretton Woods system in 1971 is a prime example. We appear to intuitively grasp that excessive monetary expansion—too much growth in general liquidity leading to high levels of debt from a collective stand-point—poses potentially disastrous economic repercussions. However, these are tremendously complex issues to tackle. The Jubilee, for instance, in Judeo-Christian tradition, was a specific time when all debts were to be automatically absolved, happening in the "Sabbath of Sabbath years," or after seven cycles of seven years. This stands as a testament to the fact that excessive debt growth is a problem that has plagued humanity for millennia.

On a global scale, it would be crucial not only to curb the growth of general liquidity but also to regulate interest rate disparities between nations. These disparities often incite unnecessary international financial capital transfers (Mark, 1934), creating suboptimal circumstances for the individual citizens of countries far removed from the epicenter of active financial dealings. On this note, as we conclude this chapter and look toward further discussion, it is worth remembering that Keynes himself ultimately abandoned his optimistic monetary reform proposal, discussed in his *A Tract on Monetary Reform* (Keynes, 1923). Indeed, later in his career, Keynes (1933, p. 181) favored the reduction of "economic entan-glement among nations" and to "let goods be homespun whenever it is reasonably and conveniently possible, and, above all, [to] let finance be primarily national."

The fundamental premise of Keynes's later views on national self-sufficiency, which align with Soddy's work, essentially alludes to a broader understanding of what is "wrong" with the modern monetary system. At the heart of the issue is the observation of a propensity toward over-capitalization, specifically the excessive growth of virtual capital primarily induced by a division between the monetary ownership of capital and the tangible responsibility of capital management. This separation leads to monetary ownership being distributed among many individuals, each acting based on their personal financial interests, without acknowledging the profound implications of money's dual nature for biophysical sustainability.

Excessive virtual capital has the potential to generate an excess of real capital. Due to its very nature as an excess, it is difficult to utilize to its full capacity. This constant surplus puts nations and their constituent individuals in a relentless search for increasingly frivolous ways to use otherwise unused real capital. As Soddy (1926, p. 251) put it: "No primitive community would reckon upon eating its ploughs if short of bread. The financial mentality of modern man prevents these elementary considerations from being properly appreciated." Seen through this lens, excessive amounts of virtual and real capital can be perceived as an unnecessary biophysical burden. They also incentivize militarism and aggression on the international stage. As Keynes (1933) diplomatically explained, the great concentration of the effort of nations and individuals on expanding virtual capital is neither a safeguard nor an assurance of international peace. Soddy (1926, p. 267) echoed this sentiment a few years prior, stating:

> An excess of capital unwanted in peace production, in time of war would find an outlet for its unused capacity. So arises the incentive towards militarism and aggression in international politics, in order to secure markets, or alternatively, as serving the same object, to fight about them.

If the "We" learn to appreciate and embrace the mentioned messages of Keynes and Soddy, the "We" must strive to establish a world where money is not characterized by an explosive nature and where financial activities remain at a community scale—where collective action and institutions of trust have a hope of functioning strongly. We must learn to think differently. In his own way, Daly (2005, p. 100) makes the call: "The global economy is now so large that society can no longer safely pretend it operates within a limitless ecosystem. Developing an economy that can be sustained within the finite biosphere requires new ways of thinking." Indeed, any new ways of thinking must include recognition of the dual nature of money and its importance for a more sustainable social-ecological interaction. Only then can the unnecessary biophysical exploitation caused by monetary aggression be minimized globally.

In Sect. 5.3 of this chapter, a redemption scheme for national bonds was presented. Many nations have been issuing national bonds to compensate for the deficit in their respective government expenditures. Outstanding national bonds represent both a monetary burden and a biophysical burden on global socioeconomic systems and the biosphere. Another more significant share of money in the system, which ultimately endangers the collective perspective on biophysical sustainability as in the dual nature of money, stems from the unnatural powers of commercial bankers. Macleod's statements concerning the situation of the United Kingdom, which can be generalized to most modern nations, are as true today as they were in the 1880s: "At the present time *credit*, in its various forms, is the most gigantic species of *property* in this country [...] and the negotiation of *debts* is, beyond all comparison, the most colossal branch of commerce. The merchants who trade in *debts*—namely, *bankers*—are now the *rulers and regulators of commerce*—they almost control the fortunes of states" (Macleod, 1883, p. 157). Similarly, Woodrow Wilson, the twenty-eighth president of the United States, who was in office for two terms spanning 1913–1921, expressed as follows his inability to control his country's total money supply through his campaign and at the start of his first term:

> The great monopoly in this country is the monopoly of big credits. So long as that exists, our [...] freedom and individual energy of development are out of the question. A great industrial nation is controlled by its system of credit. Our system of credit is privately concentrated. The growth of the nation, therefore, and all our activities are in the hands of a few men who, even if their action be honest and intended for the public interest, are necessarily concentrated upon the great undertakings in which their own money is involved and who necessarily, by very reason of their own limitations, [...] destroy genuine economic freedom.
>
> (Wilson, 1913, p. 185)

and some few pages later

> We have been dreading all along the time when the combined power of high finance would be greater than the power of the government. Have we come to a time when [...] any man who wishes to be the President must doff his cap in the presence of this high finance, and say, 'You are our inevitable master, but we will see how we can make the best of it?' [....] [W]e have come to be one of the worst ruled, one of the most completely

controlled and dominated, governments in the civilized world—no longer a government by free opinion, no longer a government by conviction and the vote of the majority, but a government by the opinion and the duress of small groups of dominant men.

(Wilson, 1913, pp. 200–201)

Early Buddhist teachings list ten bad actions, one of which is "taking what is not given" (Holmes, 1997); in other words, the act of stealing. It is notable that issuing excessive amounts of money can be perceived as a proxy equivalent to the theft of common resources. Many individuals, including many Buddhists, believe that the first of the ten bad acts, "destroying life," is the most egregious of the ten. However, the tenth act, "wrong views," is fundamentally worse. Given humankind's history of weak individualistic self-control, adding an eleventh bad act in a reformed future society seems prudent: "issuing excessive amounts of money, pegged to a positive interest." This new act could likely best be assigned the epithet "most heinous among the bad acts!"

To regain control of the money supply, currently predominantly held by a privileged group of commercial bankers, the elected representatives of democratic economic communities must have full control over the total quantity of general liquidity to be issued and its distribution among citizens. Issues associated with sovereign money will be discussed further in Chapter 8.

Appendix 5.A

It must first be noted that with a constant interest rate, i, the interest payment accruing to one over time period $(t, t + dt)$ is $i\,dt = (t + dt)i - ti$. This is the case Soddy (1926) investigated. The general case is considered in this appendix.

If the interest rate $i(t)$ is a function of time t, the interest accruing to one unit of money over the time period $(t, t + dt)$ is

$$(t + dt)i(t + dt) - ti(t) = \left\{ i(t) + t\frac{di(t)}{dt} \right\} dt = f(t)dt$$

where $f(t) = i(t) + t\frac{di(t)}{dt}$, ignoring the higher order terms $(dt)^2$ and so forth.

$$Gf(t)dt + p(1 - G)f(t)dt = dG \qquad (5.A.1)$$

and rearranging the terms in (5.A.1) we have

$$\frac{dG(t)}{dt} - (1-p)f(t)G(t) = pf(t). \tag{5.A.2}$$

The solution of the first-order ordinary differential equation $\frac{dy(t)}{dt} + H(t)y(t) = Q(t)$ is known to be $y = e^{-\int H(t)dt}\left\{\int Q(t)\, e^{\int H(t)dt}dt + C\right\}$ where C is a constant. C can be identified if the initial condition $y(0)$ is given.

In our differential equation, $y(t) = G(t)$, $H(t) = -(1-p)f(t)$, and $Q(t) = pf(t)$. Therefore, the general solution of the differential Eq. (5.A.2) is given by

$$G(t) = e^{(1-p)\int f(t)dt}\left\{p\int f(t)\, e^{-(1-p)\int f(t)dt}dt + C\right\}.$$

Note that

$$\int f(t)dt = \int\left\{i(t) + t\frac{di(t)}{dt}\right\}dt = \int i(t)\,dt + ti(t) - \int i(t)dt = ti(t)$$

and we obtain

$$G(t) = e^{(1-p)ti(t)}\left\{p\int\left[i(t) + t\frac{di(t)}{dt}\right]e^{-(1-p)ti(t)}dt + C\right\}. \tag{5.A.3}$$

Given income tax rate p on interest received as well as an interest rate function over time $i(t)$, $G(t)$ can be obtained as the right-hand side of (5.A.3), together with the initial condition $t = 0$, $G(0) = 0$. Note that $C = -K(0)$ where $K(t) = p\int[i(t) + t\frac{di(t)}{dt}]e^{-(1-p)ti(t)}dt$.
The final form of $R(t)$ is

$$G(t) = e^{(1-p)ti(t)}\left\{p\int\left[i(t) + t\frac{di(t)}{dt}\right]e^{-(1-p)ti(t)}dt - K(0)\right\}. \tag{5.A.4}$$

$G(t)$ can be divided into two parts, $G_1(t)$ and $G_2(t)$, where $G_1(t)$ represents the interest earned on the redeemed part $G(t)$ and G_2 represents the income tax on unearned income from the part of national bonds that are yet not redeemed, in other words, $(1 - G(t))$.
Then, the following two relations can be obtained:

$$\frac{dG_1(t)}{dt} = G(t)f(t) \tag{5.A.5}$$

and

$$\frac{dG_2(t)}{dt} = p\{1 - G(t)\}f(t). \tag{5.A.6}$$

Substituting (5.A.4) into (5.A.5) and (5.A.6) and integrating with respect to time t, it is straightforward to obtain both $G_1(t)$ and $G_2(t)$:

$$G_1(t) = \int G(t) \, f(t)dt$$

and

$$G_2(t) = p \int \{1 - G(t)\} \, f(t)dt.$$

If the interest rate is a given constant, we can obtain $G(t)$ using the initial condition. It is straightforward to obtain the value of C in this case, the case of a constant interest rate, $C = \frac{p}{1-p}$. The final form of $G(t)$ where $C = \frac{p}{1-p}$ is given as

$$G(t) = \frac{p}{1-p}\{e^{i(1-p)t} - 1\}. \tag{5.A.7}$$

Using the relation $\frac{1}{i} = T$, which is the period of years in which the principal is redeemed by accumulated interest payment, (5.A.7) can be rearranged in the form

$$\frac{t}{T} = \frac{1}{1-p} \ln\left(\frac{1}{p}\right)$$

where ln abbreviates natural logarithm. In a similar way

$$\frac{dG_1(t)}{dt} = iG(t)$$

and

$$\frac{dG_2(t)}{dt} = ip\{1 - G(t)\}.$$

If $G = 1$, a complete redemption is realized. The final forms of G_1 and G_2 are then

$$G_1 = \frac{1}{1-p}\left\{1 - \frac{p}{1-p} \ln\left(\frac{1}{p}\right)\right\}$$

$$G_2 = \frac{1}{1-p}\left\{\frac{p}{1-p} \ln\left(\frac{1}{p}\right) - 1\right\}.$$

References

Aliber, R. Z., & Kindleberger, C. P. (2015). *Manias, Panics and Crashes: A History of Financial Crises* (7th ed.). Palgrave Macmillan (Original work published 1978).

BEA. (2018). *National Income and Product Accounts: Table 6.16D: Corporate Profits by Industry (GDPbyInd_VA_1947–2017)*. Bureau of Economic Analysis, United States Department of Commerce. https://www.bea.gov/sites/def ault/files/2018-04/GDPbyInd_VA_1947-2017.xlsx. Accessed 26 June 2023.

BOJ. (2020). *Japanese Government Bonds Held by the Bank of Japan 2020 (日本銀行が保有する国債の銘柄別残高 2020年)*. Bank of Japan (日本銀行). https://www.boj.or.jp/en/statistics/boj/other/mei/release/2020/index. htm. Accessed 28 June 2023.

Campbell, C. (2000). The Imminent Peak of Global Oil Production. In *Feasta Review 1. Money, Energy and Growth*. Trinity College, Dublin, Ireland.

Daly, H. E. (1980). The Economic Thought of Frederick Soddy. *History of Political Economy, 12*(4), 469–488. https://doi.org/10.1215/00182702-12-4-469

Daly, H. E. (2005). Economics in a Full World. *Scientific American, 293*(3), 100–107. https://doi.org/10.1038/scientificamerican0905-100

Georgescu-Roegen, N. (1971). *The Entropy Law and the Economic Process*. Harvard University Press.

Georgescu-Roegen, N. (1979). Myths About Energy and Matter. *Growth and Change, 10*(1), 16–23. https://doi.org/10.1111/j.1468-2257.1979.tb0 0819.x

Holmes, D. (1997). *The Heart of Theravada Buddhism: The Noble Eightfold Path*. Chulalongkorn University.

Huber, J. (2017). *Sovereign Money: Beyond Reserve Banking*. Palgrave Macmillan. https://doi.org/10.1007/978-3-319-42174-2

IMF. (2020). *A Year Like No Other (2020 IMF Annual Report)*. International Monetary Fund.

IPCC. (2014). *Climate Change 2014: Synthesis Report* (R. K. Pachauri et al. Ed.). Intergovernmental Panel on Climate Change.

Keynes, J. M. (1923). *A Tract on Monetary Reform* (1st ed.). Macmillan and Company, Limited.

Keynes, J. M. (1930). *A Treatise on Money: The Pure Theory of Money* (Vol. 1). Macmillan and Company, Limited.

Keynes, J. M. (1933). National Self-Sufficiency. *Studies: An Irish Quarterly Review, 22*(86), 177–193.

Lucas, R. E., Jr. (2003). Macroeconomic Priorities. *American Economic Review, 93*(1), 1–14. https://doi.org/10.1257/000282803321455133

Macfarlane, A. (1978). *The Origins of English Individualism: The Family, Property, and Social Transition*. Cambridge University Press.

Macleod, H. D. (1883). *The Theory and Practice of Banking* (4th ed., Vol. 1). Longmans, Green, Reader and Dyer.

Mark, J. (1934). *The Modern Idolatry: Being an Analysis of Usury & The Pathology of Debt*. Chatto and Windus.

Mayumi, K. (2020). *Sustainable Energy and Economics in an Aging Population: Lessons from Japan*. Springer (Lecture Notes in Energy). https://doi.org/10.1007/978-3-030-43225-6

Mayumi, K., & Giampietro, M. (2018). Money as the Potential Cause of the Tragedy of the Commons. *Romanian Journal of Economic Forecasting, 21*(2), 151–156.

MOF. (2023). *Financial Materials (財政に関する資料)*. Ministry of Finance (財務省), Japan. https://www.mof.go.jp/tax_policy/summary/condition/a02.htm. Accessed 26 June 2023.

OECD. (2023). *Fertility Rates*. Organisation for Economic Co-operation and Development. http://data.oecd.org/pop/fertility-rates.htm. Accessed 26 June 2023.

Popper, K. R. (1945). *The Open Society and Its Enemies: The Spell of Plato* (Vol. 1). George Routledge and Sons, Limited.

Renner, A., Daly, H., & Mayumi, K. (2021). The Dual Nature of Money: Why Monetary Systems Matter for Equitable Bioeconomy. *Environmental Economics and Policy Studies, 23*(4), 749–760. https://doi.org/10.1007/s10018-021-00309-7

Ryan-Collins, J., et al. (2012). *Where Does Money Come From? A Guide to the UK Monetary and Banking System* (2nd ed.). New Economics Foundation.

Soddy, F. (1922). *Cartesian Economics: The Bearing of Physical Science Upon State Stewardship*. Hendersons.

Soddy, F. (1926). *Wealth, Virtual Wealth and Debt: The Solution of the Economic Paradox* (1st ed.). E. P. Dutton and Company.

Soddy, F. (1931). *Money versus Man: A Statement of the World Problem from the Standpoint of the New Economics*. Elkin Mathews and Marrot.

Soddy, F. (1934). *The Role of Money: What It Should Be, Contrasted with what it Has Become*. George Routledge and Sons, Limited.

Trading Economics. (2021a). *External Debt*. https://tradingeconomics.com/country-list/external-debt. Accessed 22 June 2021.

Trading Economics. (2021b). *GDP*. https://tradingeconomics.com/country-list/gdp. Accessed 22 June 2021.

UN. (2019). *World Population Prospects 2019: Total Population by Sex (Thousands)*. Population Division, Department of Economic and Social Affairs, United Nations. https://population.un.org/wpp/. Accessed 22 June 2021.

USDT & FRB. (2021). *Major Foreign Holders of Treasury Securities*. United States Department of the Treasury, Federal Reserve Board. https://ticdata.treasury.gov/Publish/mfh.txt. Accessed 22 June 2021.

Wilson, R. M. (1934). *Promise to Pay: An Inquiry Into The Modern Magic Called High Finance*. George Routledge and Sons, Limited.

Wilson, W. (1913). *The New Freedom: A Call for the Emancipation of the Generous Energies of a People*. Doubleday, Page and Company. http://arc hive.org/details/cu31924025942503. Accessed 26 June 2023.

CHAPTER 6

Expanding Debt Trap and Reviving the Biophysical View on Wealth for a More Sustainable and Equitable Future: The Buddhist Perspective on a Decent Life

I am just content with what I am decently given.
—Ryoanji Temple, Kyoto, Japan[1]

6.1 Introduction

Before getting into the subject matter of this chapter, it is of service to introduce the central concepts discussed in the forthcoming three chapters, Chapters 6 through 8, in the context of the content presented in the previous four chapters, Chapters 2 through 5. These concepts suggest a citizen's path toward renouncing the peculiar set of social convictions associated with wealth, capital, and money prevalent in modernity. Such beliefs have posed substantial obstacles to the creation of a more sustainable and equitable societal form.

The dual nature of money and the two unnatural powers bestowed upon banks, as discussed in Chapters 2 through 5, hold significant implications for future society. The dual nature of money suggests that money

---

[1] The statement is inscribed on a stone at the temple, translated here by author Kozo Torasan Mayumi.

and any form of money substitute represent *biophysical debts* at a societal level. We frequently refer to money and money substitutes collectively as *general liquidity*, thereby indicating their universal exchangeability for goods, services, and forms of liquidity different in kind. In this book, the term *money* usually, though not always, just as well abbreviates *general liquidity*.

Individual owners of money are entitled to receive goods and services in the future in exchange for their money. Producing these goods and services typically requires capital equipment, such as factories and other industrial installations, along with infrastructure like railways, collectively known as *real capital*. From a biophysical perspective, every stage of the economic process, encompassing production, distribution, consumption, and disposal, requires useful energy and materials, consequently depleting the existing stock of fossil resources and inevitably leading to a deficit of low-entropy energy and materials. Georgescu-Roegen's (1971) "bioeconomic maxim" emphasizes that the economic process invariably accompanies the irreversible loss of useful energy and materials, a concept yet to be recognized by conventional economists. The long-standing disregard for the entropic nature of the economic process has resulted in our global economic system finding itself in what Daly (2005) described as a "full world"—where excessive use of fossil fuels, mineral resources, and ecological services gravely endangers the net primary production foundation of society and gives rise to grand externalities such as climate change or widespread habitat and biodiversity loss. The profound implications of the dual nature of money for biophysical sustainability cannot be overemphasized.

Despite such severity, rejecting the misconception that money is unrelated to issues of biophysical sustainability requires extraordinary integrity and resolve. The logical and strict adherence to the corollary of the *dual nature of money* and the *bioeconomic maxim* leads to the acknowledgment that a delicate balance among three elements must be maintained, for the sake of sustainability: (1) the money stock circulating in the economy, (2) the scale of goods and service production, distribution, consumption, and disposal, and (3) the stock level of real capital.

Conversely, achieving such a delicate balance is exceptionally challenging. As money issuers, commercial banks are strongly incentivized to create increasing amounts of money, given accommodating circumstances. This temptation, rooted in the two extraordinary powers granted, must be strictly moderated if society is to seriously address issues of biophysical sustainability. There are two methods to prevent the tempta-tion. Take note that in the following discussion, the distinction between money, money substitutes, general liquidity, and real capital as a produc-tion agent is emphasized to offer a more nuanced argumentative line.

First, the dual nature of money dictates that money, indeed general liquidity, represents a collective debt to society. Financial capital or assets are, strictly speaking, not wealth. Genuine wealth decays qualitatively in strict accordance with the entropy law. On the contrary, the monetary value of financial capital, such as national bonds, can and typically does grow over time in tune with a positive return, thereby defying the entropy law. Furthermore, while the issuers of national bonds view them as debt, following conventional accounting procedures, the holders of national bonds acquired in the financial capital market record these bonds on the asset side of their balance sheets. This is indeed a peculiar accounting convention from which a serious issue emerges.

What exactly is wealth? Petty (1662/1899) once claimed that *land* (or *nature*) is the *mother of wealth*. In line with Petty's dictum, Georgescu-Roegen (1971, p. 277) argued that

> the primary objective of economic activity is the self-preservation of the human species. Self-preservation in turn requires the satisfaction of some basic needs [...]. The almost fabulous comfort, let alone the extravagant luxury, attained by many past and present societies has caused us to forget the most elementary fact of economic life, namely, that of all necessaries for life only the purely biological ones are absolutely indispensable for survival.

Economic life indeed feeds on low-entropy resources from nature. Despite these observations, conventional economists uncritically accept the notion that financial capital is an important component of wealth. On the contrary, we argue that the dual nature of money and the two unnat-ural powers given to the issuers of general liquidity pose a serious question about the nature of wealth. The main topic discussed in this chapter is the identification of what wealth is about in relation to the living of a decent life in a more sustainable and equitable society.

Second, a clear distinction must be made between real capital as an agent of production and financial capital. Real capital decays qualitatively following the entropy law, whereas the monetary value of financial capital grows with a positive return over time, all other things being equal. Real capital, as an agent of production, enhances the capacity of the real production level of goods and services due to its role in producing goods and services with less labor input. While financial capital is traded in the capital market, the main purpose of holding financial capital nowadays is not directed toward the production of goods and services but rather toward increasing the monetary value of the financial capital. It must, of course, never be forgotten that an increase in the monetary value of financial capital is nothing but an increase in the debt burden on society. While real capital is useful for increasing the production level of goods and services, the upkeep, reproduction, or expansion of real capital requires an additional entropy deficit in terms of exhaustible energy and materials. Chapter 7 deals with issues of real capital, the origin of real capital interest, and the considerable biophysical burden generated by the need to maintain real capital stock.

Third, it is important to note the two unnatural powers of money granted to banks. As previously mentioned, a subtle balance must be maintained among three elements—general liquidity, the flow of goods and services, and the stock of real capital. Considering general liquidity as a debt to society, the quantity of money and money substitutes should be minimized. This implies that money circulating in society should primarily be used to exchange goods and services, not to generate substitutes or create additional money. If the volume of money substitutes were minimized, the interest rate would drop significantly, preventing unusual outflows or inflows of foreign currencies or financial capital among nations. To achieve this, each nation-state requires a sovereign money system to reduce unnecessary financial fluctuations—common events in modern reserve banking systems. Regardless of whether it is sovereign money or not, money is a debt to society. Therefore, the unwarranted expansion of the money stock, which leads to inflation and other side effects, must always be tempered. Important topics related to sovereign money systems are discussed later, in Chapter 8.

The rest of this chapter comprises five sections. Section 6.2 explores the widespread confusion between debt and wealth, a misunderstanding that has infiltrated the perspective of individualism. If the dual nature of money is seriously considered, a radically different view of wealth naturally emerges. This confusion between debt and wealth is later depicted in relation to Japanese government bonds and treasury bills (T-bills). As of March 2022, outstanding bonds and bills in Japan total roughly ¥1,225trn, a figure that is 228% of Japan's 2021 gross domestic product (GDP). Naturally, everyone acknowledges that these bonds constitute a debt for Japan. However, it is peculiar that the holders of these bonds register such financial entities on the asset side of their balance sheets! Regrettably, we have created two perpetual motion machines, in defiance of the first and second laws of thermodynamics. And we have entrusted them to banks.

Section 6.3 delves into the gravity of debt trap, examining external debt, debt service on that debt, and its correlation to national product and income. An examination of various countries, roughly categorized into three groups, is conducted: (1) the United Kingdom, France, Germany, Sweden, and Greece, (2) Japan and the United States, and (3) Argentina, Brazil, China, India, and Indonesia, along with low-income economies. A prevalent paradox, though seemingly basic to many, asserts that the wealthier a nation, the more it can borrow, thus accumulating a larger external debt. The right to issue money as debt appears to be a key determinant in understanding this paradox.

Following this, the role of the World Bank and the International Monetary Fund is discussed in Sect. 6.4. These powerful and influential organizations forge a global economic policy consensus through weighted voting and majority rule. Two central points are: (1) the International Finance Corporation, an affiliate of the World Bank, extends attractively termed loans to multinational corporations, yielding outstanding returns, yet neglects to provide loans to local banks and private-equity firms, which might otherwise alleviate the economic plight of the impoverished, and (2) the rigid structure of the International Monetary Fund's articles, regrettably, inhibits developing nations from escaping debt trap and seemingly favors the economic policies of economically influential nations.

Section 6.5 is aimed at presenting an alternative vision of biophysical wealth. Regrettably, a head-over-heels tumbling into deep debt trap is currently occurring worldwide, supported by the triad formed by the commercial banking sector, national governments, and central banks. These three types of influential entities closely cooperate with globalist organizations like the World Bank and the International Monetary Fund toward funneling the entire world economy into a "drenched to the skin" debt-ridden state. It is highly useful to trace the economic thoughts leading to the present status of the concept of wealth, heavily distorted by financial mentality. This includes the transition process of a brief emancipation from Mother Nature as the genuine source of biophysical wealth needed for survival. This process began or at least accelerated with the Industrial Revolution, culminating in oil and natural gas civilization.

There is an urgently felt need for a drastic revision of the concept of wealth, toward the establishment of an alternative long-term vision of biophysical wealth for a more sustainable and equitable society that is at least relatively compatible with the binding biophysical constraints of Daly's (2005) full world.

6.2   Beyond the Utmost Confusion Between Debt and Wealth: The Truth of General Liquidity

Section 2.2 ("Why Does Money Exist?") described how money and credit are recording devices used to indicate past imbalances of transactions—to overcome the need for a double coincidence of wants during a barter transaction. Money and credit represent debt to be fulfilled on demand. In this regard, Macleod's (1883, p. 55) statement is essential: "If all the services exchanged in society exactly balanced, there would be no need for *money*." Macleod goes on to mention the status of the period in which he lived, where credit was the most colossal form of property, bankers were the salesmen of debts as commodities, and monetary rulers and regulators controlled the pecuniary fortunes. Not much has changed in the past century-and-a-half in this respect.

Nonetheless, the present authors find that the notion that debt can be a salable item mostly surprises the average citizen, barring any tendencies toward an insane state of mind. Euler, certainly one of the greatest mathematicians to have graced planet Earth, correctly states:

> Since negative numbers may be considered as debts, because positive numbers represent real possessions, we may say that negative numbers are less than nothing. Thus, when a man has noting of his own, and owes 50 crowns, it is certain that he has 50 crowns less than nothing; for if any one were to make him a present of 50 crowns to pay his debts, he would still be only at the point nothing, though really richer than before.
>
> (Euler, 1828, pp. 4–5)

The present authors are in complete agreement with Euler's statement, and we hope the reader is or will come to be as well. In contrast, Macleod criticized Euler's statement as follows:

> *Debt* is the abstract *personal duty* to pay: and it does not come into existence until the time for payment has come. Consequently, *the person is not*

in debt at all until the end of the year: and consequently *the debt, which does not exist, cannot be subtracted from his property. But the owner of the debt may put it into circulation: and it may be sold, transferred, or exchanged, and produce all the effects of money, any number of times, until it is paid off and extinguished.* So that there may be the 100 crowns, and the *right* to demand the 50 crowns, circulating simultaneously in commerce.

(Macleod, 1889, p. 212, emphasis added)

What gives? Has the grasp of madness taken hold of Macleod? On the contrary. But why, indeed, did Macleod attempt to contest Euler, the great mathematician?

Debts are sold, transferred, or exchanged numerous times until they are paid off and extinguished. This is due to a conventional, albeit questionable, accounting practice where the distinction between an asset and a liability does not accurately reflect common sense. This notion is echoed in Euler's statement about the distinction between an asset as a positive number and a liability as a negative number. The conventional, quite mad indeed, accounting method serves as a patch to an ill-conceived financial mentality—that debts are salable commodities expressed in positive numbers. This concept is accepted by a vast majority of the contemporary world without adequate respect to common sense.

On the other hand, where the present accounting practice is accepted without raising fundamental issues inherent to such a dubious act, it is clear that in the case of intangible financial assets, all are balanced out since one asset is entirely canceled out by one liability. It is difficult but instructive to consider these several problems concurrently, especially those associated with the gigantic species of debt circulation, which is impossible to quantify accurately.

One must remember that both the assets and liabilities sides of balance sheets are, in a sense, debts. It is a convention, not a naturally ordained rule, that allows a positive view of the asset side of balance sheets. The implications of this convention are more significant in a world with a high velocity of general liquidity exchanges, facilitated by pervasive computer networks expediting financial transactions aimed at capturing even the smallest profit margins. The scale and scope of this network are so vast that it is impossible to grasp the movements in their entirety. Note that a new form of general liquidity is nearly always created after a certain part of the existing liquidity is paid out. The crux of the issue is the right of private entities to create money out of nothing and then breed yet more money from that money—zero becomes two. Individuals must recognize that, ultimately, the creation of money generates a biophysical burden.

When a national bond, which is a debt and is accounted for as a liability with a negative sign, is sold to an individual, that individual places it on the asset side with a positive sign. Banks then proceed to provide the holders of national bonds with additional demand deposits, using the aforementioned national bonds as collateral. These acts are the start of an utter confusion. Such an accounting practice is the secret to the creation and expansion of fictitious money.

To illustrate the confusion between real wealth and debt, consider the following case example. Japan has been issuing a series of national bonds to compensate for a continuous national budget deficit, largely attributed to an aging population and sluggish GDP growth. Figure 6.1 exactly shows that debt, like Japanese government bonds and treasury discount bills (T-bills), are saleable commodities. T-bills, issued by the Japanese government to supplement a budgetary fund shortage in a fiscal year, are sold at a discount to the par value, their actual value. Not only the Japanese people but anyone on this planet must naturally and indeed correctly regard Japanese national bonds and T-bills as debt—a perfectly appropriate view of such debt instruments.

All these liabilities, essentially negatively signed debts, are listed as positively signed assets on the balance sheets of their holders. As shown in Fig. 6.1, 98% of the debt holders are money management agents. Merely 1% of the debt is held by the general Japanese citizenry! The source of such financial assets is primarily the banking sector and secondary capital markets, where the original bankmoney in the form of demand deposits is transformed into various forms of financial assets without much being erased into nothing. In this scenario, banks enjoy the ability to issue additional money by providing demand deposits to the holders of Japanese government bonds and T-bills, which can serve as collateral for the bond-holders. This mechanism allows debt to expand continuously, without end.

As emphasized in Chapter 5, a total ignorance of *collectivistic and biophysical perspectives* associated with monetary phenomena undermines our sustainability ambitions. We live, in a sense, in a mad world—a world where a total confusion between debt and wealth is uncritically accepted, where the forces pushing a billion people into the throes of absolute poverty are largely overlooked. In such a situation, the distinction between madness and sanity becomes tricky to navigate. As the

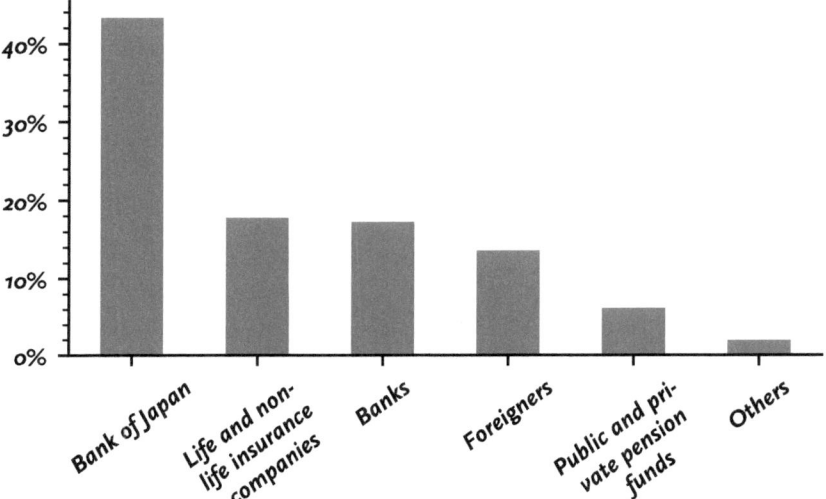

Fig. 6.1 Breakdown of the holders of Japanese government bonds and T-bills as of September 30, 2022 (*Data source* MOF [2022])

celebrated film director Kurosawa once stated, "In a mad world, only the mad are sane."

6.3 Worldwide Debt Trap

In his influential book *The Modern Idolatry: Being an Analysis of Usury and the Pathology of Debt*, Mark (1934) characterized the economic condition of nations during the 1930s as existing in a state of running solvency. A financial entity is considered to be in a state of running solvency when its total capital assets, if liquidated at current market value, would be inadequate to settle its total liability. However, this entity, one way or another, can continue its operations by either meeting, at the very least, its interest payments or by perpetually borrowing funds and capital from other financial players such as banks, thereby preventing bankruptcy. Although a routine matter for corporate entities, the concept of solvency calculations is not as prevalent at the country level. However, at that level, it can be just as informative and instructive, if not more so.

At the country level, GDP is typically used as a measure of real wealth. By no stretch of the imagination is it a foolproof proxy, but it offers a useful point of departure. Our analysis uses the external debt (ED) to GDP ratio of several European nations as an index to measure national-level monetary debt in relation to national-level real wealth. Figure 6.2 first shows ED to GDP ratios for the United Kingdom, France, Germany, Sweden, and Greece over the roughly two decades leading up to 2021. To illustrate the scale of the numbers behind the ratios, in 2017, the United Kingdom's GDP was $2.6trn and ED was $8.2trn. That same year, Germany's GDP was $3.7trn and ED was $5.2trn, while Greece's GDP was $200bn and ED was $454bn. Within the European Union, the general criterion for determining if a country has a serious budget deficit is a budget deficit to GDP ratio not exceeding 3%.[2] However, under a broader consideration, money represents debt. In this context, all the countries listed in Fig. 6.2 appear to be grappling with serious debt throes.

In recent years, Greece's high ED to GDP ratio has been substantially criticized by several economically influential European countries. The United Kingdom, despite having a higher ratio over the years analyzed, exceeding 300% most years, has largely avoided similar scrutiny. The United Kingdom's ED may be deemed acceptable because the strength of its financial sector suggests, in the eyes of creditors, that the Kingdom can safely manage such an enormous amount. A significant part of Greece's struggles stems from its inability to become a debt issuer without the consent of other economically influential countries, such as the United Kingdom.

Figure 6.3 presents the ED to GDP ratios for Japan and the United States from 2006 to 2017. In 2017, Japan had a GDP of $4.9trn and an ED of $3.6trn. The United States had a GDP of $19.5trn and an ED of $19.1trn that same year. These statistics and indeed Fig. 6.3 suggest that Japan's debt situation is far more favorable than that of the United States. However, it is important to note that Japan's domestic financial debt is not included in the ED total. The face value of outstanding

---

[2] To give an idea, the United Kingdom's deficit to GDP ratio was over 4.3% from 2009 to 2015. During that same period Greece's deficit to GDP ratio was below 3.3%. France's budget deficit to GDP ratio from 2009 to 2014 was over 5.5%, a period during which that same ratio was less than 3% for Greece. With regard to the economic criterion, it is difficult for countries such as the United Kingdom or France to condemn Greece.

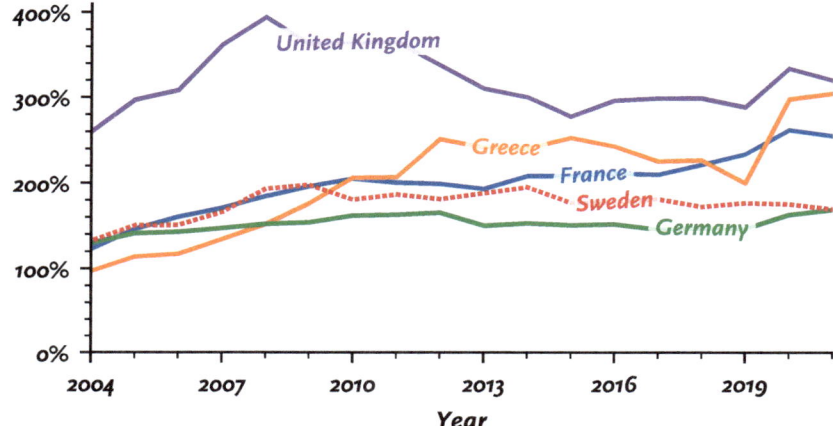

Fig. 6.2 External debt (ED) to nominal gross domestic product (GDP) ratios for the United Kingdom, France, Germany, Sweden, and Greece, 2004–2021; line dashing has aesthetic value only (*Data source* CEIC [2023])

Japanese national bonds totaled ¥1013trn in 2018, of which 46% were held by the Bank of Japan, 40.4% by Japanese banks, and just 6.4% by (external) foreign governments and agents. Regardless of who holds the debt, debt is debt. At all times, the total debt to GDP ratio for Japan from 2011 to 2018 remained above 220%, suggesting Japan is caught in a state of perpetual, running solvency, the grave situation described by Mark (1934).

Gross national income (GNI) refers to the total value of a country's GDP combined with its net income from foreign sources. It signifies the financial value of everything a country produces, no matter if it originates from within the country or is income received from abroad. In the case of poorer countries, net transfers from abroad are often significant and may play an important welfare role. Figure 6.4 illustrates ED to GNI ratios for a low-income economies aggregate—countries where GNI is less than $1.1 k per capita per annum[3]—and a group of five countries. Figure 6.5

---

[3] According to the 2021 classification by the World Bank (1) a per capita GNI of $13.2k or more is regarded as a high-income economy, such as Argentina, (2) a per capita GNI of $4.3k–$13.2 is regarded as a upper-middle-income economy, such as China and Brazil, (3) a per capita GNI of $1.1k–$4.3k is regarded as a lower-middle-income economy,

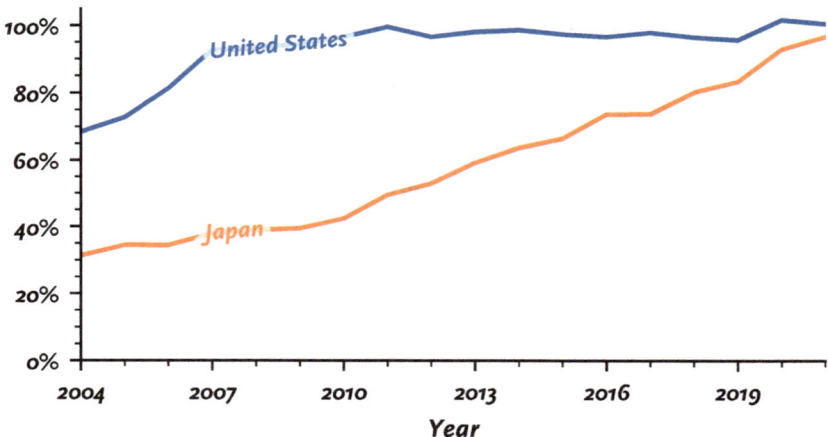

Fig. 6.3 External debt (ED) to nominal gross domestic product (GDP) ratios for Japan and the United States of America, 2004–2021 (*Data source* CEIC [2023])

then depicts the total debt service paid (TDS) ratio to ED for that same group of countries. Here, TDS is an indication of all payments required to cover the repayment of both the interest and principal on a debt over a certain time period.

In the low-income aggregate, the ED to GNI ratio proves sufficiently high, averaging 51.5% over the last three accounting years, implying that cash is insufficient to pay for the principal and interest due. As a result, the TDS to ED ratio remains low, less than 5% for most of the years assessed. China generates a relatively large GNI and accompanies that income with a relatively small ED. Therefore, for China, the ED to GNI ratio appeared relatively low, less than 15% for all years except 2014. Argentina, Brazil, Indonesia, and India all pay a high rate, in terms of TDS to ED, between 10 and 20% during the period assessed.

Table 6.1 concludes this section with a readout of ED, GNI, and TDS variables, in addition to derived ratios of ED to GNI, TDS to ED, TDS to GNI, and TDS to GDP for the most recent year for the set of countries

such as India and Indonesia, and (4) a per capita GNI of less than $1.1k is regarded as a low-income economy. Disclaimer: the provided numbers have been rounded from the originals.

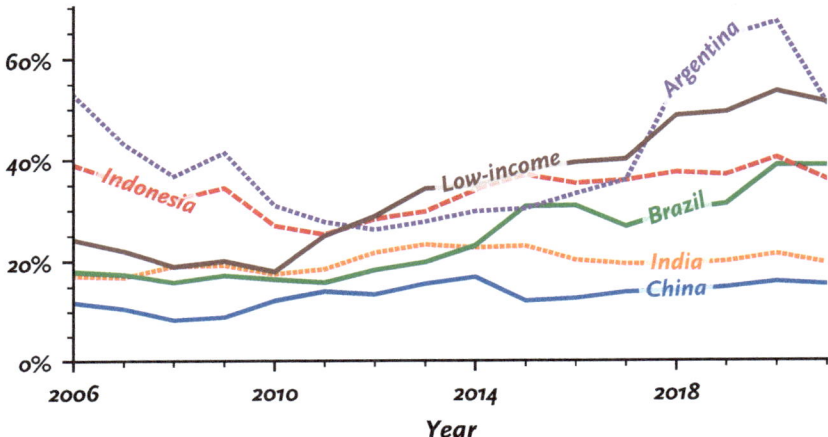

Fig. 6.4 External debt (ED) to gross national income (GNI) ratios for the low-income economies aggregate and a group of five countries, 2006–2021; line dashing has aesthetic value only (*Data source* World Bank [2023a, 2023b, 2023c])

shown in Fig. 6.4 and Fig. 6.5. Readers are invited to explore its rows. To summarize, the situation facing each of the twelve countries discussed in this section, plus those in the low-income aggregate, is different and depends on the organization of their financial markets and their stage of economic development. Nonetheless, all entities appear to be in a most undesirable state of *running solvency*.

6.4 The Roles of the World Bank and the International Monetary Fund in Accelerating the Debt Trap

Contrary to the common perception of the World Bank and the International Monetary Fund (IMF) as financial intermediaries championing global cooperation and stability, both institutions contribute, through their structural, policy, and voting mechanisms, significantly to the debt trap observed in many developing nations. In critiquing their efforts, we

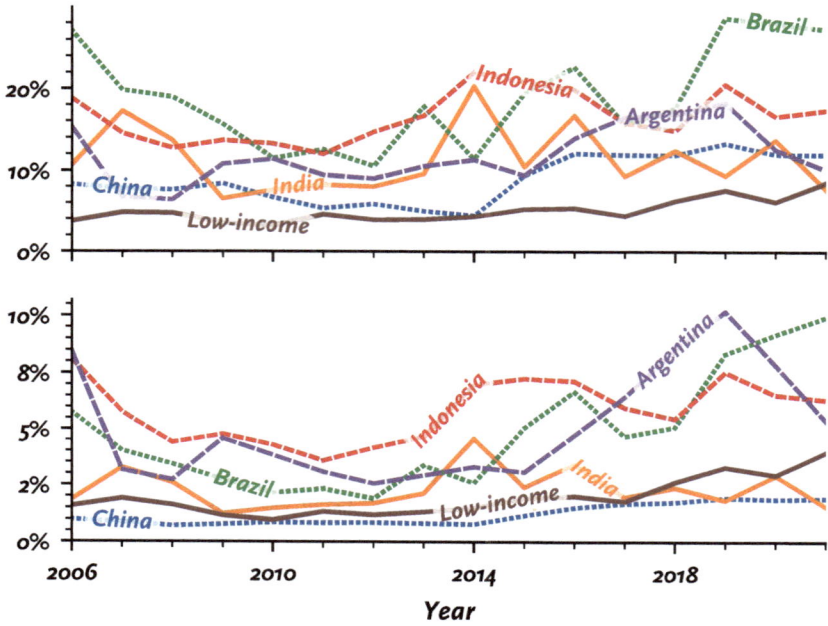

Fig. 6.5 Total debt service (TDS) to external debt (ED) ratios (top) and TDS to gross national income (GNI) ratios (bottom) for the low-income economies aggregate and a group of five countries, 2006–2021; line dashing has aesthetic value only (*Data source* World Bank [2023b, 2023c])

discuss as follows ways in which the two institutions can, in practice, exacerbate the very debt issues they strive to alleviate (see also Peet, 2009; Toussaint & Millet, 2010; Woods, 2006).

Strictly speaking, the World Bank is comprised of two entities: (1) the International Bank for Reconstruction and Development (IBRD), the world's largest development bank, and (2) the International Development Association (IDA), which offers loans to poorer nations. The World Bank Group extends the World Bank a further three entities: (3) the International Finance Corporation (IFC), which finances private sectors in developing countries, (4) the Multilateral Investment Guarantee Agency (MIGA), which promotes investment in developing countries, and (5) the International Center for Settlement of Investment Disputes (ICSID), a court that private companies can approach for conflict resolution. Despite

Table 6.1 External debt (ED), gross national income (GNI), and several total debt service (TDS) indicators for the low-income economies aggregate and a group of five countries in 2021

		China	India	Brazil	Indonesia	Argentina	Low-income
$bn	External debt (ED)	2700	613	606	416	246	250
	Gross national income (GNI)	16,800	3020	1660	1140	456	532
	Gross domestic product (GDP)	17,700	3180	1610	1190	487	563
%	ED/GNI	15.4	19.6	38.9	36.1	51.1	51.4
	TDS/ED	11.9	7.69	27.2	17.4	10.1	8.52
	TDS/GNI	1.92	1.56	9.93	6.32	5.43	4.01
	TDS/GDP	1.81	1.48	10.2	6.09	5.08	3.79

Data source World Bank (2023a, 2023b, 2023c)

being formally incorrect, the World Bank Group is often referred to simply as the "World Bank." We adopt that convention also in this work, though we focus mostly on the first and third entities enumerated.

The IRBD was established in 1944 and the IFC in 1956. Both entities have voting power breakdowns heavily skewed toward economically powerful nations, mostly in the Western World. As of June 8, 2023, the top five members in terms of voting power in the IRBD are the United States (15.8%), Japan (7.2%), China (5.6%), Germany (4.3%), and France/United Kingdom (each 3.8%). As of May 30, 2023, the top five in the IFC are the United States (18.2%), Japan (7.6%), Germany (5.1%), and France/United Kingdom (each 4.6%). In both the IFC and IBRD, a coalition spearheaded by the United States and nearly any other country from the aforelisted countries can overturn a motion they deem unfavorable.

Officially, the IFC concentrates on poverty alleviation and job creation. It can take equity participation in private companies, underwrite debentures, and make loans to private companies in developing countries without the direct financial backing of the IBRD member countries. The IFC also offers investment and asset management services to foster private enterprise development in countries lacking infrastructure or liquidity for businesses to secure financing. Each member country contributes to the

IFC's investment fund, the amount of which corresponds to the country's respective share in the IBRD fund. The IBRD, in turn, provides the IFC with favorably termed loans—charging an annual interest rate of 1% to 1.5% on the outstanding amount for the initial ten years.

Concerning the Global South, the World Bank's objective is transparent and consistent—export more, spend less. The Bank generally intervenes through structural adjustment programs, adhering to the Washington Consensus since the 1990s. Despite injecting billions of dollars, these programs have proven insufficient in subsidizing basic necessities for the poorest populations, creating jobs, or protecting local products. As a consequence of an efficiency criterion that advocates maximizing the present value of monetary investments, the IFC's funds often go toward large multinational companies—rather than the local banks and private-equity firms one might otherwise expect to better improve the economic situation of the local poor (Einhorn, 2013).

The IMF operates similarly to the World Bank regarding structural adjustment programs. Both institutions have shared origins[4] in the Bretton Woods Agreement and parallel administrative structures. In fact, if a country opts to withdraw its membership from the IMF, it will automatically forfeit its World Bank membership three months later—unless the country manages to secure a 75% share of votes within the Bank. The IMF is managed by twenty-four Executive Directors, one fewer than the World Bank, with a voting system that favors similar economically influential countries, especially the United States, Japan, Germany, France, the United Kingdom, and China, mentioned before, plus Saudi Arabia and Russia.

While the World Bank procures funds from financial markets through IFC activities, the IMF relies on member states' contributions in terms of Special Drawing Rights (SDRs) to establish loan reserves for countries dealing with temporary deficits. This system typically requires signing an agreement stipulating the measures a member country must take to qualify for the loans. A common requirement is a structural adjustment designed to stimulate exports from the member country. Toussaint and Millet (2010, p. 110) cite twenty instances of such export stimulation,

---

[4] Following Bretton Woods, the IMF and the IBRD were created for the purpose of the regulation of international finance. The IBRD is today one of two World Bank entities and one of five World Bank Group entities. The IMF and the World Bank are typically referred to as the two "Bretton Woods institutions."

including Benin and Niger. For Benin, cotton accounts for 84% of total export revenue; in Niger, uranium comprises 51% of total export revenue. According to Toussaint and Millet, opening commodity markets typically results in increased subsidies on foreign products. These imported goods often destabilize local markets.

The SDR has been the IMF's own unit of accounting since 1969. SDRs were introduced when the Bretton Woods system faced instability due to a gold deficit, linked to the increasing presence of the United States dollar in the global money market. SDRs are not considered a currency or a claim on the IMF, but rather represent a potential claim on the freely usable currencies of IMF members, currently the weighted average of five key currencies—the United States dollar, Euro, Japanese yen, Chinese yuan, and British pound. Interest is earned by all SDR holders at a uniform rate based on their respective holdings, and interest rates are determined by a seventy percent majority vote, in this way giving countries with greater economic influence an advantage. Additionally, any proposed amendments must receive approval from at least three-fifths of the IMF's members, representing at least eighty-five percent of the total voting power, to be passed.[5]

Finally, capital transfers (under Article VI of the IMF) are strictly limited to situations involving substantial or sustained capital outflows. This restriction severely affects developing countries, which typically lack sizable foreign currency reserves and cannot control the outflow of foreign capital during financial crises. Their only option for capital transfer to counterbalance outflows is a reserve tranche purchase. A reserve tranche represents a segment of the IMF member country's quota, accessible without fees or economic reform conditions. Regrettably, the reserve tranches available to these countries are often minuscule, forcing them to seek private financial arrangements with considerably less favorable terms than the IMF's conditions.

[5] Regarding how to make an amendment to IMF articles, refer to Article XXVIII of IMF procedures.

6.5   Recognition of Money as a National Debt and a Revival of the Biophysical View of Wealth for Sustainability and Equity

A deep debt trap is underway worldwide, supported in practice by the triad formed by the banking sector, national governments, and central banks, as discussed in Chapter 2. All members of the triad closely cooperate with the two Bretton Woods institutions—the World Bank and the IMF—nominally toward a sound regulation of the global economy but empirically toward a "drenched to the skin" debt status.

In this context, it is instructive to trace the economic thinking that led us to our contemporary concept of wealth—a concept heavily distorted by financial mentality and far removed from the original idea of nature as the genuine origin of wealth, biophysical and necessary for survival. This line of thought starts with the Industrial Revolution and culminates with the modern oil and natural gas civilization. Following the subsequent thought exposition, which is simply an overview of the broader discourse, it is suggested that a dramatic revision of the wealth concept is made toward establishing a long-term vision enabling a more coherent addressing of sustainability and equity goals and a higher degree of compatibility with the binding biophysical constraints in Daly's (2005) full world.

Mill (1806–1873) Mill (1866, p. 4) writes, "To be wealthy is to have a large stock of useful articles, or the means of purchasing them. Everything forms therefore a part of wealth, which has a power of purchasing; for which anything useful or agreeable would be given in exchange." Hence, according to Mill, wealth includes money. Wealth is simply that which commands purchasing power over any economic item. It is worth noting that Mill's view was quite modern for his time.

Marshall (1842–1924) Marshall describes economics as a study of how people earn income and command money over material wealth. For Marshall, economics deals not only with the study of wealth but also with the study of people. Marshall (1898, p. 37) writes, "Thus 'money' or 'general purchasing power' or 'command over material wealth,' is the centre around which economic science clusters; this is so, not because money or material wealth is regarded as the main aim of human effort, nor even as affording the main subject matter for the study of the economist." Marshall regards wealth as that which can be exchanged for money as income.

Piketty (1971–present) Piketty uses the words *capital* and *wealth* mostly interchangeably. He excludes human capital—labor power, skills, and abilities—from the purview of wealth. For Piketty, wealth is the sum of non-human assets that can be owned and exchanged in markets, including real property, real capital, and financial capital. Piketty (2014, p. 47) cautions about possible subtle distinctions between capital and wealth, stating, "By some definitions, it would be better to reserve the word 'capital' to describe forms of wealth accumulated by human beings (buildings, machinery, infrastructure, etc.) and therefore to exclude land and natural resources, with which humans have been endowed without having to accumulate them. Land would then be a component of wealth but not of capital."

Samuelson (1915–2009) and Nordhaus (1941–present) Samuelson and Nordhaus describe wealth as a stock of asset values for individuals. They argue that wealth "consists of the net dollar value of assets owned at a given point in time" (Samuelson & Nordhaus, 2010, p. 231). According to the two economists, as of 2004, about 36.3% of the "wealth" of American households took the form of financial assets.

The common denominator of these four representative understandings of wealth can be summarized as follows: wealth consists of any economic property, including money and financial assets, that possesses purchasing power useful for market transactions. Such an understanding of wealth is purely individualistic—no serious concern is given to money as a proxy for biophysical debt at the societal level, following the dual nature of money in a national economy.

From a collectivistic perspective on money, money should be used to facilitate the transfer of (real, biophysical) wealth ownership, preceding the consumption or otherwise use of that wealth. In contrast to the idea of money for money's sake and the two unnatural powers of banks, which do not treat debt or money as negative quantities, this is the original, indeed the fundamental, purpose of money. Following this original vision, an alternative understanding of the wealth concept is presented, following the ideas of Soddy and Georgescu-Roegen.

Before the Industrial Revolution, people mostly obtained the food and materials necessary for life directly from the land, primarily through net primary production (Mayumi, 1991). Net primary production ultimately constrains long-term productivity and dictates the long-term ability of both humans and other biological species to survive on Earth (Vitousek et al., 1986). Conventional economic analysis offers little insight into this basic constraint. With few exceptions,[6] notions of wealth before the Industrial Revolution largely aligned with sentiments like that of Petty (1662/1899, p. 68): "*labor* is the *father* and active principle of *wealth*, as *lands* are the *mother*."

During the transition from a wood-based civilization to an urbanized, fossil fuel-based civilization—initially coal, then oil, and now natural gas—the perception of land as a source of wealth has been gradually forgotten. To appreciate this gradual change, it is useful to consider the concept of Promethean technology. A technology is considered Promethean, analogous to a biological species, if and only if it can continue to reproduce itself while providing an energy carrier surplus—a positive feedback loop (Georgescu-Roegen, 1978). According to Georgescu-Roegen (1992), in human history, there have been only four such technologies: (1) husbandry (agriculture), (2) mastery of fire, (3) the steam engine, and (4) the internal combustion engine. These technologies share a common explosive characteristic—they open up new vistas of expansion, summarized by the sentiment "with just the spark of a match we can set on fire a whole forest, nay, all forests" (Georgescu-Roegen, 1992, p. 150). Due to the (temporary) emancipation from land brought about by the two most recent Promethean, fossil fuel-based technologies, land as a source of food and materials has largely disappeared from the public consciousness. However, it must be remembered that coal, oil, and natural gas—the energy forms required as inputs for these two most recent Promethean technologies—are, ultimately, products of land millions of years in the past.

In economics, the concept of land, Petty's "Womb of Wealth," has unfortunately been replaced by the concept of Ricardian land, defined as "the original and indestructible powers of soil" (Ricardo, 1817, p. 50). This conception is narrow in its focus and entirely divorced from biophysical reality—an illusory world where soil is inaccurately considered "indestructible." The next part of this section introduces an alternative

---

[6] A notable exception was the French school known as *physiocracy*, which, in the eighteenth century, attempted to construct their basic theory of wealth on the basis of *legal claims on properties in terms of money* (Soddy, 1926). The physiocrats, contrary to what their labeling might imply, were concerned primarily with the ownership of property as wealth rather than the physicochemical processes which bring biophysical wealth into existence. Samuels, an able historian of economic thought, writes on their framework, "[the physiocrats'] affection for private property as the dominant institutional from is clear" (Samuels, 1961, p. 96).

theory of wealth, where wealth is exclusively biophysical and adheres to the constraints imposed by the first and second laws of thermodynamics. Our formulation further emphasizes the appropriate positioning of money, which is described as "no more and no less [than] a means of effecting the transference of ownership of wealth without a *quid pro quo* in wealth" (Soddy, 1926, p. 79).

In *Politics*, Aristotle (1885) delineated the discourse on wealth into two strands: (1) wealth pertaining to the *stewardship of household riches*, and (2) wealth related to *commerce*, linked with retail trade and usury. According to Aristotle, the origin of wealth in household management is Nature, and consequently, the wealth available to households is not limitless. Nature is understood to restrict the creation of wealth. Conversely, wealth in commerce, derived through retail trade, could be abstractly accounted for as merely "a quantity of coins." As per Aristotle, the wealth emanating from commerce is boundless due to its abstract nature. Despite the absence of a limit, remember from the introduction that Aristotle vehemently condemned the unnatural process of generating money from money. Until recently, commerce was typically seen as a practice fraught with dishonesty and other immoral acts (Spencer, 1874). One can only speculate what Aristotle would think about the ethics of creating money out of nothing, an idea hardly relevant to him in Ancient Greece.

Connecting Aristotle's initial line of thought with the more recent works of Soddy and Georgescu-Roegen, it is suggested here to conceptualize wealth in terms of:

(1) a first category of wealth, comprising commodities or services with the characteristic of perishability—entities for immediate consumption that require a flow of disposable energy[7] to the user, and

(2) a second category of wealth, encompassing entities, either tangible or intangible, with the quality of durability, the use of which, while essential for the user's well-being, does not necessitate a flow of

---

[7] It would be more precise to use the term "negative entropy" from the field of non-equilibrium thermodynamics, or "free energy" in physics in general. Following Schrödinger (1944/1967), biological entities (organisms) feed on (identity-dependent) negative entropy in order to grow and survive.

disposable energy for the user to utilize at their discretion[8] later on.

The distinction between items of wealth in the first or the second categories is closely related to the entropic diffusion and decay process. In plain terms, items in the first group are referred to as perishable items, while those in the second group are known as durable items. The former items are necessarily flow elements. People, often accustomed to thinking of wealth in terms of property items as stockable entities, frequently overlook this reality. The propensity of perishable items to rot, decay, catch fire, or undergo rapid deterioration is an essential quality. When using them, they are either completely consumed or otherwise destroyed. Such wealth includes items like, for instance, according to Soddy (1926), food, fuel, explosives, and certain fertilizers.

Durable items, considered as biophysical wealth, are designed to resist wear and tear and endure as long as possible. Durable commodities are often made of refractory, resistant, or otherwise solid material substances. Examples include clothes, kitchen items, stationery, furniture, and houses. Durable wealth also encompasses a production agent—a fund in the context of Georgescu-Roegen (1971)—as well as infrastructure such as highways and railways as finished products. It should be noted that the production and maintenance of real capital and infrastructure necessitate a portion of the first category of wealth and a segment of the second category of wealth. Durable wealth also includes intangibles such as patents, which emerge using portions from both categories of wealth, and human diligence, more broadly referred to as labor.

Any given form of wealth can, and often does, at a more basic level, involve sub-forms of both perishable and durable wealth. For instance, when writing prose on paper with a refillable ballpoint pen, two entropic processes are at work: (1) the diffusion of ink onto the paper, coupled with the dissipation of a certain volatile constituent of the ink into the air, and (2) a certain fallible resistance or retardation effort of the pen itself, against the entropy law and so as to maintain the pen's material structure over a reasonable work life. The ink in the first process is a perishable form

---

[8] The use of wealth from the second category implies a transformational flow of energy that, for example, rearranges the material of the object it is being used against. Energy is dissipated when a hammer is used to drive a nail into a board, for example, but effectively no disposable energy is imparted into the user for use at their later discretion.

of wealth related to the first category, and the pen body in the second process is a durable form of wealth associated with the second category. Both forms—perishable and durable—will inevitably succumb to entropic demise, although the timescales of their demise will likely vary.

Two essential points remain. Firstly, it must be emphasized that wealth, viewed through the biophysical lens, is firmly constrained by thermodynamic laws. Consequently, money, which can be created from nothing and resist qualitative degradation, is not considered wealth. Furthermore, money is not *directly* beneficial for the user's well-being, keeping in mind that the very term weal*th* is derived from *well* as heal*th* is derived from *hale*. Regrettably, present society is governed by and for those who create societal debt, not by and for those who generate biophysical wealth (Soddy, 1926).

Lastly, it is crucial to highlight that natural resources and global commons—including ecological services like net primary production, common land or water resources, solar energy, tidal energy, and so forth—are not considered wealth in this formulation. Nor are they typically regarded as wealth in most other formulations. Although wealth indeed originates from natural resources, human diligence applied to those resources plays a significant definitional role. Moreover, for an item to be considered wealth, it must be a *finished product* in some respect—including, potentially, how one person's trash becomes another person's treasure. Commodities and forms of real capital that are not finished products are in a transitional state—on the path to becoming wealth but not yet having achieved such a status. Various services are included as long as they are economically relevant and essential for life. Medical services provide a prime example.

6.6 Conclusion

The modern economic system is a colossal apparatus busy at work generating an enormous mountain of monetary debt. This machine is adeptly manipulated by commercial banks, endowed with two unnatural powers, and other financial institutions, including central banks and the two Bretton Woods establishments. These actors seem to operate in blissful ignorance of the grave implications of money's dual nature concerning the biophysical basis of human society and long-term sustainability. Dominant individualistic perspectives—uncritically viewing debt as authentic wealth on a personal level—prevent us from acknowledging the urgently needed collectivistic viewpoints. The first step in acknowledging our ignorance is understanding the critical differences between monetary debt and wealth. While monetary debt defies the first and second laws of thermodynamics, wealth adheres to the constraints set by nature. Wealth cannot be created out of nothing and inevitably undergoes qualitative decay over time.

The confusion between debt and wealth is indeed striking. In line with widely accepted accounting norms, national bonds—universally recognized as a nation's debt—are classified as an asset by bondholders. Commercial banks naturally view the national bonds they possess as real wealth. Bondholders can, furthermore, borrow additional money as demand deposits, using the bonds ("assets") as collateral. In this manner, fictitious money tied to a positive interest rate expands exponentially. It is perhaps high time to collectively revisit the fundamentals we choose to teach and explore in economics curricula. As Leacock (1916, p. 27) famously stated in *The Apology of a Professor*, "Political Economy is that which teaches that we know nothing of the laws of wealth."

The concept of wealth introduced in Sect. 6.5 aims to establish a more rigorous definition of wealth relevant for discussions on sustainability and equity—indeed, the future of society in general. To conclude, a quote from the *Dhammapada* ("Buddha's Path of Wisdom") is fitting:

There is no satisfying sensual desires, even with the rain of gold coins. For sensual pleasures give little satisfaction and much pain. Having understood this, the wise man finds no delight even in heavenly pleasures. The disciple of the Supreme Buddha delights in the destruction of craving.

(Buddharakkhita, 1985, p. 52)

REFERENCES

Aristotle. (1885). *The Politics of Aristotle* (Vol. 1, B. Jowett, Trans.). Clarendon Press.

Buddharakkhita, A. (1985). *The Dhammapada* (3rd ed.). Buddhist Publication Society. https://www.buddhanet.net/pdf_file/scrndhamma.pdf. Accessed 26 June 2023.

CEIC (2023) *External Debt: % of Nominal GDP*. ISI Emerging Markets Group Company. https://www.ceicdata.com/en/indicator/external-debt-of-nominal-gdp. Accessed 26 June 2023.

Daly, H. E. (2005). Economics in a Full World. *Scientific American, 293*(3), 100–107. https://doi.org/10.1038/scientificamerican0905-100

Einhorn, C. S. (2013, January 2). Can You Fight Poverty With a Five-Star Hotel? *ProPublica*. https://www.propublica.org/article/can-you-fight-poverty-with-a-five-star-hotel. Accessed 26 June 2023.

Euler, L. (1828). *Elements of Algebra* (4th ed., J. Hewlett, Trans.). Longman, Rees, Orme, and Company.

Georgescu-Roegen, N. (1971). *The Entropy Law and the Economic Process*. Harvard University Press.

Georgescu-Roegen, N. (1978). Technology Assessment: The Case of the Direct Use of Solar Energy. *Atlantic Economic Journal, 6*(4), 15–21. https://doi.org/10.1007/BF02300267

Georgescu-Roegen, N. (1992). Nicholas Georgescu-Roegen About Himself. In M. Szenberg (Ed.), *Eminent Economists: Their Life Philosophies* (pp. 128–159). Cambridge University Press.

Leacock, S. (1916). The Apology of a Professor. *Essays and Literary Studies* (pp. 1–38). John Lane Company.

Macleod, H. D. (1883). *The Theory and Practice of Banking* (4th ed., Vol. 1). Longmans, Green, Reader and Dyer.

Macleod, H. D. (1889). *The Theory of Credit* (1st ed., Vol. 1). Longmans, Green and Company.

Mark, J. (1934). *The Modern Idolatry: Being an Analysis of Usury & The Pathology of Debt*. Chatto and Windus.

Marshall, A. (1898). *Elements of Economics* (2nd ed., Vol. 1). Macmillan and Company, Limited.

Mayumi, K. (1991). Temporary Emancipation from Land: From the Industrial Revolution to the Present Time. *Ecological Economics, 4*(1), 35–56. https://doi.org/10.1016/0921-8009(91)90004-X

Mill, J. S. (1866). *Principles of Political Economy with Some of Their Applications to Social Philosophy* (People's ed.). Longmans, Green, Reader, and Dyer.

MOF. (2022). *Breakdown of Government Bonds by Holder (国債等の保有者別内訳)*. Ministry of Finance (財務省), Japan. https://www.mof.go.jp/jgbs/reference/appendix/breakdown.pdf. Accessed 26 June 2023.

Peet, R. (2009). *Unholy Trinity: The IMF, World Bank, and WTO* (2nd ed.). Zed Books.

Petty, W. (1899). *The Economic Writings of Sir William Petty: Together with the Observations Upon the Bills of Mortality, More Probably by Cap. John Graunt* (Vol. 1, C. H. Hull, Ed.). Cambridge University Press (Original work published 1662).

Piketty, T. (2014). *Capital in the twenty-first century* (A. Goldhammer, Trans.). The Belknap Press of Harvard University Press.

Ricardo, D. (1817). *On the Principles of Political Economy and Taxation*. John Murray.

Samuels, W. (1961). The Physiocratic Theory of Property and State. *The Quarterly Journal of Economics, 75*(1), 96–111. https://doi.org/10.2307/188 3206

Samuelson, P. A., & Nordhaus, W. D. (2010) *Economics* (19th ed.). McGraw-Hill Irwin (The McGraw-Hill series economics).

Schrödinger, E. (1967). What Is Life? The Physical Aspect of the Living Cell. In *What is Life? & Mind and Matter* (pp. 1–96). Cambridge University Press (Original work published 1944).

Soddy, F. (1926). *Wealth, Virtual Wealth and Debt: The Solution of the Economic Paradox* (1st ed.). E. P. Dutton and Company.

Spencer, H. (1874). The Morals of Trade. *Sins of Trade and Business: A Sermon & The Morals of Trade* (pp. 29–85). W. Isbister and Company.

Toussaint, É., & Millet, D. (2010). *Debt, the IMF, and the World Bank Sixty Questions, Sixty Answers*. Monthly Review Press.

Vitousek, P. M., et al. (1986). Human Appropriation of the Products of Photosynthesis. *BioScience, 36*(6), 368–373. https://doi.org/10.2307/131 0258

Woods, N. (2006). *The Globalizers: The IMF, the World Bank, and Their Borrowers*. Cornell University Press (Cornell Studies in Money).

World Bank. (2023a). *GDP (current US$)*. The World Bank Group. https://data.worldbank.org/indicator/DT.TDS.DECT.GN.ZS. Accessed 26 June 2023.

World Bank. (2023b). *GNI, Atlas Method (current US$)*. The World Bank Group. https://data.worldbank.org/indicator/NY.GNP.ATLS.CD. Accessed 26 June 2023.

World Bank. (2023c). *Total Debt Service (% of GNI)*. The World Bank Group. https://data.worldbank.org/indicator/NY.GDP.MKTP.CD. Accessed 26 June 2023.

CHAPTER 7

Real Capital and Its Relation to Sustainability: The Dual Nature of Real Capital as Biophysical Wealth

> Like money, [real] capital is individual wealth and communal debt.
>
> (Soddy, 1926, p. 251)

7.1 Introduction

Real capital consists of wealth in the form of such entities as machinery, factories, and infrastructure ranging from highways to internet networks. Although infrastructure is often used indirectly to increase the scale of wealth production, the term "real capital" is mostly interchangeable with "agent of production" in this context, thus emphasizing the productive role it plays and its contrast with financial capital, the vast majority of which is money used for the sake of breeding more money without intending to make a substantial contribution to the production of goods and services.

Unlike the creation of money for the sake of generating more money, the creation of real capital is generally aimed at boosting the production of goods and services. Although real capital, as an agent of production, contributes to producing more goods and services, two characteristics may pose a significant biophysical burden for society.

K. T. Mayumi and A. Renner, *Reconsidering the Privileged Powers of Banks*, https://doi.org/10.1007/978-981-99-6058-3_7

Firstly, it is nearly impossible to transform real capital directly into flows of consumable goods and services. Soddy's (1926) example of the impossibility of eating one's plow when one runs out of bread is most instructive on this point. Despite the simplicity of the example, it is no laughing matter. In a modern economic system, where money can be exchanged for virtually anything, anywhere, and at any time, the underlying impossibility of this transformation in physical terms is often overlooked. Once created, real capital remains as real capital and decays qualitatively over time per the entropy law.

The general populace also tends to neglect how the economic process of production, distribution, consumption, and disposal not only produces goods and services but also reproduces and often expands the economic process itself. The process of maintaining and creating real capital is a source of further growth. However, as the stock of real capital tends to expand continually, the useful energy and material objects needed to construct and maintain real capital burden society with an additional biophysical debt. In this way, a dual nature of real capital as an agent of production emerges, similar to the dual nature of money. The importance of mineral resources for maintaining real capital stock should be noted, not just energy. Certain biophysical economists advocate for reducing the economic process solely to energy terms. In contrast, Georgescu-Roegen (1977) appropriately emphasized both energy and material (such as mineral) aspects of the economic process, notably in his so-called "fourth law of thermodynamics," which represents among other things his idea that mineral resources are crucial for the economic process.

As the stock of real capital increases due to economic expansion, the required amount of intermediate goods, which are not yet finished products, also tends to increase. These intermediate goods, associated with an increase in real capital stock, represent an additional biophysical burden on society. Following Soddy's metaphor, this burden can be conceptualized and referred to as "water in the pipes."

The remaining exploration of real capital in this chapter is divided into four parts. Section 7.2 begins with a definition of capital and a critical appraisal of the understanding of capital proposed by Keynes in his seminal two-volume work, *A Treatise on Money* (Keynes, 1930a, 1930b). The section also discusses the significant role played by "water in the pipes," a concept equivalent to Georgescu-Roegen's "process fund." Sect. 7.3 then explores a set of capital interest theories, initially criticized in Böhm-Bawerk's *Capital and Interest* (Böhm-Bawerk, 1890,

1891). These theories are (1) fructification theory, (2) capital theory, (3) exploitation theory, (4) abstinence theory, (5) productivity theory, and (6) Böhm-Bawerk's theory.

Section 7.4 presents an alternative theory regarding the origin of real capital interest, drawing on both biophysical and economic factors. The biophysical origin of real capital interest arises directly from an expansion in the production scale of commodities and a decrease in labor requirements where real capital is suitably employed within the economic process. Higher interest payments on real capital are necessitated to entice certain individuals to invest in real capital rather than enjoy the end-use of goods and services for themselves. Anticipation of scientific and technological advancements further draws these individuals to invest in real capital, considering its potential for favorable returns. Section 7.4 further shows that neither a justified level of money interest nor a universally acceptable level of monetary capital return exists—any interest or monetary capital function of time can be advocated for as long as the present value of the total interest payment or the present value of the total monetary capital return is one unit from one unit of money or one unit of monetary capital. Therefore, if the theory of monetary capital return is taken at face value, there is no fundamental difference between the various forms of real capital, which would otherwise play distinctive roles in production processes.

Section 7.5 discusses real capital and the strain it imposes on society. Real capital, serving as a key production agent, is vital to scale up the production of goods and minimize labor requirements per unit of goods production. A swift expansion in the scale of the economic process, propelled predominantly by fossil fuels through the continuous creation of real capital, burdens society with a long-term biophysical debt in terms of real capital. Several concerns arise: (1) as the stock of real capital increases, upkeep demands substantial exhaustible energy and mineral resources, which are largely irrecoverably lost, (2) scientific and technological advancements often accelerate the replacement of older capital equipment, leading to additional consumption of useful resources, (3) real capital, once established for a specific purpose, is almost impossible to directly convert into consumable commodities, (4) as the stock of real capital grows, the stock of intermediate goods correspondingly increases, amplifying the biophysical burden on society, (5) due to limitations imposed by the utilization factor of real capital, it is challenging to determine an optimal level of real capital, and (6) in the contemporary era, where new products are produced in tandem with savvy long-term marketing strategies, intentional functional decay or "planned obsolescence" is commonplace. This strategy again tends to inflate the stock of real capital.

7.2   PRODUCTIVE CAPITAL: ESCAPING THE INFLUENCE OF THE CONVENTIONAL WEALTH CONCEPT

Often referred to as equity or simply "capital" in finance, accounting, and economics, *financial capital* refers to any form of economic ownership expressed in monetary terms. It is used by entrepreneurs, businesses, and the general public to, ultimately, purchase goods and services, along with other types of conventional wealth such as equipment and land. This book proposes that a delicate balance between the production of goods and services and the stock of money (general liquidity) needs to be upheld, given the dual nature of money. An excess of financial capital, particularly money for money's sake, should be minimized as much as possible.

Financial capital is best understood in contradistinction to real capital. The role of financial capital is to motivate or otherwise facilitate the transformation of goods and services into real capital—agents of production serving as the essential driving force of economic processes. While financial capital is abstract, real capital is physicochemical, and its construction requires finished goods of the wealth type defined in Chapter 6. According to Keynes (1930b, pp. 128–129), the stock of real capital is classified into three forms:

(1) *fixed capital*, or goods in use, refers to capital used in the economic process of production, distribution, consumption, and disposal, including such things as infrastructure, railways or factories,

(2) *working capital*, or goods in process, alternatively referred to as Soddy's "water in the pipes," consists of unfinished fixed capital existing in an intermediate form, such as half-built machinery, and

(3) *liquid capital*, or goods in stock, describes fixed capital in surplus stock—finished goods not in use but theoretically capable of being utilized in short order.

First, it is unclear whether fixed capital in Keynes' sense truly includes agents of production. In this work, in somewhat of a contrast to Keynes, *only the first form of capital (fixed capital) is to be considered proper real capital.* The other two forms of capital—working and liquid—have the potential to become real capital but are not yet agents of production in the economy. Hence, they cannot truly be considered real capital. Of course, all three forms of capital degrade over time, requiring maintenance where due and eventually becoming useless. This process of decay is particularly notable in the cases of real capital (fixed capital for Keynes) and liquid capital.

In relation to the discussion of capital by Keynes (1930a, 1930b), the following remarks can be made:

(1) Keynes adopted his own definition of capital, which only accounts for goods and does not contain any financial aspects (in his terms loan capital, if a closed economic system is considered, and due to loan capital canceling out).

(2) Keynes included finished goods in his definition of liquid capital.

(3) Keynes mistakenly classified goods in process as a type of real capital when actually they are unfinished intermediary goods, as per our classification.

(4) Keynes inconsistently included land in the definition of fixed capital (Keynes, 1930a, p. 98). Such a definition is difficult to accept and easy to reject since land and capital are different types of funds, each playing a distinctive role in the economic process.

(5) Keynes did not draw a clear line between finished and unfinished goods. Instead, he defined working capital as the total of goods in the midst of production, manufacturing, transport, and retailing, including such minimum stocks, be they raw materials or finished products, which are necessary to prevent risks of process interruption or to manage seasonal irregularities.

(6) A serious issue lies in Keynes's misunderstanding about the nature of working capital and liquid capital—according to Keynes, working capital must account for the handling of seasonal stocks between harvests and also for variances in the carry-over from one harvest to another, as long as such carry-over is necessitated by the inevitable fluctuations of individual harvests around the "mean harvest."

(7) Keynes did not acknowledge the crucial difference between real capital in its role as a production agent and real capital in its capacity as goods.

It must be noted, as a disclaimer, that there occasionally exists a situation where drawing a *sharp distinction* between items belonging to fixed capital (real capital in our definition) and those belonging to liquid capital proves difficult. A hammer used in production is considered fixed capital, while a hammer in a warehouse is categorized as liquid capital. This practical difficulty should not, however, dissuade us from seeking definitional precision.

Georgescu-Roegen (1971, p. 239, emphasis added), employing language similar to Soddy's "water in the pipes" metaphor for working capital, referred to intermediate goods as "process funds":

> The role of the process fund is fundamental. It can be likened to *the water in the vertical pipe of a hand pump*. Unless the water fills that pipe, the pump is not primed; we must operate the pump for some time before we can obtain any water. If, on the contrary, the pump is primed, water starts to flow the moment we move the pump's handle.

Without such intermediate goods, production processes cannot commence the production of goods and services. Furthermore, if the scale of production is to be increased, the wealth in the pipes must also be increased accordingly. Conversely, too many intermediate goods represent a significant biophysical burden, as they are not finished goods and, therefore, cannot be considered members of the first or second category of wealth.

7.3   A Critical Review
of Capital Interest Theories

In this book, capital is viewed as a resource employed in activities that enable, reproduce, or augment productive capacity. It affords entrepreneurs, producers, and merchants command over purchasing power, which is valuable for procuring goods and services. However, using capital solely to accumulate wealth is highly questionable in moral terms. While capital, land, and labor are all agents of production, only the former is regarded as capital. Additionally, credit plays a role in the discourse of capital as a mechanism delegating purchasing power to borrowers, who then strive to provide their services to communities. To reiterate, securing capital equates to acquiring purchasing power in monetary terms, encompassing non-traditional forms like credit.

The origins of capital interest must be inherently connected to the origins of money interest, as detailed in Chapter 3. Notably, while the history of money interest extends back to Babylonian times, that of capital interest does not. The genesis of capital interest seems to unveil additional factors that cannot be solely ascribed to the origins of money interest. In the aftermath of the Industrial Revolution, three salient social-economic elements have surfaced, capable of shedding light on the additional factors influencing the origin of capital interest:

(1) A *biophysical factor*, which includes the creation of a global transportation and information processing network, coupled with a swift expansion of productive capacity in the form of facilities and machinery due to the high-scale consumption of fossil fuels and mineral resources. This element pertains to the enlargement of production scale, not just in terms of output quantity but also in the variety of new goods and services.

(2) A *monetary factor*, which involves the establishment of global financial markets and institutions to streamline commercial transactions and investments.

(3) An *anticipatory factor*, which embodies certain forecasts of future production and consumption trends conceived by capital borrowers, lenders, and the general public of industrial society, grounded in biophysical and monetary considerations.

These three intertwined factors help elucidate an alternate theory of the origins of capital interest, which will be discussed in Sect. 7.4. With them in mind, a re-evaluation is conducted on six core theories related to the concept of capital interest: (1) fructification theory, (2) capitalist labor theory, (3) exploitation theory, (4) abstinence theory, (5) productivity theory, and (6) Böhm-Bawerk's theory. The dialogue on the first five is inspired by the prominent critique presented by Böhm-Bawerk (1890) in *Capital and Interest*. Böhm-Bawerk's own theory, as discussed, is described in *The Positive Theory of Capital* (Böhm-Bawerk, 1891, p. 91). Böhm-Bawerk's definition of capital is akin to the idea endorsed by Keynes concerning goods. In fact, Böhm-Bawerk (1890, p. 6) asserted that capital is "a complex of goods that originate in a previous process of production, and are destined, not for immediate consumption, but to serve as means of acquiring further goods." Contrary to Keynes, however, Böhm-Bawerk rightly omitted land from the definition of capital.

According to Böhm-Bawerk, Turgot, deemed the greatest of the physiocrats, is generally credited with introducing fructification theory into the conversation. Fructification theory suggests that capital interest emerges from the purchase of rent-bearing land. According to the theory, capital, via the acquisition of rent-bearing land, generates the general purchasing power that economic agents can wield—useful for producing commodities from which capital owners gain profit. As per fructification theory, land, since it is traded in the market toward gaining purchasing power, can be considered a form of capital. Fructification theory and the biophysical factor appear closely related, and even fossil fuels are, ultimately, products of land, albeit those created in the distant past. The flaw in this theory stems from the reality that land as a source of rent is consistently treated as a unique fund element in economic theory, entirely separate from capital. Turgot, a physiocrat who was overly concerned about the significance of land as the ultimate source of all economic value, did not give adequate consideration to the unique role played by actual capital in enabling the large-scale production of commodities. He failed to accurately distinguish capital interest per se from rent on land.

In contrast, capitalist labor theorists support the notion that capital interest results from the unique role that a capitalist's labor plays in investment activities aimed at generating profits, based on the capitalist's motivation and their ability to anticipate future economic patterns. According to these theorists, the investment activities of capitalist labor are not fully included in the earnings of capitalists, suggesting that the labor associated with investment activities should be accounted for separately. Unfortunately, it is impossible to distinctly define the unique role of the portion of labor devoted to investment activities since the unique role of the capitalist is, in fact, already compensated for at a specific rate through the sum of amortization included in annuities. Therefore, capitalist labor theory is untenable. Additionally, there are not one but three key fund elements in economic theory: (1) labor, including the capitalist's investment of labor, (2) land, and (3) real capital used for production in conjunction with infrastructure. At the very least, each fund element must be distinctively accounted for.

Schumpeter (1951) put forth a theory that parallels capitalist labor theory, with a unique emphasis on the entrepreneur's role, contrasting the traditional focus on the capitalist's role, who provides the purchasing power for the entrepreneur. According to Schumpeter, only capitalists possess the ability to supply this purchasing power. He suggested that the core of the entrepreneur's role is to initiate new combinations, which can become a source of interest within "entrepreneurial" profit during economic development. Schumpeter maintained that without economic development, interest would not arise in a steady-state economic system, and there would be no interest payment. However, Schumpeter's theory falls short of stressing the importance of the three crucial factors related to the origins of capital interest, particularly the biophysical and anticipatory factors. This omission leaves a part of the overall picture unrepresented, yet it paves the way for entrepreneurs by providing them with a broad scope of options beneficial for executing ambitious economic development projects.

Exploitation theory attempts to explain capital interest as a forced deduction from the products of labor that capitalists seize, given that the role of workers in production is inherently limited, except for the production tools supplied by capitalists. Marx (1867/1990), for instance, dedicates a chapter[1] in *Capital* to the subject of the working day, wherein he undertakes a comprehensive analysis of labor hours. Marx postulates that due to their advantageous market position compared to laborers, capitalists consistently skim off the value created by laborers. The fundamental flaw lies in the nearly dogmatic belief that all economic products stem exclusively from labor power. Marx seems to take for granted that the institution of private property, by its mere existence, grants a particular group of people, the capitalists, sole control over the indispensable means of large-scale industrial production. Contrarily, for the production of goods and services using energy and materials, a harmonious integration of three fundamental elements—funds of land, labor, and capital—is required. These three elements are intrinsically interrelated and interdependent in both production and consumption activities.

Moreover, historical evidence collected during the evolution of capitalist society, where the biophysical factor combined with productivity-enhancing real capital has led to a remarkable reduction in labor hours and a significant enhancement in laborers' material standard of living, appears to relegate Marx's exploitation theory to a mere cynical perspective. The potentially exploitative role of the capitalist, if it exists, and the role of

---

[1] See Chapter 10 "The Working Day" in *Capital* Volume I.

capital (particularly real capital) toward an increase in the production of commodities, do not seem as tightly intertwined as assumed. The rationale provided by exploitation theory is far from convincing, as it lacks both theoretical and empirical backing.

Abstinence theory springs from a consideration of the interplay between the supply and demand of capital over time. This theory posits that humans are inherently spendthrifts who favor present enjoyment over future satisfaction. Accordingly, it suggests that the owner of capital is inclined to withhold the purchasing power of that capital without an interest payment. Thus, the concept of capital interest owes its existence to the scarcity of capital. The emergence of capital interest can be seen as compensation for postponing immediate gratification. Abstinence theory aptly elucidates the motivation of capitalists seeking higher returns on capital investment activities. However, it does possess two primary shortcomings. As Gesell (1916, 1958) posits, abstinence theory is production-oriented and tends to underestimate the joy derived from consumption activities. We argue that the anticipatory factor—for instance, the expectation of a prosperous economic future—holds more weight than current abstinence. This forward-looking perspective highlights that not only do capital borrowers and lenders, but also the general public in an industrial society, often anticipate optimistic future patterns of production and consumption, influenced by biophysical and monetary considerations. A consistent increase in production and consumption activities rooted in the ample use of dense fossil fuel and mineral resources is a common expectation, underpinning economic development considerations based on biophysical factors and a more intense use of real capital.

The fifth and final core theory, productivity theory, posits that production instruments are the source of capital interest. It is evident that biophysical factors play a crucial role in production processes—specifically, the use of certain instruments in the production of goods and services. However, productivity theory tends to underestimate the impact of capital loans on the emergence of capital interest. While profit naturally stems from the effective use of capital, given the unchanging possibility of profit production derived from capital use, interest inevitably arises from capital lending. The monetary factor and the anticipatory factor play significant roles, as, without them, investment activities through monetary and financial institutions could not be robustly operated in a forward-looking manner, based on the optimistic future perspectives of investors.

Without any theoretical and empirical proof, Böhm-Bawerk's (1891, pp. 248–249) theory of interest assumes that present goods have a higher *subjective* value than future goods of a similar kind and quantity. His reasoning is peculiar. Biophysically speaking, the owner of present goods must incur an additional storage cost to preserve those goods due to the inevitable decay of materials—an absolute certainty according to the law of entropy. Therefore, the owner of present goods naturally attributes a higher subjective value to future goods of a similar kind and quantity, as they do not need to bear any additional storage costs for present goods and can enjoy the consumption of these goods if they wish. In light of the law of entropy, perishable goods should ideally be consumed sooner rather than later, thereby avoiding storage costs. Böhm-Bawerk (1891, p. 243, emphasis added), however, asserts:

> Even in the case of those perishable goods, such as meat and drink, wood and candles, which we keep ready for immediate consumption in our domestic economy, only one portion of their use is strictly speaking, devoted to the service of the moment; *the greater part is carried over into the future.*

Continuing, Böhm-Bawerk (1891, pp. 251–252, emphasis added) ventures further astray with his statement:

> The only exception occurs in those *comparatively rare cases* where it is difficult or impracticable to keep the present goods till the time of worse provision comes. This happens, for instance, in the case of goods subject to rapid deterioration or decay, such as ice, fruit, and the like.

Commenting on this assertion, Wicksell (1893, 1970, p. 108) offers his insightful critique: "This is certainly a great exaggeration." Wicksell astutely suggests that Böhm-Bawerk's examples, such as ice and fruit, should not be considered exceptions; instead, all foodstuffs are indeed perishable goods without exception. The primary error in Böhm-Bawerk's theory appears to be a lack of adequate attention paid to structural decay, which is intrinsically linked to the law of entropy. All goods are, somewhat counterintuitively, treated as if they are durable. As such, Böhm-Bawerk's theory is not universally applicable to the concept of capital interest. Its applicability is limited strictly to the sphere of money loans, where the loaned funds have an *immediate* need for goods or investment activities.

If we accept the central premise—that present goods hold a higher subjective value than future goods—then the situation of the money borrower becomes more understandable. The money borrower, as an investor, must acquire present goods as swiftly as possible to make the most of the incoming investment funds. In this context, when converted into monetary terms, present goods should hold greater significance for the money borrower than future goods.

Perhaps Böhm-Bawerk purposely refrained from unveiling his implicit belief that a positive money interest should be socially acceptable—a belief conceived without any solid theoretical justification!

7.4   The Origin of Real Capital Interest: An Alternative, Biophysical Theory

Although Keynes (1930a, p. 98) explicitly included land in the category of fixed capital in *A Treatise on Money*, land itself and land-related properties such as infrastructure are omitted from his consideration of the origin of capital interest. Our theory of the origin of capital interest is confined to the case of real capital as an agent of production, which is directly utilized to enhance the production of goods. Indeed, the function of real capital cannot be entirely separated from the function of infrastructure, considering the comprehensive economic process of production, distribution, consumption, and disposal. However, elements of infrastructure are not contemplated in this discussion. The conversation is limited to the origin of capital interest, examining capital as an agent of production, thereby emphasizing the crucial role of real capital for productive purposes.

All forms of biophysical wealth—the first and the second categories of wealth—qualitatively degrade and decay over time due to the entropy law. The primary role of real capital is to augment the production level of both the first and second categories of wealth. The origin of money interest in this book was derived from the distinction between money and goods. Unlike goods, only money can maintain its function intact, including through occasional token replacements guaranteed within legal and institutional arrangements. This privilege, granted to money issuers and owners, represents a fundamental source of money interest.

On the other hand, as previously suggested, the biophysical origin of real capital directly stems from a scale increase in the production of commodities where real capital is conscientiously applied to the economic process in conjunction with human diligence and energy and material resource flows. With the Industrial Revolution, the large-scale, capital-intensive production of finished goods began. Without the widespread utilization of real capital, an organ of production, achieving the observed large-scale production of real wealth would have been impossible. Conversely, in our predominantly individualistic society, where a vast majority of people are focused on acquiring finished goods for their immediate enjoyment of life, there is limited interest in the growth of real capital, which enables the large-scale production of finished wealth. If there were no profitable capital interest payments higher than money interest payments, no one would invest in real capital formation activities. This factor is a key aspect of economic logic that explains why real capital interest is higher than money interest. Moreover, based on generally accepted expectations of ever-larger scales of production and consumption activities bolstered by the anticipation of continued scientific and technological advancement, continually rising real capital interest rates seem normal, incentivizing investors to invest further in real capital.

If the use of real capital is properly managed, hours invested can be dramatically and repeatedly reduced in comparison to the non-utilization alternative. The potential to increase the level of production of goods is considerable. The seemingly endless payment over an indefinite period represents a further physical basis for the origin of capital interest, defined as the hire payment for the use of organs of production during wealth production, generally at a rate much higher than money. Capital essentially multiplies human efficiency—"exosomatic" devices of real capital replace manual labor power on a large scale.

At this juncture, it is instructive to reconsider the nature of capital in the financial market, differentiating said discussion from the origin of real capital interest advanced in this section. Recall the MSA relation, which is associated with the interest payment on one unit of money principal. The present value of future interest payments (PVFIP) between an initial point of time t_0 and a final point of time t_f is represented as:

$$\text{PVFIP}\big(t_0, t_f, i(x) : x \in [t_0, t_f]\big) = \int_{t_0}^{t_f} i(x) e^{-\int_{t_0}^{x} i(\tau)d\tau} \, dx \qquad (7.1)$$

where

$$\text{PVFIP}(0, \infty) = 1 \qquad (7.2)$$

The special characteristic of the MSA relation, detailed in the above relations, is that it holds valid independently of the functional form of the interest rate over time so long as the interest rate function, $i(t)$, remains always positive. According to Soddy, Macleod used the same formulation, "on behalf of the banking sector," to evaluate capital value. Macleod's formulation for the constant return case, below, is worth considering when attempting to understand the nature of financial capital:

$$C = \int_0^\infty iCe^{-it}\,dt \qquad (7.3)$$

The capital value C is the sum of the present value of all capital returns, iC, from now to infinity. The relation, where the present value of capital return payments on one unit of capital is calculated in the capital market, is, in this way, similar to the MSA relation. After all, one unit of capital in the present capital market could be treated as essentially equivalent to one unit of money principal. Soddy properly noted that this, the banker's attitude concerning the capital interest level, does not have any physical justification. Soddy (1926, pp. 269–270, emphasis added) is, on the subject, in line with the view of the present authors and in line with this section's discussion of the origin of real capital interest:

> But it is interesting to note in passing the banker's attitude towards a sum of money in terms of that of the rate of interest, as set forth by MacLeod, though *it is a point of view with purely mathematical rather than physical justification*. Assuming a continuous growth of money with the lapse of time, the capital sum may be regarded as the sum total of all future interest payments over an infinity of time, discounted to their present-day value. But this is necessarily true *whatever the rate of [capital] interest may be*.

It should be clear by now that there is neither a strictly justifiable level of money interest nor a generally justifiable level of monetary capital return. Any given interest or monetary capital function of time can be argued for as long as the present value of interest payment or the present value of monetary capital return is one unit from one unit of money principal or one unit of monetary capital. There is one additional important point to remember. If monetary capital return theory were to be taken at face value, there would be no essential difference among the various real capital forms, which must have distinctive roles in tangible production processes. The banker's view of capital seems rather absurd and lacks a biophysical base. Therefore, the banker's view of capital is nothing but a phantom.

7.5 Real Capital and its Biophysical Burden on Society: The Dual Nature of Real Capital as Biophysical Wealth

Real capital as an agent of production is the essential element for increasing the scale of production of wealth. From the Industrial Revolution to the present day, however, thanks to the explosive nature of the steam engine and then the internal combustion engine—two Promethean technologies, drivers behind the establishment of the global transportation network—real capital investment has tended to expand beyond compatibility with other key drivers of the economy. Excessive investment in capital formation, commonly associated with an inflated monetary representation of production factors, has further instigated shifts in perceptions of what is truly produced in the economic process.

The introduction of heterogeneous factors in monetary units within aggregate production functions (Solow, 1957) has further complicated matters, as aptly noted by Daly (1997). This homogenization of inputs into monetary units obscures the biophysical limitations of production activities and conceals sustainability concerns (Gowdy, 1997). The misrepresentation caused by portraying the production process in financial terms is an inherent part of the weak sustainability understanding, traditionally embraced by neoclassical economists, often adopted by ecological economists, and centrally defining the constant value rule: "the total value [expressed in monetary terms] of all capital stocks [should] be held constant, man-made and natural" (Pearce et al., 1990, p. 10).

Georgescu-Roegen identified an even more substantial analytical and conceptual error within the conventional approach, critical for the development process: "It is high time, I believe, for us to recognize that the essence of development consists of the organizational and flexible power to create new processes rather than the power to produce commodities by materially crystallized plants" (Georgescu-Roegen, 1971, p. 275). He denoted this paradigm of power as the Π-*sector*, suggesting that "an economy can 'take off' when and only when it has succeeded in developing a Π-sector" (Georgescu-Roegen, 1971, p. 275).

The Π-sector concept is linked to the question of what is produced in the economic process. Some researchers studying the functionality of social-economic processes seem unclear about what is produced, really and biophysically, by the economic process. Georgescu-Roegen posited that the economic process not only yields goods and services but also, at a more fundamental level, replicates the very procedures necessary to generate such goods and services. In other words, the economic process has the vital role of self-reproduction. From the viewpoint of the entire social-economic system, the combined action of the productive economic sector and the final consumption sector must be acknowledged. In Georgescu-Roegen's words, the economic process has the goal to reproduce and augment various production agents—real capital, delineated concurrently at different levels and scales—by utilizing the available wealth flows (Mayumi, 2009).

In this way, overcapitalization can be seen as a typical consequence of the modern economy, properly emphasized by Keynes and Soddy, as mentioned in Sect. 5.4. The question that emerges is then: what is the biophysical burden of real capital creation in sustainability terms?

Real capital, like money, exhibits a dual nature. During real capital formation, useful energy and materials are invested. Biophysically speaking, such energy and materials can never be totally recouped. Maintaining real capital in a productive and efficient status requires additional energy and materials. Furthermore, scientific and technological advances tend to make old capital obsolete sooner rather than later. This leads to an increased speed of replacement of old capital equipment with new capital, thereby accelerating the consumption of energy and material resources. Consider Japan as a case study. Tanikawa et al. (2021) showed that components of in-use stock in Japan changed from 17.2 Mt in the year 1990—details of buildings at 7.5 Mt, roads at 4.0 Mt, and infrastructure at 5.7 Mt—to 31.4 Mt in 2015, with details of buildings at 11.5 Mt, roads at 10.3 Mt, and infrastructure at 9.3 Mt. The in-use stock of Japan increased by more than 82% between 1990 and 2015 despite Japan's aging demographic. The maintenance and expansion of such a considerable infrastructure stock will likely prove exceedingly troublesome in the long run.

The biophysical debt created by capital creation and maintenance cannot be repaid in the form of finished goods, let alone money. Real capital is inherently attached to a particular production process or a set of closely related processes. The proper use of real capital is similarly limited by its application. The direct transformation of real capital into perishable and durable goods is difficult to achieve—the by-now proverbial attempt to convert a plow into bread is futile. The monetary mindset of contemporary citizens obstructs these fundamental considerations from being appropriately understood. In an environment where production and distribution are rigidly governed by money, adequate differentiation is not made between plows and bread, as both are equally interchangeable for money.

Semi-manufactured goods—alternatively referred to as working capital or "water in the pipes" by Soddy and "process fund" by Georgescu-Roegen—also increase with the stock of capital. Therefore, an escalation in the stock of semi-manufactured goods indicates an additional, significant biophysical burden for society.

There is another issue not directly related to the biophysical burden. Any accumulation of a production agent beyond a certain limit comes at the expense of leisure, in the sense that labor is needed to increase the capital utilization factor. A per unit reduction in labor is realized, but in total, more work is required.

The mechanisms of production generate finished wealth, satisfying various human needs and desires. However, an excessive accumulation of fixed capital is problematic from a biophysical perspective. The future profusion of finished goods will largely depend on the amount of new capital (excluding financial capital) to be created and how it will be utilized. There must be a point where further capital accumulation diminishes rather than enhances wealth, on average, and not contingent on the specific ownership of the accumulated capital. Thus, social forms of ownership cannot resolve this biophysical problem, which is closely related to the well-being of future generations.

From a consumer's present perspective, which would be more desirable: (1) a certain capital stock fully utilized, or (2) a relatively larger capital stock with a slightly lower average utilization factor per stock element but similar total output? The first solution, less adaptable but more efficient, seems more immediately appealing. There does, however, exist a noticeable tendency toward overcapitalization—as the wealthy become wealthier, they begin investing their money in increasingly frivolous overcapitalizations. The typical decision made by a proverbially rich person is not based on whether more capital is needed or desired by society but rather on their own individual whims.

These trends are particularly significant in our fast-paced, consumerist society. Planned obsolescence, a business strategy that involves designing products with a limited lifespan—thereby intentionally creating a need for consumers to replace purchased products more frequently than otherwise necessary—serves as a clear illustration. One of the more notable examples is the frequent release of new versions of information and technology products such as smartphones, laptops, or the software they run. Certain well-known tech companies have been criticized for intentionally designing products that are difficult to repair or upgrade internally, thereby encouraging consumers to purchase new versions instead of repairing older models. These companies have also faced large settlements for issuing software updates that intentionally and subtly slow down older devices, a form of imposed functional decay that incentivizes users to acquire a newer model, no matter how marginal the upgrade might be. In the realm of apparel, fast-fashion retailers produce inexpensive clothing designed to be worn briefly before falling apart or going out of style. These examples merely scratch the surface of a widely used business strategy that significantly boosts corporate profits while amplifying the use of valuable resources and costing consumers billions of dollars each year.

7.6   CONCLUSION

Real capital contributes significantly to the increase in the flow of goods and services. It also considerably enhances labor productivity by reducing labor hours. Acknowledging these two biophysical factors, the interest rate of real capital is typically expected to be substantially higher than that of money. Additionally, most people lack a compelling incentive to invest their money in real capital formation, the results of which usually materialize following a gradual increase in the production of goods and services. If investors were not offered a significantly higher interest payment, real capital formation would unquestionably be impeded.

While an increase in real capital genuinely contributes to wealth accumulation, an excessive increase, incompatible with population size, imposes an additional biophysical burden on society. This means that real capital, like money, has a dual nature. While money and real capital represent forms of wealth for individuals in society, they can also be perceived as a biophysical burden at the societal level.

However, a crucial contextual difference exists between the dual nature of money and that of real capital for society. Monetary debt can be extinguished, but the biophysical debt represented by real capital can never be repaid in money. The state must undertake the monetary redemption of excessive capital indebtedness as a trustee of those without property, correcting for income inequality. This monetary transfer signifies a marginal resetting of the "balance sheet" between the poor, who lack substantial access to capital interest, and the rich, who participate in the capital market and earn corresponding interest. However, this transfer is the maximum the state can do and falls short of settling the biophysical debt.

The undeniable fact that biophysical debt can never be recuperated was illustrated by Georgescu-Roegen (1979, p. 17, emphasis added):

> Nature does not have a check-out line for us to pay for the resources we take out; money royalties are set up by people, not by nature. On the other hand, resources in situ, being irreproducible, cannot have a cost of production on which to base a price determination. To be sure, there is the elementary economic principle according to which the value of any irreproducible object—whether some coal in situ or the Mona Lisa of Leonardo da Vinci—is its auction price. But this principle must be corrected by adding 'provided that absolutely everyone interested in the object is allowed to bid.' For if only my neighbor and myself were to bid on the Mona Lisa, I might perhaps have it for only a few dollars, if my neighbor happened not to like Renaissance art. Therefore, in order to establish a *valid* price for any resource according to the above principle, *all future generations should also be allowed to bid*. The earth is as much their inheritance as it is ours. And since they cannot be present to bid, we can have no valid price for the resources in situ, and hence for any commodity produced with their aid.

The above statement by Georgescu-Roegen is a cornerstone of his bioeconomic paradigm, and understanding it is crucial. For a meaningful discussion about sustainability and equity, it is essential that we, as citizens, learn to reinstate a practice of careful consideration of biophysical concerns.

REFERENCES

Böhm-Bawerk, E. V. (1890). *Capital and Interest* (W. Smart, Trans.). Macmillan and Company.

Böhm-Bawerk, E. V. (1891). *The Positive Theory of Capital* (W. Smart, Trans.). Macmillan and Company.

Daly, H. E. (1997). Georgescu-Roegen versus Solow/Stiglitz. *Ecological Economics, 22*(3), 261–266. https://doi.org/10.1016/S0921-8009(97)000 80-3

Georgescu-Roegen, N. (1971). *The Entropy Law and the Economic Process.* Harvard University Press.

Georgescu-Roegen, N. (1977). The Steady State and Ecological Salvation: A Thermodynamic Analysis. *BioScience, 27*(4), 266–270. https://doi.org/10. 2307/1297702

Georgescu-Roegen, N. (1979). Myths about Energy and Matter. *Growth and Change, 10*(1), 16–23. https://doi.org/10.1111/j.1468-2257.1979.tb0 0819.x

Gesell, S. (1958). *The Natural Economic Order* (Revised English ed., P. Pye, Trans.). Peter Owen Limited (Original work published 1916).

Gowdy, J. M. (1997). The Value of Biodiversity: Markets, Society, and Ecosystems. *Land Economics, 73*(1), 25–41. https://doi.org/10.2307/3147075

Keynes, J. M. (1930a). *A Treatise on Money: The Applied Theory of Money* (Vol. 2). Macmillan and Company, Limited.

Keynes, J. M. (1930b). *A Treatise on Money: The Pure Theory of Money* (Vol. 1). Macmillan and Company, Limited.

Marx, K. (1990). *Capital: A Critique of Political Economy* (Vol. 1) (B. Fowkes, Trans.). Penguin Books (Penguin Classics) (Original work published 1867).

Mayumi, K. (2009). Nicholas Georgescu-Roegen: His Bioeconomics Approach to Development and Change. *Development and Change, 40*(6), 1235–1254. https://doi.org/10.1111/j.1467-7660.2009.01603.x

Pearce, D. W., Barbier, E., & Markandya, A. (1990). *Sustainable Development: Economics and Environment in the Third World.* Earthscan.

Schumpeter, J. A. (1951). *The Theory of Economic Development: An Inquiry Into Profits, Capital, Credit, Interest, and the Business Cycle.* Harvard University Press.

Soddy, F. (1926). *Wealth, Virtual Wealth and Debt: The Solution of the Economic Paradox* (1st ed.). E. P. Dutton and Company.

Solow, R. M. (1957). Technical Change and the Aggregate Production Function. *The Review of Economics and Statistics, 39*(3), 312–320. https://doi.org/10. 2307/1926047

Tanikawa, H., Fishman, T., Hashimoto, S., Daigo, I., Oguchi, M., Miatto, A., Takagi, S., Yamashita, N., & Schandl, H. (2021). A Framework of Indicators for Associating Material Stocks and Flows to Service Provisioning: Application for Japan 1990–2015. *Journal of Cleaner Production, 285,* 125450. https://doi.org/10.1016/j.jclepro.2020.125450

Wicksell, K. (1970). *Value, Capital and Rent.* A.M. Kelley (Reprints of Economic Classics) (Original work published 1893).

CHAPTER 8

Sustainability and the Road to Sovereign Money

But of the existence of a real conspiracy—a conspiracy of silence—on all monetary problems, in the Press and on political platforms, among editors, publishers and economists, who more than any others ought to be alive and awake to their infinite importance—there can be no question whatever. It exists, and anyone who has tried to call attention to the evils of the present system will affirm it.

(Soddy, 1926, p. 291)

A Banker's Conspiracy! The idea is absurd! I only wish there were one!

(Keynes, 1963, p. 178)

8.1 Introduction

Split-circuit circulation, the dominant arrangement in the reserve banking system, involves the circulation of money in two separate circuits—a public circuit and an interbank circuit. In the public circuit, bankmoney in the form of demand deposits circulates among non-banks. In the interbank circuit, a circuit that includes transactions of currencies with foreign central banks, money in the form of central bank reserves circulates among banks (Huber, 2017). A failure to understand the split-circuit arrangement prevents understanding money circulation in general.

© The Author(s), under exclusive license to Springer Nature Singapore Pte Ltd. 2023
K. T. Mayumi and A. Renner, *Reconsidering the Privileged Powers of Banks*, https://doi.org/10.1007/978-981-99-6058-3_8

For a money system to be a sovereign money system, single-circuit circulation is necessary. It must be emphasized, however, that most proponents of sovereign money systems either overlook or deny a fundamental aspect of money's nature—namely, that money, including any form of near substitute (general liquidity), is debt at the societal level. Huber, for example, while rightly endorsing the need for a general understanding of the split-circuit arrangement, states, "Donating money is just a gift anyway" (Huber, 2017, p. 94), and, "Sovereign money circulates as a liquid asset only" (Huber, 2017, p. 145). Two additional works referenced therein share a similar view on the relationship between money and debt. First, Walsh and Zarlenga write:

(1) "money and debt are two different things, that is why we have different words for them. We pay our debt with money" (Walsh & Zarlenga, 2012, p. 2), and
(2) "it is a huge error to then define the '*nature*' of money as debt" (Walsh & Zarlenga, 2012, pp. 2–3).

Second, Knapp (1924) concludes that money issued by modern states is, in the eyes of the law, generally not a debt, despite good intentions politically for it to be so. The "debt" that money represents, officially to the issuing state, is found to ultimately not be intended to be paid by the state. In this context, it is argued that it would be more accurate to understand money as "free[ing] us from our debts" (Knapp, 1924, pp. 50–52). Similar opinions are expressed by the proponents of *modern monetary theory*, which justifies limitless government spending toward achieving full employment (Dyson & Hodgson, 2016; Roberts, 2019). Despite and in response to these assertions, we believe that a sovereign money system can never be established until the dual nature of money—including its relation to matters of biophysical sustainability—is understood.

The question is as timely as ever as societies contemplate the possibility of phasing out physical currency in favor of digital currency. If such a development were to occur within our current two-circuit money system, it would represent a further expansion of the power of commercial banks and their affiliates—another setback toward the potential future achievement of a sovereign monetary system.

In light of this, the present chapter discusses three aspects central to achieving sovereign money systems at the nation-state level. Section 8.2

reports, perhaps surprisingly to some readers, that in the cases of the United States and Japan, constitutional law does not grant any institution(s) the right to issue legal tender. Stating the obvious, there is no article that permits commercial banks to issue legal tender. Despite this, bankmoney in the form of demand deposits in the current accounts of bank customers is widely used as a means of tax payment, not only in the United States and Japan but in most other modern nations as well. Following this point, Sect. 8.2 presents nine fundamental elements associated with the creation of a sovereign money system within any given state. These nine elements include the establishment of a fourth government organization responsible for the issuance of money—a fourth organization in principle independent from the classical three branches of government: legislative, executive, and judicial. Among various other tasks, this fourth organization is responsible for declaring and disseminating that money is, by nature, a debt to a nation.

Section 8.3 begins with an evaluation of 100% plans, which aim to raise the fractional reserve ratio to 100%. However, as long as the current split-circuit system is maintained, reserves are not used for *all forms of deposits*. Banks take advantage of the fractional reserve system due to the exclusion of the client money rule, a highly beneficial aspect of bank privilege. Section 8.3 then offers a practical guide for transitioning to a sovereign money system. The fundamental points are summarized into four elements: (1) the customer accounts at any commercial bank should be removed from the bank's balance sheet, (2) central banks must create accounts for all such customers, (3) central banks must grant liabilities to commercial banks as sovereign money, after determining the amount of customer liabilities held by commercial banks, and (4) central banks must settle all payments from all customers, as the central bank has already created and issued sovereign money tied to the prior liabilities of the commercial banks. In this way, Ruskin's golden rule of economics can be fully realized. Namely, in an economy, one must strive to avoid fictitious elements, such as fictitious money created by commercial banks.

Following, Sect. 8.4 introduces a vertically integrated production system involving n producers, a system typically seen in the automobile industry. This system illustrates several vital elements for the effective management of a sovereign money system, where there is a drive to increase the production of completed wealth. In this setup, all producers, except the top producer, create unfinished wealth for the next highest producer in the sequence. Examination of this system is designed to prompt reflection on nine significant issues: (1) additional unfinished wealth must be maintained in the system where wealth production is scaled-up in relation to complicated and indirect production procedures, (2) a fair and appropriate distribution of sovereign money loan allocation schemes across the entire industrial structure should be democratically arranged, (3) when finished wealth is ready for sale, money distribution should be executed promptly, (4) a close coordination of money distribution between production and consumption is necessary, (5) time delay is a crucial factor when real capital and infrastructure are to be built prior to the commencement of actual wealth production, (6) the presence of several different time scales, related to the production and consumption of a variety of finished wealth items, should be considered, (7) the entire spectrum of finished wealth, unfinished wealth, real capital, and infrastructure must be compatible with the stock of sovereign money circulating in a society, (8) different money turnover rates linked to each type of wealth as well as various forms of monetary payments and receipts should be coordinated concurrently, and (9) regular surveys of household accounting books should be conducted to reflect income distributions and to establish a proper representative basket of commodities and services for determining the general price level for a nation.

The section also proposes the creation of a new institution for data and information analysis, aiming for the correct and systematic management of the sovereign money system. Several additional points are made related to cautionary aspects of a properly managed sovereign money system. To conclude, Sect. 8.5 emphasizes that a democratically determined collective purpose concerning money creation and deletion is not entirely compatible with individual motivations. Most other activities are left to individuals.

8.2   A Sovereign Money System to Be Stipulated by Constitutional Law

Money can be considered at the community level as debt—not solely monetary debt, but also, and more pertinently for discussions of resource sustainability, biophysical debt. Consequently, all social-economic actors must anticipate a governance structure that determines who should be responsible for issuing legal tender. It is only natural for members of civil society to expect their country's or nation-state's constitution to contain articles outlining who has the authority to issue legal tender.

However, this expectation often does not align with reality. For instance, Japan's Constitution has no such set of articles. Only two articles are loosely related to the topic. Article 83 declares, "The power to administer national finances shall be exercised as the Diet shall determine," while Article 85 asserts, "No money shall be expended, nor shall the State obligate itself, except as authorized by the Diet" (MOJ, 2023). Unfortunately, these articles pertain only to the national budget and do not cover the broader issues of money issuance. The Constitution of Japan is silent on the subject of seigniorage that results from money creation, including but not limited to who should receive it. The current seigniorage that accrues to private commercial banks as a result of their creation of money with positive interest is, quite remarkably, not officially sanctioned.

Only two Japanese laws address the issuance of coins and banknotes. Article 4 of the *Act on Currency Units and Issuance of Coins* permits the Japanese Government to manufacture and issue coins, while Article 46 of the *Bank of Japan Act* stipulates that the Bank of Japan is responsible for issuing banknotes, which serve as legal tender. While coins and Bank of Japan notes constitute only a minor part of Japan's contemporary money supply compared to the substantial volume occupied by bankmoney, there is, in fact, no Japanese law that defines whether bankmoney should be officially considered legal tender. Bankmoney, in the form of demand deposits, is practically accepted as a tax payment method in Japan—but it lacks legal authorization.

In the United States Constitution, two sections address the issuance of money, albeit ambiguously. Article I, Section 8[1] states that Congress, the United States government's legislative body, has the power to coin money. Section 10[2] asserts that no state shall coin money, emit bills of credit, or make anything but gold and silver coin a tender in payment of debts. Adhering *strictly* to these provisions, it appears incongruous to consider the now ubiquitous Federal Reserve Notes as legal tender. Timberlake (1989, p. 320) summarizes this somewhat serious, unauthorized state of legal tender issuance, deducing from his constitutional review that "the U.S. government has never had any license to create money." Surely the absence of a government body explicitly authorized to create money for United States citizens is rather extraordinary.

---

[1] See Article I, Section 8, Clause 5 (Art. I §8 Cl. 5).
[2] See Article I, Section 10, Clause 1 (Art. I §10 Cl. 1).

Despite the ambiguity in the constitutional articles of Japan and the United States about who is responsible for the issuance and distribution of money, our discussion on the dual nature of money suggests that the organization(s) deserving authorization to issue, retire, and distribute money should, in a republic form of government, represent the people's sovereignty. Almost a century ago, Soddy (1926/1961, p. 13) echoed a similar judgment, asserting that the "only way banking today can be made safe for both the banker and the nation is for the nation to be the banker." In the context of the United States, this suggests that the right to issue money should be vested in an organization authorized or established by Congress.

In our view, there are at least nine fundamental elements associated with the notion of a sovereign money system for any given nation-state. These nine elements must be stipulated in constitutional form within the legal framework of each state prior to entering the sovereign money system.

(1) The nation-state establishes only one organization entitled to issue, distribute, and eliminate money, stipulated in the constitution and democratically managed on behalf of national citizens as sovereign monetary power, independent of legislative, executive, and judicial powers—in this way, just one single circuit of money circulation is established.

(2) Only the money—coins, banknotes, digital cash, and money on account in any form of deposit in the nation—created, distributed, and eliminated by said organization is to be accepted as legal tender in the state.

(3) The said organization must determine the monetary unit of accounting for the authorized currency.

(4) The said organization is responsible for disseminating to the citizenry that the true society-level identity of money is not only monetary debt but, more importantly, biophysical debt.

(5) The said organization must carefully control the total money stock to stabilize the domestic general price level—defined in the second element—so that money is basically used for wealth transactions, as described in Chapter 6.

(6) The said organization must pay due attention to the economic distributional fairness of money issuance, deletion, and distribution.

(7) The level of interest must be carefully reduced to zero to dramatically reduce transactions bent on increasing "money for money" in the national and international economy.

(8) Tax payments and other pecuniary transactions must be made only by the legal tender issued by the organization.

(9) The current accounts of bank customers must be taken off the balance sheets of the banks.

While the society-level identity of money as monetary and biophysical debt is often overlooked by proponents of sovereign money systems, including the "modern money theorists," element (4), the core idea of which is represented by the dual nature of money, is perhaps the most important element of a sovereign money system. Furthermore, in the design of the sovereign money system, there is no such thing as "[t]aking the benefit from money creation, the *seigniorage*" (Huber, 2017, p. 144).

From a long-term, large-scale sustainability perspective, money creation, a form of virtual wealth, is debt creation. However, it appears to be a necessary evil for large-scale human society, vital for facilitating the smooth exchange of goods and services. If properly managed, a sovereign money system can work to stabilize the general price level to ensure money retains stable purchasing power. Regional sub-systems would not be a possibility. As Keynes (1933) endorsed in "National Self-Sufficiency," monetary issues should fundamentally be controlled individually at the nation-state level.

Concerning these nine points, it is informative to examine how national bonds are being issued on a large scale under the current central bank reserve system to compensate for an *eternal budget deficit* and support the split-circuit money system controlled by commercial banks. An examination, taking Japan as a case example, helps illustrate why establishing a sovereign money system is advantageous. A thorough interpretation of Article 5 of Japan's Public Finance Act is crucial to accurately evaluate fund provision operations carried out by each country's or region's central bank. The core issue is that while Article 5 of the Public Finance Act prohibits the Bank of Japan from underwriting public bonds at the time of their issuance, it does not forbid the Bank from underwriting national bonds post-issuance. The Bank of Japan often exploits this underwriting practice of national bonds. A notorious example can be seen in the current state of the Bank of Japan's quantitative easing policy, initiated in April 2013, under which a vast number of national bonds are purchased back from commercial banks, intended to create more liquidity and previously shown in Fig. 4.4. Despite its shortcomings, this policy remains in effect, even after a decade.

If a sovereign money system is established in the future, the existing Article 5 of the Public Finance Act of Japan will become unnecessary. However, unless money is recognized as a form of debt, the expansion of the money stock could prove unstoppable. It is important not to forget the maxim that money, at the societal level, is nothing but debt.

8.3   A Practical Guide for Transitioning to a Sovereign Money System

The current two-tier system obscures an essential defect of the fractional reserve banking system. In a sovereign money system, there would be only one money circuit system. The two-tier banking structure consists of (1) a public circulation of money, the vast majority of which comprises demand deposits in current accounts at commercial banks, and (2) an interbank circulation of money in current accounts at the central bank, where circulation is based on central bank reserves flowing at an extremely high velocity, often involving currency exchanges with foreign central banks.

Since the onset of the Great Depression in 1929, numerous scholars have endorsed plans to adopt a 100% money system. Two of the most notable scholars are Soddy (1926) and Fisher (1936). Soddy's original proposal was adapted and refined by Knight (1927), leading to the conception of the Chicago Plan (Phillips, 1995). Despite significant publicity, this plan was never implemented. Fisher (1936, p. 154), following Soddy's logic, optimistically stated that the "100% system would reduce this risk to zero in the case of the checking-deposit business."

All 100% plans fundamentally rely on raising the fractional reserves ratio to 100%—as if reserves were used for *all forms of deposits*. However, such an assumption is not accurate. Unless all forms of deposits in the banking sector are gathered in a designated "safe place," any 100% plan is ill-advised. As long as the current two-tier system is maintained, new reserves and cash will continually appear in circulation and disappear from circulation. Commercial bank customers do not safely hold their money and will not do so unless customer accounts are entirely removed from the balance sheets of banks. Presently, banks leverage the fractional reserve system to their advantage, specifically by exclusion of the client money rule, a considerable privilege granted to commercial banks. All accounts of commercial bank customers are blended in the bank's current account at the central bank. This practice results in a mixer within which the explicit identification of the various accounts of customers is essentially impossible. As long as the reserve system is maintained, commercial banks will persist in creating credit in the form of demand deposits independently, and central banks will follow suit. Advocates of a 100% reserve system seemingly have not considered that the banking sector collectively creates primary credit, which is not responsible for the 100% coverage of all subsequent deposits and their virtual circulation in the market. As a collective, the commercial banking sector possesses a remarkable ability to create and retract money.

In summary, a 100% plan that does not *abandon the fractional reserve banking system*, such as in those plans optimistically envisioned by Soddy and Fisher, could never realistically ensure a risk-free situation for bank customers.

How long would it take for a nation-state or country to transition to a sovereign money system? The answer depends heavily on the maturity time schedule of the various forms of debt owed to the banks, accumulated before the transition day. What is easier to say is what would be needed on transition day. At a specified time on that day, all demand deposits in the current accounts of bank customers are to be declared legal tender. Simultaneously, the current accounts of bank customers are to be removed from the bank's own balance sheets, following the abolishment of the privileged abilities to defy the two natural laws and the exclusion of client money rules. The entire spectrum of regulations associated with commercial banks, the respective central bank, and related organizations would need to be simultaneously modified and duly stipulated in law to facilitate a smooth transition procedure and to realize the nine fundamental elements associated with the notion of a sovereign money system, introduced in Sect. 8.2.

While the current accounts of bank customers are no longer filled with debt owed to the banks, the transitory liability to the banks—the existing stock of liquid demand deposits before the transition day—must be gradually settled following the transition. Each bank's transitory bank liability would have to be calculated, duly mediating further interest payments. Of course, the corresponding amount due from the commercial banks to the central bank, if any, must be subtracted from the transitory bank liability. The central bank is to issue sovereign money equivalent to the corresponding amount due from the banks to the central bank in order to not reduce the total stock of sovereign money. Only if and when the transitory bank liability is entirely eliminated, depending on the structure of maturities, would the transition from the current system to a fully sovereign money system be completely accomplished. At the same time, the system of deposit guarantees in the present world would become a *fiche* for museum display.

When a customer attempts to deposit money into a bank in the form of savings and time deposits, the money is directly transferred into the on-balance bank account from the customer's off-balance account. On the other hand, when a bank lends money to a customer, that money is be transferred from the on-balance account of the bank to the customer's off-balance account. These cases are discussed under the assumption that customers hold bank accounts even after the transition day. However, it would be possible to have a sovereign money system where a customer can choose to bank either with commercial banks, the central bank, or both.

After the transition day, any monetary transactions between the banks and their customers will be conducted exclusively in terms of sovereign money, which, of course, is to be reused as many times as possible. The fractional base of minimum and excess reserves of commercial banks, however, will be eliminated since such money is irrelevant to the sovereign money system. Minimum reserve requirements will be canceled both as an asset and as a liability on both the commercial banks' and the central bank's balance sheets, resulting in no loss or gain for either party. It is important to understand that in a sovereign money system, without the presence of fictitious money linked to the fractional reserve system, savings and time deposits may not necessarily be merely inactive money for societies.

An essential part of a sovereign money system is that there would no longer exist duplicative flows of "fictitious money." As Ruskin (1877, p. 171, emphasis added) states, "care in nowise to make more of money, but care to make much of it; remembering always the great, palpable, inevitable fact—*the rule and root of all economy—that what one person has, another cannot have.*"

The essential practical steps for transition day can be succinctly summarized as follows:

(1) customer bank accounts are to be removed from the bank balance sheets,

(2) the central bank is to offer accounts to such customers,

(3) concerning the transition from customer-bank liabilities to bank-central bank liabilities, the central bank will convert those liabilities created by commercial banks as fictitious money into sovereign money, and

(4) regarding loans, customers are expected to repay sovereign money to the central bank, which was previously owed to commercial banks. The central bank is obligated to nullify payments received, as the central bank has already created and distributed sovereign money associated with the previous liabilities, which equates to the same amount of sovereign money.

In this manner, Ruskin's golden rule of economics may finally be realized. The process of the fourth item listed above requires emphasis. If this item were overlooked, banks would surely engage in the widespread creation of fictitious money in the period leading up to transition day. This additional sovereign money, given by central banks to commercial banks, could lead to significant profits for individuals involved with commercial banking, as well as their close associates. Money, even sovereign money, is a societal debt. This critical aspect is notably absent in discussions supported by Huber and proponents of "modern monetary theory." Specifically, the theory seems to endorse limitless government spending to maintain full employment (see Dyson & Hodgson, 2016; Roberts, 2019), entirely neglecting the intrinsic nature of money as a societal debt.

It must also be emphasized that the sovereign money system outlined in this book is not related to the nationalization of the private banking sector. Rather, in the system described, private banks are collectively stripped of several powers, including the ability to create demand deposits from nothing, later profiting from a positive interest rate on those funds, and the exception to the client money rule. Private banks must manage customer current accounts separately from their own funds. Naturally, the fractional reserve system will vanish. Under this new sovereign money system, private banks remain free to offer customers account management utilities and various payment services. They may also grant loans—utilizing their own money, *not fictitious money generated out of thin air*.

Modern industrial corporations no longer rely heavily on bank credit. They typically finance their current expenditure from their current earnings. When they require more than mere bridge funding from banks, they turn to secondary credit sources. This could involve issuing corporate bonds or securing loans from funds in a multitude of manners. Moreover, several large corporations now operate their own banks. Sony serves as a prime example of this trend.

In a sovereign money system, nations do not need to issue bonds to cover government budget deficits. Outstanding national bonds can be gradually redeemed by employing the strategy of discounting bond principals. This way, all national bonds would eventually vanish from capital markets, as proposed in Sect. 4.3. However, each nation must remember that sovereign money equates to sovereign debt. Consequently, care must be taken to avoid generating money beyond the level of wealth production. A strict correlation must exist between the production of goods and services and the money stock, representing the virtual tokens used in exchange for goods and services. Minimizing the stock of financial assets, which could compromise biophysical sustainability, must also be a priority.

Nations can then focus on maintaining the domestic stability of goods and services prices. Keynes's (1933, p. 181, emphasis added) preference for minimizing "economic entanglement among nations" is reiterated here, along with his encouragement to "let goods be homespun whenever it is reasonably and conveniently possible, and, above all, [to] *let finance be primarily national.*" Establishing a sovereign money system would be particularly advantageous for economically disadvantaged countries with weak currencies currently dominated over by economically advanced nations. Disturbing capital flows would occur less frequently than in today's monetary and financial system, characterized by severe exchange rate fluctuations and widespread stock market volatility.

8.4   Points of Caution for the Proper Management of a Sovereign Money System

The practical steps toward a sovereign money system proposed in the previous section could be achieved relatively quickly, within a few years after the transition day. This, however, is conditional on whether *the citizenry genuinely supports the concept of sovereign money, thereby tempering the long-enjoyed privileges of banks*. A national referendum would need to be organized on the issue.

The practical steps described represent only the first facet. Establishing a robust and resilient sovereign money management practice is the second challenging task at hand. Managing a sovereign money system, particularly with respect to changes in the money stock, is indeed difficult. It involves avoiding abrupt changes in the general price level or instigating severe conflicts among political, social, and economic agents. Money holders and money system managers can exert significant power over others in various ways. It must be remembered that the act of redistributing money is essentially an altering of power relations among political, social, and economic participants. Lord Acton's (1887) famous maxim aptly summarizes this concern:

> Power tends to corrupt and absolute power corrupts absolutely. Great men are almost always bad men, even when they exercise influence and not authority; still more when you superadd the tendency of the certainty of corruption by authority.

Before delving into a set of significant issues for collective consideration, it is beneficial to discuss a simple mechanism of how an increase in sovereign money supply could correspond to an intended rise in finished wealth without inciting disruptive changes in the general price level. This mechanism, a slightly expanded version of one posited by Soddy (1926), is simplistic yet, hopefully, effective in illustrating several key points and unresolved questions relevant to the appropriate management of the sovereign money system. Readers should comprehend the nuanced nature of sovereign money management, which extends far beyond the strategy of merely altering governmental expenditure structures and tax rates—strategies commonly proposed by certain advocates of sovereign money systems. A continuous, iterative process of trial and error, coupled with an examination of plausible consequences across diverse money systems, should be shared as common knowledge among global citizens, including future generations, in pursuit of a more sustainable and equitable organizational form.

The primary objective of presenting this mechanism is to conceive of a society where money is primarily utilized to exchange goods and services without intending to increase ownership of other financial capital—in essence, money for the sake of money. For simplicity of argument and without loss of generality, the units of wealth and the units of money are adjusted so that one unit of money corresponds to one unit of wealth. In this manner, money and wealth can be treated as equivalent, in a manner of speaking, safely disregarding the dimensional aspects of money and wealth as if there were no fundamental difference between the two. The mechanism is constructed under the assumption that capital utilization in the considered economic system is sufficiently low and that the unemployed labor force is sufficiently large, so as to increase both unfinished (intermediate goods) and finished wealth production. Under these assumptions, the considered system can increase finished wealth without having to construct real capital and related infrastructure.

Consider a vertically integrated production system composed of n different producers, denoted as $M_1, M_2, \ldots, M_n$. The producer M_n provides one form of finished wealth, while the other producers, $M_1, M_2, \ldots, M_{n-1}$, produce unfinished wealth, or in other words, intermediate goods. This type of production system is common in industries like automotive manufacturing, reminiscent of a Ford-inspired assembly line in some particular division of the industry. The production system aims to produce an additional $S_1 + S_2 + \ldots + S_n$ units of finished wealth. For this purpose, the first producer, M_1, receives a sovereign money loan equivalent to S_1 to procure raw materials, secure funds for other expenses like wages and profits, then convert these materials into the first stage of unfinished wealth S_1 for the second producer M_2. It should be noted that after the first round, M_1 does not need an additional money loan. Conversely, the second producer, M_2, requires a sovereign money loan of $S_1 + S_2$. Out of the loan $S_1 + S_2$, S_1 is used to purchase the unfinished wealth S_1 from M_1 and S_2 is used to secure money for other expenses, including material inputs and wages for the production of additional unfinished wealth $S_1 + S_2$. Just like before, after this round, M_2 does not require an additional loan. This iterative production process continues until the final producer in the sequential composition, M_n, produces their additional $S_1 + S_2 + \cdots + S_n$ as finished wealth. M_n receives a loan equivalent to $S_1 + S_2 + \cdots + S_n$, out of which $S_1 + S_2 + \cdots + S_{n-1}$ is used to buy unfinished wealth from M_{n-1} and S_n is allocated for such expenses as wages and individual-level profits. At this point, the finished wealth $S_1 + S_2 + \cdots + S_n$ is ready for market sale, and following this stage, none of the producers $M_1, M_2, \cdots, M_n$ requires an additional loan.

Table 8.1 summarizes the process up until the additional finished wealth $S_1 + S_2 + \cdots + S_n$ is ready for sale. Out of the new loan totality

Table 8.1 Loans, payments, unfinished wealth, and finished wealth within a vertically integrated production system

Producer	Sovereign money loan	Payments for materials and other items	Unfinished wealth	Finished wealth
M_1	S_1	S_1	S_1	0
M_2	$S_1 + S_2$	S_2	$S_1 + S_2$	0
M_i	$S_1 + S_2 + \ldots + S_i$	S_i	$S_1 + S_2 + \ldots + S_i$	0
M_{n-1}	$S_1 + S_2 + \ldots + S_{n-1}$	S_{n-1}	$S_1 + S_2 + \ldots + S_{n-1}$	0
M_n	$S_1 + S_2 + \ldots + S_n$	S_n	0	$S_1 + S_2 + \ldots + S_n$
Total	$\sum_{i=1}^{n} i\, S_{n+1-i}$	$\sum_{i=1}^{n} S_i$	$\sum_{i=1}^{n-1} i\, S_{n-i}$	$\sum_{i=1}^{n} S_i$

$\sum_{i=1}^{n} i\, S_{n+1-i}$, given to the producers in aggregate, payments used for each producer $\sum_{i=1}^{n} S_i$ are transformed into finished wealth $\sum_{i=1}^{n} S_i$. In this way, additional unfinished wealth $\sum_{i=1}^{n-1} i\, S_{n-i}$ must always be maintained within the system—"water in the pipes" leading up to an increase of $\sum_{i=1}^{n} S_i$ in finished wealth.

Several points of reflection can be identified in relation to the simple scheme presented, associated with sovereign money distribution. Nine such points of crucial concern are discussed in the following.

(1) A substantial level of unfinished wealth, equal to $\sum_{i=1}^{n-1} i\, S_{n-i}$, must be maintained in the system when scaling up the production of wealth by $S_1 + S_2 + \ldots + S_n$. This reality echoes the understanding of the modern economic process presented in Chapter 7, where the process is understood to be primarily involved with the (re)production of processes themselves, not necessarily directly related to increasing production of finished wealth for the sake of finished wealth. Not only money but also an additional labor force is required for the maintenance and management of such unfinished wealth. Concerning sovereign money, the system requires a loan of $\sum_{i=1}^{n-1} i\, S_{n-i}$, corresponding to the unfinished wealth created by all producers except the top producer M_n. Complicated and roundabout production procedures that extensively use real capital and infrastructure tend to decrease the relative share of finished wealth in relation to unfinished wealth production, which must

be maintained in the system. Reflecting on the decreasing share of finished wealth, more money in relative terms must be secured to maintain an increasing share of unfinished wealth stock in the system. It is urgent to recognize the biophysical burden of the fact that unfinished wealth has now disproportionately increased beyond what is necessary, compared to finished wealth production. This fact seriously undermines biophysical sustainability as well as monetary sustainability due to the dual nature of money, where production levels are expected to be increased.

(2) The total loan to be provided to n producers is $\sum_{i=1}^{n} i S_{n+1-i}$. Identifying a series of sovereign money loans to be allocated to each producer is a challenging task. More generally, determining how such loans of sovereign money are allocated across the whole spectrum of industrial activity is an imposingly formidable challenge. Correct and fair identification of loan allocation schemes would need to be democratically and fairly arranged.

(3) At the moment when additional finished wealth $S_1 + S_2 + \ldots + S_n$ is ready for sale, consumers *must have received* additional sovereign money $S_1 + S_2 + \ldots + S_n$ to purchase the newly finished wealth $S_1 + S_2 + \ldots + S_n$. While money is required for the production of wealth, it is also necessary for consumption. Money is required to prevent an accumulation of goods in the system—avoiding a glut. It goes without saying that accumulated unfinished wealth must also be, without delay, continuously advanced up the production ladder.

(4) Points (2) and (3) strongly indicate that proper coordination between the production of wealth and the consumption of wealth in terms of sovereign money distribution is absolutely necessary for sovereign money systems to function well, avoiding disturbing adjustments in general price levels. While this statement may appear obvious, without careful, close coordination of the production and consumption of wealth through the judicious distribution of money on both sides, sound management of a sovereign money system cannot be realized.

(5) When new processes of production are urgently necessary to increase the level of wealth, a delay time is encountered, corresponding to the construction of real capital in the form of factories and equipment directly used for the production of finished wealth, as well as related new infrastructure, indirectly used by producers.

Once again, sovereign money loans or distribution must be allocated to the concerned producers for the construction of the new infrastructure. Such a mechanism operates perhaps on a larger scale than the previous one discussed. Toward this mechanism, well-organized coordination of money distribution for various activities *over time* is required. That is, sovereign money is necessary for the construction of new infrastructure, for the construction of real capital for a certain set of producers, for producing unfinished and finished wealth, and finally, for purchasing freshly finished wealth.

(6) Thus far, no consideration has been given to *the existence of various inherent time scales* associated with the production and consumption of a variety of finished wealth forms. These scales cannot be easily adjusted in accordance with human desires due to natural, technological, and behavioral constraints. These constraints are strongly tied to various characteristics of the diverse forms of finished wealth. For example, a radish cannot be conjured from the soil within a twenty-four-hour span. Additionally, the pattern of money use related to radish consumption is dictated by human preferences and whims—perhaps at a certain point, people prefer to avoid consuming radishes, fancying some other pungent, edible root instead. It is, therefore, crucial to study how money circulates in relation to each form of wealth—from the starting point back to the starting point. Each form of wealth has its own inherent time scale. Assembling the necessary data for such a study is, of course, a very difficult task. On this point, a brief discussion is made toward the end of this section, addressing the challenge of obtaining the necessary data and information.

(7) The entire spectrum of finished wealth, unfinished wealth, real capital, and infrastructure must be compatible with the sovereign money stock circulating in a society, which disallows fictitious money flows issued by private actors. If a sovereign money system operates effectively under the statistical support of the general price index and other data sets, all that is required is to create new money if the price level tends to fall and unsalable finished wealth begins to accumulate. Conversely, in a situation where the price level tends to rise, and the inventory level of finished wealth decreases, it is necessary to remove parts of the circulating money until the equilibrium-level general price is restored. Such a system of money management should reflect the population size, its structure, and

standards of living, along with the presumably stable preferences of all economic agents in the respective community.

(8) Over a century ago, Bilgram (1921, p. 760) presented an alternative formulation of the quantity theory of money that included "the volume of bank credit subject to check." His attempt at reformulating that theory was highly stimulating to his contemporaries. Nevertheless, the velocity of circulation of currency and bank credit represents only the *average* number of times the total currency or bank credit changes hands in a year. What is actually necessary for the identification of the turnover rate of money is the average period of complete circulation back to the starting point, corresponding to the way each type of finished wealth traded in the market is produced and consumed. Furthermore, information is needed on the frequency with which money in various forms—wages, profits, and so forth—is disbursed among economic agents and how often money is used for payments of various types of finished wealth and services. Unless such information is securely provided and well organized, the proper management of the sovereign money system in question will remain a challenge.

(9) Historically, certain governments have issued money without the intention of increasing the production level of wealth. This course of action might be taken in the aftermath of a period of warfare under the assumption that people's habits concerning money use remain relatively stable in the short term. The primary consequence of such money issuance, inflation, is easy to anticipate, as Keynes (1923) discussed in his article "Inflation as a Method of Taxation." *Regardless of the organization issuing money, such as commercial banks or the entity proposed in this chapter*, the process of money issuance results in the transfer of real wealth from the owner of the money to the issuing bodies. This effectively redistributes real wealth proportionately to the size of the money supply before and after issuance. If this type of money issuance is repeated, the citizenry learns to alter their money use habits. For instance, they might reduce money hoarding despite significant inconvenience or purchase luxury items to evade depreciation losses, where possible. Consequently, the velocity of currency circulation dramatically increases. Unless the sovereign money system is managed appropriately, especially regarding the careful maintenance of general price stability, severe distributional consequences

could ensue. We agree with Keynes's analysis up to this point. However, his analysis is somewhat unsatisfactory in its continuation since it does not pay enough attention to the systematic consideration of how to select commodities and services in the price basket used to determine the general price level. For selection purposes, regular surveys of household accounting books must be conducted in relation to a diverse group of employees from various industrial sectors, representative of the population's income distribution and spending habits.

The nine points discussed up to this point suggest that a new institution should be created to manage data and information associated with the proper management of the sovereign money system. This institution should be created under the authorization of the four key governmental powers—legislative, executive, judicial, and monetary. Private agents from various economic hierarchies must be actively involved in this institution's formation and practical management. The institution must take responsibility for acquiring time series data and conducting analytical and statistical research on, at the very least, the following items: (1) the population in question, including its structural changes, (2) capital utilization factors and unemployment in various industrial sectors, (3) inventory distributions of all types of finished and unfinished wealth, (4) various forms of infrastructure associated with industries and non-economic sectors such as the household sector, (5) wages and the profit distribution of industrial sectors, (6) the spectrum of household accounting books in relation to various employees of industrial sectors, reflecting income distributions and spending habits, (7) the status of sovereign money circulation across different sectors, (8) the general price level, including the general index of financial asset prices and land-related properties, (9) the structure of expenses and taxes of the public sector, (10) various forms of tax structures, including corporate taxes, (11) the standard of living index of different income groups, (12) practices of money hoarding and retention of earnings by companies, and (13) energy and material consumption as well as disposal patterns of the societal metabolic profile. This list is not exhaustive. Any data and associated information collected must be organized in a comprehensive, multi-scale system of accounts. This information will then inform the issuance and deletion of money, ensuring it is properly managed.

Information gathered by the institution should ideally be shared with the respective institutions of other societies to enhance mutual aid among different societies and improve the knowledge base of the entire spectrum of nation-states. This approach aims toward better management of sovereign money, thereby achieving sovereignty over monetary and financial matters. It is hoped that, in this way, each nation-state will enforce a policy aimed at stabilizing the general price level, thus minimizing the influence of international financial markets prevalent in the current world economy. Simultaneously, the most important function of money—exchange for goods and services at a stable price level—will be effectively maintained within each society. The unnecessary hoarding of money at home and in companies as retained earnings would be minimized, except in situations of absolute necessity. In a sovereign money system devoid of fictitious money, money must circulate openly and freely for the exchange of goods and services.

Perhaps the most pressing issue to address before considering the endorsement of concepts related to sovereign money is establishment of the legitimacy and fairness of the actual money supply. Reflect on how, whenever a vacuum for bureaucratic power expansion forms within a political institution, this void tends to fill rapidly with newly spawned bureaucratic activities. Hayek (1990), a staunch advocate of free banking policy, offered a stringent critique of the unwarranted expansion of public expenditure via government money creation, pinpointing government monopoly as the catalyst for unnecessary inflation. The post-disaster reconstruction efforts following the Great Tohoku-Kanto Earthquake in Japan exemplify some of the complications involved. Out of the overall reconstruction endeavors, the Board of Audit of Japan deemed 326 out of 1,401 "reconstruction projects," which totaled ¥1.3trn, to be unsuitable. Over 12% of the reconstruction fund was eventually directed toward projects unrelated to earthquake damage (Mayumi, 2020). This type of scenario is common after a large injection of general liquidity, highlighting the importance of discussions on the distribution of freshly minted sovereign money. How to strike a delicate balance between the production of goods and services and virtual wealth, as described by Soddy and *without destabilizing general prices*, is a moot point. This principle applies to the goods and services that make up gross domestic product accounts—commonly the focus of economists like Hayek—and to other assets, such as land-related and financial ones.

The redistribution of money resulting from money creation further empowers those who receive a larger share compared to those who receive a smaller one. Following an act of money creation, the power structure of an economy adjusts. When more money is created, adjustments to the power structure are typically not a central concern, as each economic actor is expected, usually, to have more money than before. However, in the case of an aging population, the distribution of less money overall can lead to potentially more significant changes in power structure relations, possibly resulting in acute conflicts among economic actors.

8.5 Conclusion

When Georgescu-Roegen (1979, p. 17) writes, "Nature does not have a check-out line for us to pay for the resources we take out," he does not imply that natural resources are entirely free for the taking, in line with some ubiquitous "five-finger discount." Every action comes at a cost, and a proper understanding of the entropic nature of the economic process is indispensable to grasp the essence of the dual nature of money, which is the central theme of this book. The dual nature of money reflects the biophysical reality that, contrary to individualistic perspectives of money as a form of wealth, it must be considered as collective biophysical debt at the societal level due to the entropic nature of all economic activities. These activities inevitably require the irrevocable consumption of exhaustible energy and materials to produce wealth, ultimately exchangeable for money. The dual nature of money argues that giving the two unnatural powers of money to the private banking sector *is a risky move* and that reclaiming such powers for the nation's citizenry implies the implementation of a sovereign money system.

In international law, the respect for the sovereignty of political entities is generally considered to be enshrined in the long-standing principle of "Westphalian sovereignty," which promotes a certain sense of legal equality and protects against interventionism. The sentiment is incorporated into the Charter of the United Nations with phrases such as, "Nothing […] shall authorize the United Nations to intervene in matters which are essentially within the domestic jurisdiction of any state" (UN, 1945, p. 3, art. 2–7). Despite such noble intentions, in the modern day and particularly when it comes to issues of money systems, the principle of sovereignty can hardly be said to apply. This is especially true considering the close affiliation and shared post-World War II origin of the

United Nations, the International Monetary Fund, and the World Bank, discussed in Chapter 6.

Having given due recognition to this fact of the matter, it is surprising to see Keynes (1963, p. 178) proclaim his view: "A Bankers' Conspiracy! The idea is absurd! I only wish there were one!" Keynes would likely have at least known of Soddy's (1926, 1934) work on money, Soddy being at Oxford between 1919 and 1936, Keynes 100 kilometers away in Cambridge. Keynes's statement is completely against Soddy's sincere plea for radical reform of monetary systems, reprinted in this chapter's epigraph. Unfortunately, sincere calls for reform have been systematically ignored due to *a conspiracy of silence* among most political and economic powers, as well as the press—the so-called *fourth estate*. Echoing Soddy, Mark (1934, p. 275) writes:

> Just as the mental processes of the developing lunatic are extremely subtle and complicated, so the technical involutions of present economic theory and practice have become so highly elaborated in their obstinate perversity that it is almost impossible for the ordinary sane intelligence to make head or tail of it. However distasteful and unprofitable a study of these same perverse developments may seem to be, it is now compellingly necessary for the ordinary intelligence to undertake it.

It is high time the citizenry awakes from their slumber!

Wealth, biophysical in nature as defined in Chapter 6, is the result of power over nature. Power over nature means that human diligence, in coordination with Promethean technology and utilizing energy and materials, can create finished goods for human purposes under the constraints set by nature, including the first and second laws of thermodynamics. Ultimately, production processes generating wealth, both perishable and durable items, cannot defy these laws of thermodynamics. On the other hand, money and money substitutes, as currently understood, have a truly remarkable ability to defy both the first two laws of thermodynamics. These unnatural powers are entrusted to private banks, implying great economic, social, and political power over the citizenry. Nightmarish situations such as the Merchant of Venice's "pound of flesh" or those depictions where young daughters of a poor family in the Edo (1600–1868) or Meiji (1868–1912) period are taken by a brothel as "payment for family debt," commonplace on Japanese television, are brought to mind. In the modern day, tragedies indeed similar in kind, though often more subtle or at least out of sight, pervade nations the world over. Debt is nearly always serious business.

The sovereign money system proposed in this chapter is intended to change the role of money from having power over human beings to having the power to facilitate a smooth exchange for goods and services, belonging to wealth. Money should not be used to breed money from money, an act deemed most unethical by Aristotle (1885), among many others. While such a role of money does, *on aggregate*, correspond to the quantity theory of money in classical economics, *the true identity of money and money substitutes is nothing but debt to societies*. This simple and basic point is *widely overlooked at present*, not only in conventional economics but also in classical and heterodox economics. Soddy is perhaps the only scholar of exceptional note to properly recognize money as debt, proposing to flip its sign from negative to positive. Soddy referred to the total quantity of money as *virtual wealth*. All citizens belonging to a nation—*collectively, not only as individuals*—must learn to behave as if virtual wealth were debt, the sole purpose of which is to facilitate smooth transactions of goods and services. The citizenry as a collective must learn to pay due attention to maintaining compatibility between the production level of wealth and the stock of virtual wealth.

Of course, such monetary reform treads a thorny path since money issuance, elimination, and distribution are always closely related to the economic and political powers hierarchically organized in any given society. The proper management of a sovereign money system is certainly a formidable task for a society—emphatically so for economically advanced nations weighed down by aging populations, sluggish economic growth, perpetual budget deficits, and the increasing issuance of national bonds. Notwithstanding, it is an essential element of our survival.

References

Aristotle. (1885). *The Politics of Aristotle* (Vol. 1) (B. Jowett, Trans.). Clarendon Press.

Bilgram, H. (1921). The Quantity Theory Scrutinized. *Journal of Political Economy, 29*(9), 757–766. https://doi.org/10.1086/253393

Dyson, B., & Hodgson, G. (2016). *Accounting for Sovereign Money: Why State-Issued Money is Not 'Debt'*. Positive Money.

Fisher, I. (1936). *100% Money* (Revised edition). Adelphi Company.

Georgescu-Roegen, N. (1979). Myths about Energy and Matter. *Growth and Change, 10*(1), 16–23. https://doi.org/10.1111/j.1468-2257.1979.tb00819.x

Hayek, F. A. (1990). *Denationalisation of Money: The Argument Refined* (3rd ed.). The Institute of Economic Affairs.

Huber, J. (2017). Sovereign Money: Beyond Reserve Banking. *Palgrave Macmillan*. https://doi.org/10.1007/978-3-319-42174-2

Keynes, J. M. (1923). Inflation as a Method of Taxation. In *A Tract on Monetary Reform* (1st ed., pp. 41–62). Macmillan and Company, Limited.

Keynes, J. M. (1933). National Self-Sufficiency. *Studies: An Irish Quarterly Review, 22*(86), 177–193.

Keynes, J. M. (1963). The Consequences to the Banks of the Collapse of Money Values. In *Essays in Persuasion* (pp. 168–178). W. W. Norton and Company, Incorporated.

Knapp, G. F. (1924). *The State Theory of Money* (H. M. Lucas, Trans.). Macmillan and Company, Limited.

Knight, F. H. (1927). Review of "Money: Wealth, Virtual Wealth and Debt" by Frederick Soddy. *The Saturday Review of Literature*, p. 732.

Lord Action. (1887). *Acton-Creighton Correspondence*. Online Library of Liberty. https://oll.libertyfund.org/title/acton-acton-creighton-correspondence (Accessed 26 June 2023).

Mark, J. (1934). *The Modern Idolatry: Being an Analysis of Usury & The Pathology of Debt*. Chatto and Windus.

Mayumi, K. (2020). Sustainable Energy and Economics in an Aging Population: Lessons from Japan. *Springer (lecture Notes in Energy)*. https://doi.org/10.1007/978-3-030-43225-6

MOJ. (2023). *The Constitution of Japan (日本国憲法)*. Ministry of Justice (法務省), Japan. https://www.japaneselawtranslation.go.jp/ja/laws/view/174 (Accessed 28 June 2023).

Phillips, R. J. (1995). *The Chicago Plan & New Deal Banking Reform*. M.E. Sharpe.

Roberts, M. (2019). Modern Monetary Theory: A Marxist Critique. *Class, Race and Corporate Power, 7*(1). https://doi.org/10.25148/CRCP.7.1.008316

Ruskin, J. (1877). *Unto this Last: Four Essays on the First Principles of Political Economy* (2nd ed.). George Allen.

Soddy, F. (1926). *Wealth, Virtual Wealth and Debt: The Solution of the Economic Paradox* (1st ed.). E. P. Dutton and Company.

Soddy, F. (1934). *The Role of Money: What it Should Be, Contrasted with what it Has Become*. George Routledge and Sons, Limited.

Soddy, F. (1961). *Wealth, Virtual Wealth and Debt: The Solution of the Economic Paradox* (3rd ed.). Omni Publications (Original work published 1926).

Timberlake, R. H. (1989). The Government's License to Create Money. *Cato Journal, 9*(2), 301–321.

UN. (1945). *Charter of the United Nations and Statute of the International Court of Justice*. United Nations.

Walsh, S., & Zarlenga, S. (2012), *AMI's Evaluation of "Modern Monetary Theory" (MMT)*. American Monetary Institute. https://monetary.org/ima ges/pdfs/AMI-Evaluation-of-MMT.pdf (Accessed 26 June 2023).

CHAPTER 9

Conclusion: Toward a Pathway of Responsible Development

Monks, there are these three things which shine forth for all to see, which
are not hidden. What three? The disc of the moon shines for all to see: it
is not hidden. The disc of the sun does likewise. The Dhamma-Discipline
of a Tathāgata shines for all to see: it is not hidden. These are the three
things.

—Tika Nipāta (Woodward, 1932/2006, p. 261)

9.1 Conclusion

On November 21, 2022, two economists from the Federal Reserve
Bank of New York ("NY Fed") published a timely article entitled "How
Do Deposit Rates Respond to Monetary Policy?" (Kang-Landsberg &
Plosser, 2022). Although the NY Fed raised the targeted rate range for
federal funds[1] to intensify the effect of tight monetary policy, deposit rates
did not rise to the anticipated degree. In November 2022, the targeted
rate of the federal funds was elevated by an impressive 3.75% compared to
the rate in January 2022. On the other hand, the average deposit rates in
November 2022 were only 0.24%, a marginal increase of 0.18% from the

---

[1] This encompasses the interest paid to banks on reserve balances, the primary credit
rate provided to banks, and the award rate given to participants who invest in the
overnight reverse repo market.

K. T. Mayumi and A. Renner, *Reconsidering the Privileged Powers
of Banks*, https://doi.org/10.1007/978-981-99-6058-3_9

0.06% rate observed in January 2022. It is remarkable to observe such a poor understanding of the current system of monetary and financial markets at the Federal Reserve Bank.

Readers familiar with the theoretical, historical, and empirical analysis presented in this work will easily recognize why the NY Fed's policy on the federal funds rate did not significantly influence deposit rates under the current reserve banking system. These rates are essentially determined by the banking sector's money issuance and deletion initiatives. Workers at the NY Fed still seem to believe in the fatal myth that their "proper" manipulation of the federal funds rate plays the central role in determining bank customers' deposit rates.

A second example of the poor performance of the policy approach adopted by central banks is evident in the case of the Bank of Japan's quantitative easing policy, initiated in April 2013. It is worth noting that as of June 2023, this policy remains in effect with no substantial changes. The Bank of Japan's primary commitment is the achievement of a 2% increase in the general price level through the Bank's purchase of massive amounts of national bonds from commercial banks, unfortunately for the Bank creating an equivalent increase in the monetary base. A lesser-known fact is that the 2% targeted inflation rate set by the Bank of Japan is identical to the rate once attempted by the NY Fed shortly after the collapse of Lehman Brothers. The Bank of Japan's policy represents an indiscriminate imitation of the NY Fed's subpar policy (Conti-Brown, 2016, p. 143).

The consumer price index in Japan was 96.9% in 2013, for example, compared to the index in 2015. If the quantitative easing policy of the Bank of Japan were successfully realized, the index in 2020 was supposed to have been $96.9 \times 1.02^7 = 111.3\%$. The actual index in 2020 was only 101.7%, considerably lower than the targeted index rate. After over a decade of general failure to achieve the inflation rate goal, the 2% target inflation rate was suddenly and emphatically achieved following the cost-push inflation consequence of the February 2022 commencement of the Russo-Ukrainian War. At the time of writing, one of the central lessons from that war appears to be that renewable energy by itself is nowhere near capable of supporting our current industrial society, which is heavily dependent on fossil fuels and locked in with age-old Promethean technology. The European energy crisis triggered by that war first presented itself as a dramatically increased share of energy expenditure within the household budget, gradually causing an increase in general price levels. Japan also experienced a general price level hike, initiated by an increase in imported raw materials from other countries and ultimately following a similar pattern as the European one. The Statistical Bureau of Japan announced on January 20, 2023, that, in relation to one year prior: (1) the general price index had increased by 4.1%, (2) the electricity price had increased by 21.3%, and (3) the natural gas price by 33.3%. What the Bank of Japan's quantitative easing policy failed to achieve for nearly ten years materialized extraordinarily quickly, independently of the Bank of Japan's policy.

As first suggested in Chapter 8, independently of money issuance organizations like commercial banks and the new organization proposed in the sovereign money system, the process of money issuance leads to a transference of real wealth from the owner of money to the issuing bodies, thereby *redistributing real wealth in proportion to the amount of money holdings*. That is conceivably the general effect of increasing money stock in macroeconomic analysis, where works of conventional economics such as Keynes (1922, 1923) are generally not seriously concerned with the distributional ramifications of inflation.

Notwithstanding, it is worth investigating the distributional effects associated with the phenomena of inflation, which are crucial in relation to the core ideas of this book. It is not well-recognized, even among contemporary ecological economists, that Georgescu-Roegen investigated several distributional aspects of inflation, for example, in his paper "Structural Inflation-Lock and Balanced Growth," being Chapter 7 of *Energy and Economic Myths: Institutional and Analytical Economic Essays* (Georgescu-Roegen, 1976). A brief discussion inspired by this work is in order.

When new money is injected into the economy, an unequal distribution, favoring one group or another, is inevitable. This results in a new constellation of relative prices, and despite the uncertain final effects, it is evident that the creation of new money, regardless of who initiates it, devalues the existing money, *ceteris paribus*. It is evident that commercial banks can manipulate the process of devaluation and appreciation of existing money by creating money or deleting money with their two unnatural powers. Consequently, an increase in living costs due to inflation tends to disproportionately affect lower-income groups, most of whom have rigid contract patterns that do not automatically adjust to inflation. Individuals in this situation often find themselves unable to afford many items, whether for subsistence needs or protection against currency depreciation. In cases where the items are necessary for survival, such individuals might resort to borrowing money from commercial banks or other mainstream lenders, as black-market rates are generally prohibitively high. The current world situation in mid-2023, more than a year into the Russo-Ukrainian War, is typical—a higher inflation rate is accompanied by a higher interest rate implemented by the policy of the Federal Reserve Bank and the European Central Bank.

Similarly, seniors who live off pensions or savings often find themselves in the same predicament, lacking effective economic means to combat inflation. As famously quoted by President Johnson, inflation is "the pickpocket of the poor" (Georgescu-Roegen, 1976, p. 163). Inflation acts as a "tax on the poor"—a unique levy, which is not collected in money or kind, but rather a covert tax that effectively transfers funds to privileged individuals who have the ability to increase their salaries or implement other inflation protection measures.

The primary objective of an "inflation policy," whether intentionally or not, is typically to protect wealthy individuals and favor lenders. The latter group can exploit periods of inflation by lending to those without other options, ensuring they secure several sureties and set favorable interest rates. Often, the wealthy and the lenders are the same individuals. Inflation policies create serious economic problems for the poor. We believe that readers will come to reconsider the distributional implications of such unfair policies of the Federal Reserve Bank, for example, an entity which *adamantly* adheres to continuous inflation.

Even when a nation imposes a cap on money interest rates, it is challenging to avoid adverse consequences. As it is generally understood, an interest rate cap applies to regular money and capital markets. When introducing the cap, the government assumes the responsibility of supplying the monetary capital the business sector requires. Simultaneously, the government usually infuses a substantial amount of new money directly into commercial banks and other financial institutions—an act akin to a conjuring trick. Readers will recall the example of the Bank of Japan's quantitative easing policy that started in 2013, which intends to give sufficient liquidity to the industrial sectors by purchasing the national bonds of Japan from commercial banks. The liquidity created by that policy did not effectively influence the investment activities of industries, resulting only in an increase in the monetary base. The interest rate for the loan created in this manner is, of course, tied to the official legal interest rate. Considering the depreciation of money through inflation, the actual interest rate is usually negligible or even negative. A similar situation is currently prevailing in 2023. Conversely, the demand for low-cost loans with negative interest is practically infinite, so banks ration their loans, employing a selective criterion. A common example is the deliberate restriction of personal loans to lower-income customers, the very group for whom the interest rate cap was initially established. This practice effectively denies these poorer individuals access to loans, meaning the principle of *"borrowing now and repaying later in depreciated currency"* cannot apply, once again favoring the wealthy.

Thus, higher-income individuals often reap the lion's share of profits from a government injection of money and the associated inflation period. Contrary to conventional understanding, the income inequality aspect of money distribution and inflation truly matters. The variety of issues linked with inflation needs to be recognized and communicated to citizens clearly and transparently. An example of this approach can be found in the early teachings of Buddhism about the three things that shine, as endorsed in the scripture of *Tika Nipāta*, quoted in this chapter's epigraph.

Our discussion of inflation is closely tied to the broader issue of general price levels. For the sake of simplicity, let us assume there are price-level indices for three categories: (1) goods and services, (2) land-related assets, and (3) financial assets. Any increase in the money supply invariably leads to a relative increase in these three price indices. The specific increases depend on the percentage of the liquidity increase spent on each category.

Since the 1980s, what we have been witnessing in economically advanced nations, largely due to global banking deregulation, can be interpreted as follows: (1) On the demand side, relative to supply, there is a disproportionate demand increase for financial assets, sometimes followed by additional demand for land-related assets, itself juxtaposed with a relatively stagnant demand increase for goods and services. This reflects a situation where the consumption of basic items needed for a decent life is reaching a saturation point. (2) On the supply side, there is a disproportionate increase in the supply of financial assets linked to money creation by traditional banks and the creation of derivatives and other financial instruments by shadow banks.

As a result, an increase in general liquidity has led to noticeable increases in the prices of financial assets, often coupled with spikes in housing market prices, as we observed in the early 2000s. In this context, economically advanced nations that have recently engaged in quantitative easing policies targeting a mild-level 2% inflation policy appear to have overlooked financial inflation, currently evident in global stock markets, and the resulting rise in income and monetary wealth distribution inequalities.

The traditional scope of the "price index in economics" is too narrow. There is an urgent need for us to develop a new framework based on three indices founded on a paradigm of sustainability and equity (Mayumi, 2020).

Money is a legal entitlement to receive goods and services corresponding to an equivalent value of the purchasing power of money when presented in the market—money indeed exerts a strong legal power over others. The issuance of money out of nothing and the dutiful accruing of money from money over time are the two unnatural powers bestowed upon banks. More precisely, banks *collectively* can potentially create two units of money out of nothing—one unit of money principal in defiance of the first law of thermodynamics and one unit of interest payment in defiance of the second law of thermodynamics. The latter phenomenon is illustrated by the Macleod–Soddy–Allais (MSA) relation. In the context of this banking privilege, it is no wonder that the stock of money tends to increase continuously. One could even appreciate Macleod's (1883, p. 157) statement, made 140 years ago:

> At the present time, *credit*, in its various forms, is the most gigantic species of *property* in this country: inferior only, if it be inferior, to the *land* in magnitude: and the negotiation of *debts* is, beyond all comparison, the most colossal branch of *commerce*. The merchants who trade in *debts*— namely, *bankers*—are now the *rulers and regulators of commerce*—they almost control the fortunes of *states*.

In relation to this quote, it must be remembered that land-based properties are closely tied to debt in terms of general liquidity. Mark (1934, p. 272) described the situation similarly:

> *[A]ll of us are now living participants in a vast psychological drama of idolatry*, the writer has no doubt whatever. The fact that the primitive scene included priests, incantations, living sacrifice, and the worship of a visible image of gold, in no way differentiates it from the modern situation, where the idol is simply a universal psychological fixation whose name is—Debt.

In truth, in the wake of Macleod and Mark, the situation of the banking sector's collective dominance has further progressed. Shadow banking has been a key component of the regulated banking system for over three decades, particularly through increasing access to money substitutes. These substitutes do not directly relate to demand deposits in terms of securitization, repurchase agreements (repos), derivatives, and other financial market activities. None of these activities were accessible to commercial banks before 1980, except repos (Fein, 2013). While it is essential to emphasize the distinction between monetary and financial intermediation, it can be argued that such a distinction does not make much sense in the case of shadow banks. Contrary to popular belief, shadow banks do not create demand deposits; instead, they accelerate the circulation of debts in the form of deposits and bank refinancing activities. The current societal arrangement is dominated over by the banking sector and shadow banks to a degree much more pronounced than the situation described by Macleod in the late nineteenth century.

Furthermore, such a difficult situation is significantly accelerated by active participation in increasing general liquidity by all governments, central banks in nations and regions, as well as the International Monetary Fund (IMF) and the World Bank. Most economically advanced countries are in the habit of issuing enormous quantities of national bonds, thereby complementing eternal budget deficits, as seen in cases like the United States and Japan. These national bonds, acting as a form of debt, play a crucial role in the capital market and make a considerable contribution to increasing the general liquidity stock.

Central banks appear to erroneously believe in the positive role of interest rate policy to control the money supply, as suggested at the start of this chapter. On the contrary! As the money supply is proactively and predominantly controlled by the banking sector, how can the central bank regulate the money supply closely through interest rate policy? In this context, the banking sector leverages another myth tacitly supported by central banks—the myth that the reserve banking system continues to function as originally intended by early proponents.

This belief in the myth has led some scholars, including Soddy (1926) and Fisher (1936), to propose the concept of 100% money. A further myth! Advocates of a 100% money reserve system overlook that the banking sector still collectively generates primary credit, which is not required to have 100% legal coverage regarding the implied deposits creation and their virtual circulation. Consequently, the interest rate policy adopted by central banks is far less impactful than popularly believed.

The role of the IMF and the World Bank, in collaboration with economically advanced nations and regions, to increase global debt, as outlined in Chapter 6, is even more surprising. The IMF and the World Bank can hardly be tolerated where transitioning to a sovereign money system is the goal. Both institutions oppose the concept of Westphalian sovereignty, purportedly enshrined in the charter of the ironically-related United Nations.

In the current global scenario, we seem to accept being heavily in debt, ignoring the ultimate consequences of our actions in terms of biophysical sustainability. Such repercussions are gradually but consistently coming into focus, presenting significant challenges such as climate change and biodiversity collapse—global tragedies of the commons foreseen by Hardin (1968). What the dual nature of money suggests is a contrasting implication of money for individuals and society as a whole. While money is considered a form of wealth for individuals, it is a source of *biophysical debt for the community to which those individuals belong.*

Money essentially embodies a promise to pay in terms of existing goods and services or the provision of future goods and services, thereby putting society as a whole into long-term biophysical debt. Georgescu-Roegen (1971) accurately grasped the essence of the modern production process as a deficit in terms of low-entropy resources since exhaustible energy and mineral resources are irrevocably lost during production, resulting in fewer exhaustible resources remaining.

If we are to take a global orientation emphasizing collective perspectives seriously, a discussion of the dual nature of money would lead to a drastic revision of both the definition of wealth and the biophysical implications of real capital for sustainability.

The accepted definition of wealth includes various forms of money substitutes, such as equity and other types of financial assets. Any form of general liquidity is, after all, a biophysical debt due to the dual nature of money. If such a biophysical view of debt, associated with the existence of the dual nature, is accepted, the recent trends of money and money substitute expansion must be approached with caution. Georgescu-Roegen (1971) asserted that, fundamentally, the primary purpose of economic activity is the self-preservation of the human species. The main objective of any given economy is the self-preservation of the community it serves. Self-preservation, of course, requires the satisfaction of basic needs. Among these needs, the purely biological ones are of utmost importance for survival. Particularly, net primary production is the most vital source of biological items for human life—*the source of genuine wealth* for human survival, the determiner of essential primary industrial sectors such as agriculture, fishery, and forestry (Vitousek et al., 1986). Money and money substitutes cannot be considered genuine wealth, and the definition of wealth in modern economics must be critically re-evaluated, as suggested in Chapter 6. In a more sustainable and equitable future society, owning a significant amount of wealth in terms of money and money substitutes should hardly be seen as a feather in one's hat.

Two points are underscored regarding the dual nature of real capital, emphasized in Chapter 7. Real capital, while important as an agent of production, imposes a significant biophysical burden in terms of entropy (Georgescu-Roegen, 1971). Firstly, real capital qualitatively degrades over time, thereby generating a need for maintenance and disposal. As Soddy (1926) noted, energy and materials used to construct real capital can never be fully recovered due to the law of entropy. Secondly, once created, real capital is difficult, if not impossible, to transform into consumable goods, a form of genuine wealth. In this context, Soddy (1926, p. 251, emphasis added) points out, "No primitive community would reckon upon eating its ploughs if short of bread. *The financial mentality of modern man prevents these elementary considerations from being properly appreciated.*" The financial mentality mentioned above and discussed throughout this book predicates itself on unwavering faith in the universal exchangeability of money and money substitutes for genuine wealth.

Three types of dual nature, related to money, wealth, and real capital, necessitate the maintenance of a delicate balance between money stock, wealth flows, and real capital stock. After all, all three items represent debt to society, where both conventional and heterodox economists have largely overlooked the biophysical aspects of these items. To maintain a balanced relationship among money, wealth, and real capital, the proper management of money within a sovereign money system is not only indispensable but also essential.

We, the authors, endorse a balanced view of money systems based on the dual nature of money, wealth, and real capital. This view complements mainstream individualistic perspectives, which drive economic affluence, with a correspondingly firm emphasis on collectivistic perspectives. Adopting a collectivistic perspective means establishing and properly managing into the future a sovereign money system. This is our central message. It is a matter of urgency that we rescind the two unnatural powers bestowed on the banking sector, and to smoothly transition to a democratically organized sovereign money system.

In contrast to our message and in closing, consider the famous statement of Adam Smith (1776/1976, pp. 477–478) in *The Wealth of Nations*: "By pursuing his own interest he frequently promotes that of the society more effectually than when he really intends to promote it. I have never known much good done by those who affected to trade for the public good."

With which notion are you, the reader, more sympathetic?

REFERENCES

Conti-Brown, P. (2016). *The Power and Independence of the Federal Reserve*. Princeton University Press.

Fein, M. L. (2013). The Shadow Banking Charade. *SSRN Electronic Journal* [Preprint]. https://doi.org/10.2139/ssrn.2218812

Fisher, I. (1936). *100% Money* (Revised edition). Adelphi Company.

Georgescu-Roegen, N. (1971). *The Entropy Law and the Economic Process*. Harvard University Press.

Georgescu-Roegen, N. (1976). *Energy and Economic Myths: Institutional and Analytical Economic Essays*. Pergamon Press.

Hardin, G. (1968). The Tragedy of the Commons. *Science, 162*(3859), 1243–1248. https://doi.org/10.1126/science.162.3859.1243

Kang-Landsberg, A., & Plosser, M. (2022). *How Do Deposit Rates Respond to Monetary Policy?* Federal Reserve Bank of New York. https://libertystreetec onomics.newyorkfed.org/2022/11/how-do-deposit-rates-respond-to-mon etary-policy/ (Accessed 22 June 2023).

Keynes, J. M. (1922, July 27). Inflation as a Method of Taxation. *The Manchester Guardian Commercial (Reconstruction in Europe Supplement)*, 268–269.

Keynes, J. M. (1923). Inflation as a Method of Taxation. In *A Tract on Monetary Reform* (1st ed., pp. 41–62). Macmillan and Company, Limited.

Macleod, H. D. (1883). *The Theory and Practice of Banking* (4th ed., Vol. 1). Longmans, Green, Reader and Dyer.

Mark, J. (1934). *The Modern Idolatry: Being an Analysis of Usury & The Pathology of Debt*. Chatto and Windus.

Mayumi, K. (2020). Sustainable Energy and Economics in an Aging Population: Lessons from Japan. *Springer (lecture Notes in Energy)*. https://doi.org/10.1007/978-3-030-43225-6

Smith, A. (1976). *An Inquiry into the Nature and Causes of the Wealth of Nations*. University of Chicago Press (Original work published 1776).

Soddy, F. (1926). *Wealth, Virtual Wealth and Debt: The Solution of the Economic Paradox* (1st ed.). E. P. Dutton and Company.

Vitousek, P. M., Ehrlich, P. R., Ehrlich, A. H., & Matson, P. A. (1986). Human Appropriation of the Products of Photosynthesis. *BioScience, 36*(6), 368–373. https://doi.org/10.2307/1310258

Woodward, F. L. (2006). *The Book of the Gradual Sayings: (Aṅguttara-Nikāya) or More-Numbered Suttas* (Vol. 1). Pali Text Society (Translation Series, 22) (Original work published 1932).

Index